A WOMAN OF ADVENTURE

A WOMAN OF ADVENTURE

The Life and Times of First Lady Lou Henry Hoover

Annette B. Dunlap

POTOMAC BOOKS
An imprint of the University of Nebraska Press

 Potomac Books is an imprint of the University of Nebraska Press.
Manufactured in the United States of America.

∞

Library of Congress Cataloging-in-Publication Data
Names: Dunlap, Annette, 1955–author.
Title: A woman of adventure: the life and times of First Lady Lou Henry Hoover / Annette B. Dunlap.
Description: [Lincoln]: Potomac Books, an imprint of the University of Nebraska Press, [2022] | Includes bibliographical references and index.
Identifiers: LCCN 2021038782
ISBN 9781640125155 (hardback)
ISBN 9781640125223 (epub)
ISBN 9781640125230 (pdf)
Subjects: LCSH: Hoover, Lou Henry, 1874–1944. | Hoover, Herbert, 1874–1964. | Presidents' spouses—United States—Biography. | Girl Scouts of the United States of America—Biography. | California—Biography. | BISAC: BIOGRAPHY & AUTOBIOGRAPHY / Women | SOCIAL SCIENCE / Philanthropy & Charity
Classification: LCC E802.1.H75 D86 2022 |
DCC 973.91/6092 [B]—dc23
LC record available at https://lccn.loc.gov/2021038782

For Bill

CONTENTS

LIST OF ILLUSTRATIONS

Following page 134

ACKNOWLEDGMENTS

I would not have undertaken this work had it not been for the prodding of my friend Michelle Gullion, the Archives Director and Curator for the First Ladies National Historic Site and National First Ladies' Library in Canton, Ohio. "She is an underrated first lady," Michelle told me. When Michelle says a first lady is 'underrated,' she knows whereof she speaks. The thesaurus does not contain enough accolades to bestow upon Craig Wright, archivist extraordinaire, at the Herbert Hoover Presidential Library in West Branch, Iowa. Craig scanned folders, responded to emails, and answered questions faithfully throughout this seven-year project.

Craig's colleagues at "The Hoover" also deserve their share of praise: Matthew Schaefer and Spencer Howard responded to questions in Craig's absence and tolerated my "first in, last out" visits to the library. Thomas Schwartz, director of the Herbert Hoover Presidential Library, supported and encouraged me during my visits to Iowa. Elizabeth Dinschel fed my interest in decorative arts and Lou's involvement with the Girl Scouts. Marcus Eckhardt was gracious enough to share some of Lou's beautifully constructed gowns and dresses and her clothing diaries from her White House years.

Special thanks go to Jerry Fleagle, President of the Herbert Hoover Foundation, Delene McConnaha, Academic Programs Manager, and the board of the Foundation for awarding me research grants to help defray my expenses in researching this book. As always, a shout out to the Cumberland County Public Library and Information Center, North Carolina, for its speedy and dependable interlibrary loan service. My appreciation goes to my daughter, Julia Seymour, and my husband, Bill Dunlap, who reviewed the manuscript and provided valuable feedback.

As always, there are insufficient words to express my love and appreciation for my husband of forty-one years, Bill Dunlap, who has learned that when I am "in the zone," he should not interrupt me with his joke of the day.

INTRODUCTION

Lillian Moller Gilbreth was no stranger to the Hoover White House. The first woman elected to the National Academy of Engineering, Gilbreth joined the Hoovers for a weekend at their Shenandoah retreat, Camp Rapidan, in summer 1930. Lou Henry Hoover chauffeured her friend from Washington to the Virginia countryside in her Cadillac, and the canny first lady used the time alone to recruit her passenger to become a part of the Girl Scouts. Gilbreth, a widow with twelve children, felt she had more than enough on her plate and respectfully declined.

However, Lou was nothing, if not persistent. The following January, she invited Gilbreth to a White House tea. The occasion was a meeting of national Girl Scout leadership, and Lou seized her moment. She announced that she would enroll Gilbreth in the Scouts then and there. Gilbreth had no choice but to rise and recite the Girl Scout oath.

Henrietta Bates Brooke had a similar experience with Lou over a decade earlier. When Girl Scout founder Juliet Gordon Low asked Lou to become commissioner for the District of Columbia scouts in 1917, Lou demurred. She was in the middle of transitioning her residences from London and California to Washington, where her husband had just taken an appointment as Food Administrator with the Wilson Administration. Lou thought of Brooke. She found her friend confined to bed with an attack of appendicitis. It was an opportunistic moment for Lou, and she made the most of it.

Persuasiveness. Cajoling. Friendly arm-twisting. These words are not typically associated with Lou Henry Hoover. Nevertheless, a careful look at her legacy reveals that she had honed these tools to a fine art. They are the tools of a politician, the gifts of someone who knows how to read the moment—the skills of someone who understands who can help further a cause and who is best left unapproached.

Those who have written about Lou have emphasized her independence and her organizational talent. They lauded her relief work during World War I and her efforts on behalf of the Girl Scouts which spanned two decades. During her years as the wife of a cabinet secretary, Washington society loved Lou. The same people resented her during her four years in the White House. Americans knew little of her private philanthropy, her underlying optimism, and her bountiful energy. She hated the press because of the things they wrote about her husband (although a good percentage of what was reported was grounded in truth), and she refused to give interviews. Despite her talents, she failed to understand the importance of owning her story and controlling her image.

Lou Henry Hoover found ways to maintain her independence and put her organizational savvy to work. She pursued a degree in science when it was considered a "man's field." She thought that marriage would open career doors for her in what seemed to be a union of equals, only to discover that society expected her to fulfill the role of the wife who furthered her husband's career. She was blindly devoted to a man who took her loyalty for granted. In response, she cultivated a network of female friends who stepped into the role of household management, leaving her free to pursue her agenda.

The Girl Scouts of America consumed a good portion of that agenda. Founded in 1912, Lou was one of the guiding hands who molded the scouts into an organization which fostered physical fitness, academic achievement, and self-esteem. Lou successfully traversed the societal tightrope that accused the Girl Scouts of encouraging young women to develop masculine traits. She did it by publicly emphasizing the girls' homemaking skills while quietly working to develop curricula and programming that introduced girls to the sciences, the environment, and the arts.

Lou Henry Hoover's contributions to American life expand beyond her four years as the nation's first lady. During the First World War, she was instrumental in employing British women whose husbands and fathers had gone to war. She helped fund a hospital to care for the wounded. She traversed the submarine-infested ocean to raise funds on behalf of her husband's work to feed starving Belgium, which Germany had invaded at the very start of the war.

When Herbert Hoover accepted appointments in the Wilson and Harding administrations, Lou took stock of what could help women in Washington. She provided a haven for socializing for women who had relocated to the nation's capital to work for the federal government during the war. In addition to her role in the national Girl Scout organization, Lou became a Girl Scout troop leader, which continued even after she became the first lady. She advocated for women's physical fitness and amateur athletics to encourage health and well-being.

As the First Lady, Lou was the first presidential wife to address the nation by radio. She used the new medium as a bully pulpit to promote her husband's efforts to address the pain caused by the depression, encouraging volunteerism and community cooperation. She took an avid interest in the White House, researched the provenance of its furnishings, and continued the work of historic preservation that had begun under Grace Coolidge's leadership. A strong advocate of the arts, Lou brought some of the most talented European and American musicians to the White House during her four-year tenure.

She was not idle during her post-White House years. She opened the doors of her home to Stanford students, especially to young women, whom she continued to mentor and support as they strove for independence and opportunity in what was still very much a man's world. She was influential in establishing two new curriculum programs at Stanford—physical therapy and music. Her philanthropy continued, now much of it channeled through the Salvation Army, whose work she had come to admire. She once again took up the cause of her beloved Girl Scouts, serving one more term as its national president.

By today's standards, Lou Henry Hoover died young—at sixty-nine years of age. Except for Patricia Nixon, she is the last first lady to predecease her husband. Lou's reticence about publicizing her accomplishments and the national and world events that marked the last, post-White House decade of her life provided no opportunities for the American public to understand what a truly remarkable person she was. Lou Henry Hoover is not only an underrated first lady, but she is an underrated American. Hers is a story of courage, fortitude, and optimism. She deserves to have it told.

CHAPTER 1

Avid Outdoorswoman

Seventeen-year-old Lou Henry owned a share in a gold mine. The rediscovery of gold near the southern California town of Acton in 1890 had revived prospecting, and Lou's father, Charles, decided to try his luck with part ownership of the Union mine. The Union, located on the north slope of Mount Gleason, was one of two state-of-the-art mines that contained a stamp mill—a device that pounded rock into powder, allowing for easier extraction of the metallic ores. Charles Henry divided his stake with his elder daughter.

Lou and her father worked the mine in the summer of 1891. The lithe, athletic girl with expressive blue eyes, dark hair, and a distinctive gap between her two front teeth became familiar to other prospectors. She made friends easily, and people were attracted to her warmth and sincerity. Miners welcomed her visits, took her down the shafts of their mines for inspections, and taught her about mining the precious metal. Lou thrived on the physical activity, and she fearlessly accompanied her father into their mine to conduct routine inspections.

Lou would have happily spent the entirety of her summer days alongside her father. But her mother, Florence, expected Lou to assume a portion of housekeeping and meal preparation responsibilities in the large, multi-room tent serving as the Henrys' summer home. Florence also expected Lou to keep an eye on her nine-year-old sister, Jean. Lou detested the drudgery of cooking and housekeeping, and she resented her mother for confining her to the tent with those chores.

The Henrys had moved to Whittier, California, twenty miles southeast of Los Angeles, in 1887. The move was the family's fourth attempt to find a climate that would ease Florence Henry's chronic bronchitis and offer a better income for Charles. Charles Delano Henry and Florence Weed Henry were both born in Wooster, Ohio. Charles is first listed in the 1870 census as an unmarried grocery store clerk in Fostoria, Ohio, located approximately one hundred miles northwest of his native Wooster. By 1872, Charles had moved to Waterloo, Iowa, where he found work at the First National Bank.

Florence traced her ancestry to the Revolutionary War, where a Weed ancestor served as a coroner. The Weeds gradually migrated westward, starting in New Hampshire, migrating through Massachusetts and New York, and settling in Ohio and Iowa. Florence's immediate family moved to the rural community of Shell Rock, located near Waverly, twenty-five miles north of Waterloo, in 1872, where she taught school. Charles and Florence renewed an acquaintance from their Wooster days, and the couple married on June 17, 1873.

Waterloo lay along the banks of the Cedar River in northeastern Iowa, where the river demarcated the town's social and economic divide. The western side of Waterloo developed as the town's commercial center and became home to successful merchants and professionals. The eastern side was less affluent, and evidence suggests that Lou was born in this part of town on March 29, 1874, nine months after her parents' wedding. She was simply named Lou, an unusual, single, unisex name for the era. Family lore contends that Charles announced his intentions to rear his elder daughter as a boy, a decision to which Florence initially agreed.

In 1879, with five-year-old Lou in tow, Charles and Florence moved to Corsicana, Texas, fifty-five miles south of Dallas. Charles had secured a position in a bank in Corsicana, and the couple hoped that Texas's more arid climate would benefit Florence. Lou recalled that she and her family received the famed southern hospitality, although that warmth quickly turned to ice if someone were to say, "Why, we always did so-and-so in the north." Roses and lilies had already bloomed when the Henrys arrived in Corsicana in early spring. Snow had still been on the ground when the family left Iowa. Years later, Lou dared to insist that Texas's monstrously sized watermelons tasted better than California's famed melons. It was also Lou's first experience with a large African American population and the racism that characterized the Jim Crow South.

The Henrys' stay in Corsicana lasted approximately twenty months. They returned to Waterloo in 1881 and moved into a house on Fifth Street, on the west side. Here, Lou's only sibling, Jean, was born on June 30, 1882. "I even had a delightly [sic] little baby sister come to live with us while we were there!" Lou wrote in her diary. The 'delightly little baby sister' would struggle to find her own identity outside of the giant shadow cast by her big sister.

Five years later, the family left Iowa permanently for Clearwater, Kansas. The stay was so short-lived that her parents never enrolled Lou in school. Charles arrived in Kansas with two other business partners and the plan to start a new bank, but the town proved too small to support three investors. Offered the opportunity to help found a bank in the newly forming town of Whittier, California, and to serve as the bank's chief operating officer, Charles jumped at the chance.

The year 1887 was pivotal in Whittier's history. Jacob Gerkens, a German immigrant, first started to settle the area in 1868 when he purchased 160 acres of public land for $234 from the US government under the Homestead Act. The land changed hands several times, and by 1887, a group of Quakers settled in the community and purchased an additional 1,259 acres. The Quaker group acquired the land as the Pickering Land and Water Development Company. It attracted other members of the Society of Friends [the formal name for the Quakers] from the East Coast, who bought lots from the company sight unseen. Not limiting itself to co-religionists, the company invited all "fair-minded people" to settle in the new town. Whittier's growth was further assured when the Southern Pacific Railroad built the first railroad spur to the town that same year.

Agriculture was Whittier's main industry. The mild climate allowed nearly year-round planting and a diversity of crops that ranged from traditional row crops such as barley and corn to vegetables such as cabbage and tomatoes. Peanuts were also planted in the region, but within a decade of the founding of Whittier, citrus had become the primary agricultural enterprise. A cannery allowed local processing, and a lumber mill and a grist mill soon followed as the town grew.

Quaker culture permeated the town. Lou's schoolwork includes essays about the Quaker founder George Fox, the Pennsylvania colonist William Penn, and the town's namesake, poet John Greenleaf Whittier. Growing up in Whittier a generation after Lou, the writer M F K Fisher described Whittier's Friends as "a little smug . . . probably because they still felt, after a few generations, like refugees from a scorned and even persecuted minority group."[1]

George Fox founded the Religious Society of Friends, or Quakers, in England in the mid-seventeenth century. Ridiculed by the Puritans and the Anglicans, Fox and his followers became known as Dissenters for their arguments against the need for a church hierarchy. Fox believed that every man and woman could have a personal relationship with Jesus Christ without the need for an intermediary.

The most radical of Fox's views was his commitment to complete egalitarianism. He preached that people should not oppress others because of their gender, race, or class. It was one of several Quaker teachings well-absorbed by Lou. Writing at the age of fifteen in support of universal suffrage, she observed of disenfranchised women: "To be classed with the idiot, maniac and 'jail-bird,' far below the roughest, least intelligent scamp can by no means be overlooked."

The equality of women in the community likewise gave her a keen eye toward the irony of male-female stereotypes. "Mama and I went to church with Mr. and Mrs. Wiggins," she noted in her diary. "Papa and Jean stayed home because Papa didn't have time to 'change his clothes.' Talk about a '*woman's* pride.'"

Lou's upbringing fit in well with Quaker tenets. As she became old enough to learn the skills, Charles Henry taught his daughter how to fish, ride a horse astride a saddle, and hunt. Lou was a skilled horsewoman by the time she was a teenager, and she continued to ride mountain trails into her early sixties. She was a crack shot with a rifle—a skill that would come in handy when her compound was under siege during China's Boxer Rebellion. As Lou matured, Florence Henry despaired of her daughter's lack of femininity. She criticized Lou's preference for worn, sometimes torn, blouses and skirts, urged her to wear gloves, and encouraged her daughter to wear hats to protect her complexion. As a teenager, Lou was too interested in hiking, horseback riding, and hunting to devote time to fine clothing.

The men in Lou's life included classmates and family friends, and they treated her as an equal. Mark Watson, a summer neighbor of the Henrys on Mt. Gleason, loaned Lou his shotgun for the summer, a transaction that she recorded matter-of-factly in her diary as if it were an everyday occurrence. "Went down to the gunsmiths [sic] this morning, and left Mark Watson's gun, after it was repaired, at the Chamber of Commerce . . . Went down this afternoon to get my own rifle, it has been put in thorough order." When another neighbor borrowed Lou's rifle and shot a rabbit with it, Lou's father showed her how to skin it and cut it into pieces.

Lou had completed her first year at Los Angeles Normal School in June 1891, where she enrolled following high school graduation. The three-year institution trained its students to become teachers and would eventually become the world-renowned UCLA. She gravitated toward classes in the sciences and "physical culture," as the term for physical education was then known. The science outings to collect specimens combined social activity, outdoor challenges, and the study of nature. Describing her class's first "botanizing excursion," Lou recorded:

> Miss [Della] Palmer and I are a good match for climbing, we beat all the others to pieces. We found lots of flowers, lupines, primroses, forget-me-nots, etc.,—brakes and ferns, maidenhair and baby blue eyes, lizards and frogs, Jerusalem crickets. Came home with our arms full of flowers, and our shoes covered with dust, and altogether a disrespectable looking crowd. But we're going again whenever we get a chance.[2]

The group went again in early May, and for Lou, it was another glorious day:

> Lola McLellan, Claribel Ellis, Lizzie Pepper, Wilhelmine Gifford and I went botanizing. . . .walked a long ways, climbed big hills, thought of walking to Garvanya, explored deserted castles and most wonderful cañons, saw snakes and told "snake stories," fell down hillsides and stepped on cactus and did many other delightful things, including gathering some specimens.
>
> "[D]rove part of the way up [in horse and wagon]," she wrote of another outing, and then climbed the rest of the way—went far above the falls, which is the largest I have ever seen. Della Palmer and I were the only girls who climbed down to the very brink of the falls.[3]

At the start of her second year at LA Normal, Lou organized a chapter of the Agassiz Association. Louis Agassiz was a Swiss-born naturalist and scientist, best known for his studies of extinct marine life and his understanding of the ice age in the life of the Earth, resulting in his theory of continental glaciation. He revolutionized the teaching of the natural sciences, emphasizing evaluating observed phenomena rather than gaining knowledge from textbooks.

Agassiz traveled to the United States in 1846 to study the nation's geology and natural history and deliver lectures at the Lowell Institute of Boston. Following the delivery of a series of lectures in Charleston, South Carolina, and other cities, he accepted a professorship at Harvard University and founded the Museum of Comparative Zoology in 1860. One of his pupils was David Starr Jordan, destined to become the first president of Stanford University and a close friend of Lou and her husband, Herbert Hoover.

The Agassiz Association was a union of local societies, each formed to study nature through personal observation. The associations became popular in the late 1880s and were strongly promoted across the United States into the 1890s. In addition to Lou's group of women friends, four faculty members, including her beloved zoology and drawing teacher, Sarah Monks, served as honorary members. The initiation fee was fifty cents, and the group met once a week after school in the little room adjacent to the school's museum. The group's purpose was to make regular additions to the school's collections by taking excursions to all the neighboring vicinities and getting a collection of live pets. The meetings were to be "strictly parliamentary until business disposed of and then 'delightfully informal.'" Lou was confident that " [w]e are going to make it a success." The local Agassiz Association would be the start of Lou's long and effective work as an organizational leader.

Lou entered college when public thinking about physical activity for women was in the process of a transformation. History credits Catharine Esther Beecher with founding the movement to encourage girls to be physically active in the middle of the nineteenth century. She was the daughter of Dr. Lyman Ward Beecher and the half-sister of Harriet Beecher Stowe, author of *Uncle Tom's Cabin,* and Henry Ward Beecher, pastor of Brooklyn's Plymouth Church and, along with Harriet, a noted abolitionist.

Trailblazing was clearly in the family blood. Catharine was one of the first advocates for equality in women's education. She founded Hartford Female Seminary, where she implemented several of her groundbreaking approaches to education. In her 1865 textbook on physical education, entitled *Physiology and Calisthenics for Schools and Families,* Beecher argues that girls ruined their health with tight corsets, poor diets, and culturally imposed "fragility." Lou would continue to echo Beecher's ideas throughout her life as she fought stereotypes about the connection between women's brains and bodies.

Lou was a stellar pupil in her first year at LA Normal. She ranked number one in her class over the three trimesters. Most of Lou's grades were in the high 90s, with the exception of her music grade, an 82. Music was the only class in which she struggled and the only one that she regularly complained about in her diary.

Lou had the joie de vivre of a young woman who had everything going for her. Her days were filled with attending school, completing her assignments, visiting friends, frequenting dances, attending church, and fulfilling her family obligations as the elder daughter. Her hectic life had its own rhythm, anchored in the security of her family.

On December 9, 1891, Lou arrived home from school to learn that the culmination of her father's frequent train trips to Monterey had resulted in the organization of the new Bank of Monterey. Charles was appointed bank treasurer (the modern-day equivalent is Chief Operating Officer). He, Florence, and Jean would relocate to the town, not far from San Francisco, sometime after the first of the year. Lou, who would turn eighteen in March, was to remain in Los Angeles to continue at LA Normal.

The news hit like a thunderbolt, and it came just as Lou was preparing for her end-of-term exams. Her grades suffered. She knew that she would not be first in her class and hoped that she would come out either second or third—"more than I deserve considering the amount I have studied." Her ranking was even lower than she anticipated, as she did not record it in her diary. "Went to school this morning for our standings. Mine were not particularly brilliant, but not a disgrace by any means."

Lou's natural optimism warred with a sense of foreboding. Florence arranged for Lou to board at Mrs. Ward's, where several other classmates rented. Told of the arrangements, Lou commented that it would be "perfectly glorious to be with Lola [McLellan], but I scarcely fancy the rest of it."

Lou saw her family off on their move to Monterey on the two o'clock afternoon train on Sunday, January 31, 1892. The day before their departure, Charles and Florence watched Lou perform with a dance group. After the performance, she and her father walked downtown and spent time together. "I am all alone now," the seventeen-year-old Lou observed in her diary on

Sunday evening, the idyllic summer on Mount Gleason now a distant memory. She spent the remainder of the afternoon visiting with a male friend of Lola's and fixing up her part of the room. Lou did her best to keep a positive attitude. "I rather think I shall like it here, tho' I don't think if it were not for Lola." Within a few days, Lou's climbing companion, Della Palmer, joined them at the Ward home, and two other girls, Minnie Gifford and Claytie moved in. Lou never mentioned Claytie's last name. The five formed a tight-knit group of girls who socialized, completed schoolwork, and attended church together.

Although surrounded by friends, Lou's separation from her family created a feeling of loss. Detailed descriptions of the physical environment, horseback rides, and mountain climbs are absent from her diary entries. The arrangement curtailed Lou's physical activities in a way that she had never before experienced. The feeling of isolation, underscored by an uneasy relationship with her landlady, came to a head as Lou prepared to leave for the end-of-term break.

Mrs. Ward summoned Lou in the living room, where she "and I had a long talk this afternoon, on a peculiar subject, so I had to rush around to make the train."

Lou is uncharacteristically vague in her diary about the encounter. However, she did not return to Mrs. Ward's at the start of the third trimester. Lou moved into a room with Lola at Mrs. Hathaway's. At the end of the month, Florence wrote Lou that she would spend the rest of the term at the home of Mrs. Cooley, whom Lou described as lovely. It appeared to work well for Lou. "It is so good and quiet here," she wrote. "No one around but just the two of us."

Lou attended church regularly with her new landlady, maintaining a habit that Florence had instilled. The Henrys were eclectic in their choice of denominations, attending the Methodist, Episcopal, Presbyterian, Unitarian, and Congregational churches. There is no mention of attending Quaker meetings.

Lou was as observant and analytical about matters of faith as she was about the natural world. She had strong opinions about the various ministers whom she heard preach. "I went to church with Mrs. Cooley this morning. This afternoon I went over for Flora, and we went downtown and met Edith, and all went to hear Mr. Mills, the evangelist. He is certainly wonderful if for no other reason than that he has none of that unwholesome excitement that usually characterizes one of his class."

The Women's Christian Temperance Union (WCTU) was well organized and active throughout the United States in these years. Founded in 1873 by Frances Willard, an educator at Northwestern University in Evanston, Illinois, the WCTU had gained a steady and committed following across the country. The WCTU's goal was to encourage people, especially young people, to take a pledge that they would either stop drinking or never begin to drink alcohol. Although we have no confirmation that Lou ever made a formal pledge, she did not drink alcohol, and she attended some of the WCTU's meetings during her time at LA Normal. "Went to St. Paul's this morning and to a temperance service at Fort St[reet] Methodist this evening. The latter was splendid." However, Lou was not above poking fun at the volume used by temperance preachers to get their message across: "There is a temperance meeting downstairs, and I have full benefit of it up here."

When the spring term ended in June, Lou packed her belongings and joined her family in Monterey. She was thrilled to be reunited:

> We did very little but talk this morning; there was so much to talk about. Jean and I walked down the beach with Papa's lunch. Monterey is such a funny old place,—all adobes and crooked streets, and funny places. I think I will like it very much,—it is so picturesque. We came back with Francis and Addie Malarine,—Spanish girls,—Addie is a little older than Jean, Francis younger than myself,—but they are lovely girls, and already great friends of Jean's, so suppose they soon will be of mine. Quite romantic. Mr. and Mrs. Roderick were here to dinner. She stayed nearly all evening.[4]

Lou faced a major decision for her final year of normal school. She had thrived at Los Angeles Normal, developed a close group of friends, and received encouragement and support from her teachers. But there was no question that she was homesick. Her spring 1892 diary entries are peppered with the phrase, "When Mama went away." After one trip home, Lou wrote, "Have enjoyed this vacation at home so much. Almost wished I would miss the train, but didn't."

San Jose (SJ) Normal School was only seventy miles from Monterey. Lou agonized over the decision to enroll there. She knew that the school would accept her upon a recommendation from LA Normal's principal, Professor Ira More. Lou pored over SJ Normal's catalog and went to visit its campus. Her cousin, Arthur Weed, was a student at the school, and he introduced her to several other "Normalites," as Lou called them. Even with the "lovely company" she enjoyed during her visit, she wrote, "Won't commit myself in regard to SJ Normal."

Others made every effort to help Lou feel comfortable about a possible transition. Her friend, Frank Naylor, accompanied Lou as she met faculty members at the school and introduced her to Mrs. Elwood, who boarded students. "It is a very nice house, and lovely people," Lou commented. Her positive attitude may have been because she and Frank had gone hunting earlier that morning.

Geography was the deciding factor to enroll in SJ Normal. The trip between Los Angeles and Monterey in the early 1890s was lengthy and difficult, involving a train ride from Los Angeles to the coast and then a boat ride that lasted more than twelve hours.

Lou's typical ability to adjust readily to new surroundings seemed to have abandoned her in her early days at San Jose. "There are so many, many little things to tell about school that I really cannot attempt to record them. New girls and teachers and rules and studies innumerable are too much for one person to keep account of."

In her first few months, Lou complained about being "unlucky." She lost her purse and inexplicably tore a pocket in her gym dress. She was often late for class and frequently forgot her notebooks or had failed to complete her assignment. Lou was not the same conscientious and attentive student who had entranced her teachers at LA Normal. In later years, Lou's absent-mindedness was the "tell" that she was stressed.

Lou eventually became accustomed to the new routine and the new faces. She described various teachers as "so nice," and commented on how hard some of her courses were. Notably absent were details about hours spent in the gymnasium and physical activity. It appears that San Jose Normal did not have as developed a physical education program as did LA Normal.

However, San Jose did offer something that Lou had not experienced in Los Angeles—a series of talks known as University Extension Club Lectures. Dr. John C. Branner gave the first lecture on November 2, 1892, on the chemical agents in geology. Branner was a professor of geology at the newly established Leland Stanford Junior University, located about twenty-five miles away in Palo Alto.

Branner's lecture sparked something in the young woman who had spent a summer working a gold mine. She returned the following Wednesday evening to hear a talk on the "mechanical work of water in geology," followed by a third lecture, on November 16, about the "Geological Agency of Heat."

Nothing in Lou's diary, other than her decision to return for the entire lecture series, suggests that the topic piqued her interest. The day after the first lecture, she commented on the outcome of the 1892 election: "Nothing particularly said over election—result, Cleveland pretty certain. Couldn't write anything on "Why I am a Republican" in rhetoric; consequence of election, I suppose."

Lou never finished the essay on why she was a Republican, but what she did write reveals some interesting self-awareness about her choice of political affiliation (even though women could not vote at the time):

"My home was in a part of the country where a Democrat was as much of a curiosity as a secessionist. There was always a link of similarity between them in my mind, and after I had been fully assured that they were not one and the same thing, it was some years before I could believe that they were not at least the very nearest first cousins." It was an echo of what she recalled from her short time in Corsicana, Texas, many years earlier.

By the close of her first term at SJ Normal, Lou had become fairly well-integrated into school life. She was asked to lead a pedagogy class in the professor's absence, and spent hours in the photography lab, printing her photographs. It was the beginning of a lifelong fascination with photography that would eventually include an interest in motion pictures and a love of taking home movies.

Lou graduated from San Jose in the spring of 1893. She had worked at her father's bank the summer before as an assistant cashier. In the absence of a teaching contract, Lou started to work there again. Banking appealed to her analytical and systematic mind, but Lou quickly discovered that she would not advance into management because she was a woman.

She was only at the bank a short time before the school board offered her a job teaching seventh- and eighth-grade students whose teacher was leaving to get married. The school board subsequently decided that she was too inexperienced to teach the older students, dashing Lou's dreams of fulfilling work. The board instead assigned her to a third-grade class. "I had been very much taken with the children of the 7th and 8th grade age and thought that I was going to have them in geography and history and higher arithmetic," she wrote. Instead, much to her chagrin, the school board assigned her to "the babies whom I simply hate to teach!"

A Catholic school gave Lou a contract to teach "furthering the scholastic progress of some forty exceedingly infantile personages among whom are representatives of Spain, Mexico, Portugal, Italy, Austria, England, Ireland, and various other nationalities not to mention native Americans probably better known as Indians."[5]

Lou realized that she would not be satisfied as a teacher, and her gender prevented her from pursuing banking as a career choice. Branner's lectures fascinated her. She had experienced one small part of geology in her work in the mine on Mt. Gleason, but now she had a glimpse of how much more she could learn. Lou sought out the Stanford University professor. Would the school accept a woman interested in majoring in geology? Dr. Branner assured Lou that a woman would be welcome. Stanford accepted her application, and she enrolled in fall 1894, a member of the school's fourth incoming class and its first woman student to major in geology. Little did Lou Henry know that a summer mining experience and a passion for science would set the course for the rest of her life.

CHAPTER 2

The Frustration of Being a Groundbreaker

Leland Stanford Junior University had yet to graduate its first class when Lou entered as a freshman in fall 1894. Founded in 1885 by railroad baron Leland Stanford and his wife Jane, the school was established as a memorial to their son who had died of typhoid fever at the age of fifteen. The new institution operated under a philosophy radical for universities and colleges of the era. Where most private colleges in the United States were single sex, Stanford began as a co-educational institution. While the majority of private institutions of higher learning, including the venerable Harvard, Yale, and Princeton, had a church affiliation, Stanford was secular. In its early years, thanks to the Stanfords' determination that "the children of California would become their children," the school was tuition free. Stanford's ethos promoted practicality and the making of "cultured and useful citizens."

Lou moved into Roble Hall, the campus dormitory assigned to women. Florence Henry considered the dormitory housing acceptable, but she had concerns about the propriety of Lou participating in the field trips that were an integral part of the geology curriculum Branner had designed. "How many do you expect to go on this outing—and how many ladies—how many of the professors and if none of their wives go, who is to chaperone such a club, for there is such a thing as propriety to be seen to, even if you are university people, isn't there?" Florence asked Lou.[1] (Lou apparently did not respond.)

Sue Dyer, a pre-med student who met Lou at Stanford and maintained a lifelong friendship, remembered asking one of her male classmates how he felt about having a female in his assaying class. "Oh, Lou Henry—why we would rather have her than not," he replied. As Sue observed, "She was one of them."[2]

And yet, she was not "one of them." At the end of her freshman year, Branner arranged summer fieldwork for his male students. He found Lou a job cataloging rocks in the laboratory. After having spent a summer working a gold mine, she was miserable being confined in a lab.

Branner encouraged her to pursue laboratory research with an eye toward teaching. His guidance was grounded in the precedent set by Florence Bascom. Bascom was born in Massachusetts in 1862, and she had earned her bachelor's and master's degrees from the University of Wisconsin. Bascom was the first woman to receive a PhD from Johns Hopkins University (1893). When Lou entered Stanford, Bascom had already been teaching at Ohio State University and had founded the Geology Department at Bryn Mawr College. In 1896, she was the first woman to receive an appointment as an assistant geologist with the US Geological Survey, and she contributed a substantial body of work to the Survey's study of the Mid-Atlantic region. Lou had been made aware of Bascom's accomplishments because a small piece from a local California newspaper was clipped and is a part of her archives.[3]

Lou is unusually quiet in her diary regarding her reasons for dismissing Branner's career guidance. Perhaps Lou's disappointing experiences in an elementary school classroom blinded her to the differences between young children and college-aged students, and she was determined never to teach in any setting. Or, Lou may have felt that she could not count on her parents' support for a lengthy educational career, concerned that Florence might press her toward marriage instead of funding further education. Lou expressed her frustration about the laboratory work to her parents, and Florence suggested that she come home for the summer and entertain her father—a job for which she would be paid. There is no question that Lou, while she adored her father, found that option less desirable than being in the laboratory.

Early in her freshman year, Branner introduced Lou to Herbert Hoover, a senior who was a member of Stanford's initial, "pioneer," class. Herbert Clark Hoover, known as Bert, or Bertie to family and friends, did not appear to be interested in Lou initially. But after lunching with her at the Branners' home, he became one of the men who waited in Roble Hall's reception room for Lou to come downstairs and visit with him.

Sixty years later, Bert recounted in his memoir: "As I was Dr. Branner's handy boy in the department, I felt it my duty to aid the young lady in her studies both in the laboratory and in the field. And this call to duty was stimulated by her whimsical mind, her blue eyes, and a broad grinnish smile that came from an Irish ancestor."[4] It was a disingenuous statement, for it was Bert who needed help. He had reached his senior year and had yet to pass freshman English composition, a requirement for graduation—and a subject in which the whimsical Lou Henry excelled.

Bert was born in West Branch, Iowa, on August 10, 1874, the second of three children born to Jesse and Huldah Minthorn Hoover. The couple's first child, Theodore (Tad), was born January 28, 1871. A daughter, Mary (May), was born on September 1, 1876.

Around the time of Bert's birth, Jesse sold his blacksmith business and began selling and repairing farm implements and home accessories. "A generation later," Lou wrote, "he no doubt would have been called a mechanical engineer." Jesse's business was sufficiently profitable that he purchased a third, spacious home on one acre when Bert was about five years old.

Bert was an active boy who enjoyed the outdoors more than he liked doing his schoolwork. His parents enrolled him in school at the age of five, making him the youngest child in the class. He excelled in math but was otherwise considered an average student. Bert's recollection of his earliest years is filled with happy memories of a young boy who enjoyed playing ball, swimming, and running around outside. All that changed when Jesse contracted typhoid fever from a contaminated water supply and died on December 13, 1880. He left a small estate, and the family received the proceeds from the sale of his implement business. Huldah diligently managed the monies and supplemented the family income by raising vegetables, taking in boarders, and sewing.

West Branch is a tiny town nestled in the eastern Iowa hills surrounded by hundreds of acres of corn fields in all directions. Like Whittier, the town had been founded by several Ohio families as a Quaker enclave sometime between 1850 and 1851. The community was identified as the western branch of the Red Cedar Meeting of the Society of Friends church. West Branch was named for both its geographic location on the west branch of the Wapsinonoc Creek and its designation in the Quaker church.

Bert struggled with the discipline, silence, and waiting that characterized Quaker life and worship. Quaker services did not include musical instruments or singing. Bert recalled the church as [having] "the solemnity of the long hours of meeting awaiting the spirit to move someone." Those familiar with the service "will know the intense repression upon a ten-year-old boy who might not even count his toes."[5] Huldah Hoover traveled frequently through the region as an itinerant preacher, where she was invited to speak at neighboring communities. She also gave messages at the Friends' quarterly and annual meetings. In February 1884, Huldah walked home from a meeting in the town of Muscatine, four miles from West Branch. She contracted a cold that quickly turned to pneumonia that proved fatal. The mother of three died on February 24, 1884.

The church elders decided it would be too much of a financial burden to ask one family to assume responsibility for all of the children, so the elders sought separate households for each. Bert's teacher, Miss Mollie Brown, was willing to take him into her home, but she was rejected as a suitable candidate because she was unmarried. Bert was sent to live with his uncle Allan Hoover, who lived on a farm a mile from West Branch. May went to live with her grandmother Minthorn, and Tad moved into the home of his uncle Davis Hoover.

Bert's brief interlude with his Uncle Allan's family was one of happiness and satisfaction for the young, bereaved boy. The wide expanse of the farm gave Bert ample opportunity to play ball, fish, and explore the woods when he was not in school or assisting with chores. Life with his uncle opened Bert's eyes to the economic uncertainties of farm life. "We did not know of the mortgage on Uncle Allan's farm," Bert recalled, "which was a constant source of anxiety and a dreadful damper on youthful hopes for things that could not be bought."[6]

Bert's time on Uncle Allan's farm was short-lived. Within the year, Huldah's brother Henry John Minthorn wrote his West Branch relatives to ask that Bert be sent to live with him as a substitute for his deceased son, who had been the same age as Bert. Minthorn may also have asked for Bert, and not the older Tad, because he felt a connection to his younger nephew. Bert had suffered from a severe case of the croup at the age of two. Jesse and Huldah hovered over the sick bed, watching their young son suffer and finally stop breathing. Jesse Hoover declared his young son dead. Providentially, it was at this moment that Minthorn arrived and restored the toddler's life with mouth-to-mouth resuscitation.

Born in 1846, Henry John Minthorn was two years older than his sister Huldah. He was a student at the State University of Iowa in the early 1860s, where he encountered a Union Army recruiter. In violation of the Quaker's pacifistic principles, Minthorn answered the call to enlist and joined the Army during the latter part of the Civil War. He served less than a year and was discharged in November 1865, never having seen battle.

Minthorn was a man of tremendous energy, drive, and wide-ranging interests. Following his discharge from the Army, Minthorn completed his education and taught in Iowa and Michigan. He entered medical school at Jefferson Medical College, in Philadelphia, Pennsylvania, in 1873 and completed his medical degree in 1877.

Minthorn combined both his education and medical professions to make sufficient income for his family. He served as a physician and school administrator for the Bureau of Indian Affairs first in Oklahoma, and then in Oregon. Minthorn finally settled in Newberg, Oregon, in 1885, with his wife, Laura and his three daughters to become the superintendent of the newly established Friends Pacific Academy (known today as George Fox University). He also continued as a physician.

In Minthorn, Bert encountered a man with strong opinions and enormous drive, and who was more demanding than Uncle Allan. Bert's daily chores included feeding Minthorn's team of ponies twice daily, milking the cow, and splitting firewood. On one occasion, when Bert forgot to water the ponies, Minthorn awoke him at midnight and demanded he perform the chore immediately. Although Minthorn had served in the Union Army in violation of Quaker teaching, he was a devout adherent to the faith. His family's Sunday regimen involved attending meeting, spending time in quiet reflection, and reading a required religious text before retiring to bed in the evening. For a boy who found joy in the flexibility of a life lived primarily outdoors in a farming community, Bert struggled to adjust to the more structured life of the Minthorn household.

Bert sometimes accompanied his uncle on his physician rounds, where he was exposed to Minthorn's views about his patients, often expressed in frustrated outbursts. "He told me much of physiology, health, and sickness," Bert recalled. "He did it mostly by way of explosions over the neglects which made them sick. The vigor of his disgust was equaled only by his determination to take no payment from poor non-Quaker families whom he called 'white trash.' The Quakers always paid their bills."[7]

Minthorn's worldview became the building blocks of Hoover's own philosophy—one that he would encase in the belief of American exceptionalism. Even though Bert's career took him all over the world and exposed him to a myriad of cultures, Bert maintained that Americans were superior. His attitudes influenced his treatment of the Chinese he was hired to work with and the Australians whose mines he would oversee. It would be an underlying reason for his aloofness toward the British and other Europeans. Over time, Lou, who had been raised with a more accepting view toward different races and nationalities, would absorb and reflect her husband's prejudices.

Bert quit high school at age fifteen to work as the office boy in a new Quaker land settlement company Minthorn started in Salem, Oregon. The position consisted of an eclectic set of responsibilities and put him in daily contact with a variety of people who were not his uncle's patients. The experience was good for the naturally shy and socially awkward young man. And, due to the nature of land company work, Bert was schooled in the art of dealmaking. He used that skill to his advantage as an adult to build his wealth.

Bert enrolled in night classes in a recently opened business college. The lone instructor saw Bert's potential and privately tutored him in higher mathematics. A Salem woman, Jennie Gray, introduced Bert to the wonders of English literature by handing him a copy of Walter Scott's *Ivanhoe*. The novel was vastly different from the religiously oriented fiction works that had been required reading in the Minthorn home. The exposure to a new type of literature transformed Bert into a voracious reader. He devoured Scott's other works, as well as those of Dickens.

The Quakers who ran the land office were Republican, but that did not deter a group of local Democrats led by "an elderly, retired, argumentative [man] named Hobson and his helpers" from stopping by the office in the evenings to debate heatedly past and current presidents and their actions. "Free trade and protection always raised high decibel levels," Bert recalled. "The debate invariably ended with complete disgust of each one at the obstinacy and low intelligence of his opponent."[8]

The older adults welcomed young Bert into their midst. He formed friendships with Charles Moore, one of the partners in the land-office business, Bill Hindricks, the sole reporter of the Oregon *Statesman*, and Laura Hewitt, the office's stenographer. Almost forty years later, these three would become the core of the committee that launched Bert's presidential nomination in Oregon in 1928. The land office was also where he became acquainted with Robert Brown, an engineer from the eastern United States, who visited the Salem office from time to time. Brown pushed Bert to consider attending college. He suggested engineering–a natural fit for a boy who excelled in mathematics.

Taking Brown's suggestion seriously, Bert visited the foundry, sawmill, and repair shops in Salem with an eye toward pursuing a degree in mechanical engineering. He redirected his ambitions after visiting a mining prospect in the Cascades. A discussion with the prospect's engineer opened Bert's mind to the possibilities of a career in geology and mining engineering. Seeing his seriousness, the Minthorns looked for a college opportunity and secured a scholarship for him at Earlham College, a Quaker school in Indiana. Bert looked over the Earlham curriculum and discovered that it did not offer engineering. He voiced his strong objection to attending Earlham. After considerable effort, Bert managed to get his relatives to agree.

An advertisement for the entrance exam for the soon-to-be-opened and tuition-free Leland Stanford University caught his eye. A determined Bert signed up for the entrance examination scheduled in Portland, Oregon, in the face of strong family opposition about his attending an institution with no religious affiliation. They changed their opinion when they learned that Joseph Swain had been hired as a mathematics professor at Stanford, and that he would administer the exam. Swain was "a well-known Quaker," and "his association with the otherwise suspiciously godless institution served to overcome that family hurdle."[9]

Bert's strength in mathematics was evident on the exam, but he did not do well enough in his other subjects to merit immediate admission to Stanford. The combination of his early departure from high school and his indifference toward non-mathematical subjects showed up in his test results. But this was a case where timing was everything. Stanford needed to attract students for its first incoming class.

Swain was impressed by the earnest young man who sought a career in engineering. For his part, Bert was willing to accept his failure and move on. Embarrassed by his evident scholastic shortcomings, he was diffident toward Swain as the professor questioned Bert about his financial situation and his goals.

Stanford was tuition free, but students needed to pay their room, board, and personal expenses. Bert's resources were limited. He had a few hundred dollars from his father's insurance policy that were being held for him in escrow by Laurie Tatum, the West Branch attorney who administered his parents' estates. Bert had some savings from his salary at the land office. Swain suggested that Bert plan to get a job and recommended that Bert use his nest egg to move to Palo Alto. Swain would help him engage a tutor, and Bert would re-take the entrance exams in the subjects in which he was deficient.

Bert arrived in Menlo Park, California (there was no train station at Palo Alto at the time), in the early summer of 1891 with $210 in his pocket—$160 in savings and a fifty-dollar gift from the Minthorns–plus two suits of clothes and a bicycle. Bert boarded at Adelante Villa, an older home that had been converted into a boardinghouse to accommodate early arrivals to the new campus. The two women who owned the boarding house, one of whom Bert identified as Miss Fletcher, were his primary tutors. Swain assisted in preparing the earnest Bert for his entrance exams, as did David Starr Jordan, the one-time student of Louis Agassiz, whom Leland Stanford had recruited to become the president of the new university.

The work ethic instilled by Minthorn paid off. Bert groomed horses and drove to Menlo Park by horse and buggy to pick up groceries and mail for Jordan. He often drove the university president from his home to his office on campus, giving the shy, somewhat insecure young man an opportunity to build a friendship with a man whose temperament differed markedly from his uncle's.[9]

By the end of the summer, Bert passed his entrance exams in algebra, geometry, literature, and American history. He needed one more exam, and opted for physiology, the study of the workings of the human body. It was a subject which Minthorn apparently expounded on at great length in his carriage rides with his nephew. "My association with my doctor uncle stood me in good stead," Bert acknowledged. "For by polishing a sound memory and boning all night on two textbooks on physiology, I triumphantly passed in that subject."[10] There was still a condition to Bert's admission to Stanford: Having failed English composition, he would need to pass the class to graduate.

John C. Branner was a professor of geology at Indiana University when Starr asked him to establish a Geology Department at Stanford. Branner was a good role model to replace the stern and exacting John Henry Minthorn. Branner was sympathetic to his students and took a strong interest in their work. His warm personality inspired loyalty and affection. And he clearly had a bit of the matchmaker in him when he paired Bert with Lou.

Bert has spent his first three years at Stanford building a reputation as a political organizer and hard worker. He pulled together the disparate groups of students that represented the less-than-affluent into a powerful political bloc, known as the "barbs" (short for barbarians), that eventually took control of student government. Bert was elected treasurer for the students' organizations—a position created by the newly ratified student constitution that he had a direct hand in drafting. The constitution recommended centralizing the budgets of the various student-led groups under one office, an early indicator of Bert's organizational preferences. Between his student responsibilities, his various jobs, and his studies, it would have been unsurprising if Hoover had graduated Stanford without having had a serious romantic relationship. Lou's arrival on campus changed all of that.

Lou brought the social polish to Bert's rough edges. Her keen mind and intense interest in the world around her matched Bert's own inquisitiveness. His Quaker upbringing—with its emphasis on equality of men and women—allowed Lou her independence without Bert considering her a threat to his own ambitions. It may be a cliché to suggest that they were two halves of a whole, but in the years before Bert entered public service, Lou and Bert experienced a companionship and closeness that was rare in an era that promoted separate spheres of influence within the bond of matrimony for men and women.

The two kept their relationship low-key. "We knew there was somebody... but Lou was friendly with everybody," Sue Dyer observed. Judging from her correspondence with her parents, it is a safe assumption that Lou had not shared her feelings about Bert.

Stanford offered Lou a robust intellectual education well beyond her normal school experience. Pedagogical techniques had formed the basis of Lou's teacher education. As a senior at SJ Normal, Lou took spelling tests as if she were in elementary school. The chemistry class covered material at a basic level. In contrast, Lou's chemistry notebooks from Stanford are filled with equations and analyses of the behavior of compounds. Stanford challenged Lou to study the classics and ponder the works of relatively current poets, including Lord Byron and Alfred, Lord Tennyson. In her lecture notes, she quoted from her professor: "You can't begin to live a youthful life until after it is all over, and then you live it in retrospect." Her observation to that comment: "How strange youths of 16 always talk about memories!"[11]

Lou's campus social life included membership in Kappa Kappa Gamma (KKG), one of the first "women's fraternity" organizations (the word 'sorority' was not used at the time). Women's fraternities promoted the education and empowerment of women—the same messages of intrinsic value and self-worth that Charles Henry had inculcated into his daughter. Lou developed several lifelong friendships with other members of KKG, including a close relationship with (Lucy) Evelyn Wight.

Lou and Evelyn met at the beginning of Lou's sophomore year at Stanford. Evelyn had been the Grand President of KKG from 1890–1892, and she had come to Stanford for a graduate degree in education. She was three years older than Lou, but they both shared a love of the outdoors and a hunger for education. Evelyn became a regular companion on Lou's geology overnight outings.

Lou's communication with her parents dropped off as her campus activities increased. When Lou complained in one of her occasional letters home of having walked to the mailbox only to discover no note from home, Florence replied with a tone of asperity, "Your tale of woe has been listened to. It does seem too bad that you had to walk so far and so often to be only disappointed at not receiving a letter, but it only lets you know how often I have been disappointed at not hearing from you oftener."[12]

The preponderance of Florence's letters during Lou's Stanford years were newsy and informative. In contrast to Lou's teenage diaries that chronicled so many of her mother's ailments, Florence writes of being busy with church, visiting, sewing, and helping Charles from time to time at the bank by rolling silver or counting money.

Her letters are peppered with questions about what Lou wore to various campus social events. Florence admonished her daughter to buy a nice dress to wear to an upcoming reception, be sure to insert the underarm pads that Florence had sent her to hide unsightly perspiration in her shirtwaists, and to wear attractive hats and appropriate gloves at campus events. Florence's underlying tone is an expectation that Lou would bring home a suitable beau whom she planned to marry. Lou was having fun being sociable with her fellow men without attaching strings to the relationship.

Lou returned for her sophomore year at Stanford with her little sister in tow. Jean had lost a year of school in Monterey, due to what appears to have been a serious stomach ailment. The Henrys enrolled her in Castilleja, a private, non-sectarian girls' school located in Palo Alto, where she could catch up from her missed academic year and study violin. The two sisters shared a room in a boarding house near the Stanford campus.[13]

Lou was now a full-time student at Stanford and a full-time parent to Jean. The semester had barely begun when Florence expressed concern about Jean's schoolwork load and instructed Lou to meet with Jean's teacher to increase her assignments. From a distance, Florence and Charles gave guidance on how long Jean should practice the violin. They urged Lou to be sure Jean kept up her grades and reminded Lou to see that Jean took advantage of musical events that she would never have experienced had she stayed in Monterey.

A few short weeks into the semester, Jean's stomach began to bother her again. Florence wondered why the symptoms had recurred. "Now Lou, please remember the cream of tartar and not let my baby have such a bad derangement of the stomach, and take some yourself, occasionally."[14]

The responsibility for her ailing sister came at an inopportune time for Lou, as she struggled to overcome the gender barriers in geology. She had hoped to be hired to replace Bert as Branner's lab assistant. The position went to a male student. Lou was left to wonder if she had not been given the post because she was a woman, or if it was because Branner understood how overscheduled Lou already was as she juggled her studies, her campus activities, and care for Jean. Branner and his wife had opened their home to the two sisters as a home-away-from-home. They cared for Jean so that Lou could go on the overnight Geology club outings and attend dances.

Jean's presence in Palo Alto underscored the passive-aggressive battle between Lou and Florence over Lou's lifestyle and her purpose in attending Stanford. "Does having the care of Jean take enough time or thought from your own work that you feel you cannot do as much, or as well as last year? I am perfectly happy to have you both away—in thinking you are where you can have such self-improvement."[15] Florence wrote Lou. In Florence's mind, Lou's self-improvement was to take her appearance seriously and attract a man of means who would want the benefits a well-educated woman could bring to a marriage. Lou, as evidenced by her frustration with missing out on the lab assistant job, wanted a career.

Rather than admit to her parents that she was overwhelmed, Lou decided the best thing for her to do was to quit school. Charles, forward-thinking and more in tune than Florence with his daughter's ambitions, disabused Lou of the idea in a strongly worded rebuff.

> Do not think for a moment of giving up school, you have just arrived at the point where you can begin to put your knowledge to practical use. If Dr. Branner pays you out of his own pocket, you should do just as you have decided to, while if he is allowed an assistant and the University pays the bill he should present it and pay you. Dr. Branner can be of great help to you in your studies, while you are at the University—and to giving you a position when you are through there, it will be another benefit to you to do his work without pay, and have the extra attention he will give you in your studies, than to pay you for every little bit you do, that is, of course provided, that you do your work properly and satisfactorily to Dr. Branner . . . You must have your heart in your work and studies—an interest in what you are doing—an object to be gained and not be satisfied until you have gained that object.[16]

Charles wrapped up his argument by challenging Lou to decide what she really wanted to do. If she had lost interest in studying geology, then she needed to pack her bags and come home and quit spending the money to attend Stanford. She needed to think of the example Lou would set for her sister if she were to quit. "I know you will set a good example for your little sister to follow—but try to keep her in music."[17]

Lou did not suggest quitting in her subsequent letters home, but she was still balancing the demands of her school schedule and Jean's health. Jean stayed out of school for several days in mid-November when her stomach once again troubled her, and Lou did not attend class so she could nurse her sister. Florence finally understood that things in Palo Alto were not going well for either daughter. "Lou, you wrote as if you were out of school two days on account of Jean not being well. I think it is time something should be done. You never lost a day at school (that I can remember) at such a time, and if Jean is so miserable that both of you are kept out of school, this thing must be attended to."[18]

Lou returned to Palo Alto for her spring term without Jean in tow. Lou moved back into Roble Hall and assumed a variety of leadership roles on campus. She had been elected vice president of Stanford's Women's Athletic Association in the fall of her sophomore year, and now Lou was free to fulfill her obligations in that role. She attended hops, musicales, and theater performances and served as a hostess at graduation ceremonies. Stanford's ethic of practicality and public service were already ingrained in Lou from her upbringing, but she now solidified those traits as a young adult and used them as a base from which she would serve and lead throughout the remainder of her life. She never again wrote a letter home saying she was thinking of quitting school.

Bert had graduated in June 1895, and a tough economy made it difficult for him to find remunerative work. The country was still reeling from the depression that had begun two years earlier, and there was little capital investment of any kind. Bert took a job pushing ore carts in the Reward mine in Nevada City, Nevada, for which he was paid two dollars for a ten-hour shift. When the ore in that mine played out, Bert took a job at full miner's wages at the nearby Mayflower mine.

By Christmas 1895, he had accumulated one hundred dollars, and Bert took his savings and returned to the San Francisco area. Both of his siblings had moved to California. His brother, Theodore, who had enrolled at Stanford, had quit school to provide support for himself and the boys' sister May. Bert offered to help and to assist Theodore with completing his studies.

Bert made an appointment to see Louis Janin, a mining engineer to whom he had been introduced several years earlier through his summer work with Dr. Waldemar Lindgren and the U.S. Geological Survey. Janin asked Bert to lunch at his club, where, as Bert recalled years later, Janin spent "enough on that lunch to keep me for a week."[19] Janin was not hiring engineers, but he did need an office assistant. Bert told Janin he knew how to type and asked for the position. Janin hired him, and a few days later, Janin dispatched Bert to Colorado on a mining assignment.

Upon completion of the Colorado work, Janin promoted Bert to assistant manager and sent him to a mine in Steeple Rock, New Mexico. In October 1897, the British firm Bewick Moreing and Company sent Janin a cable asking for a recommendation for an engineer familiar with American methods of gold mining. Janin offered the position to Bert. The salary was six hundred dollars a month, three times Bert's current salary. Bert had one important stop to make before sailing for Australia. He traveled to Monterey to meet Lou's parents. It is presumed that Lou and Bert came to an "understanding" during that visit.

Lou Henry became the first female to receive a Bachelor of Arts degree in geology from Stanford when she graduated in June 1898. The announcement in the San Francisco *Call* failed to put the "Miss" in front of her name. When one reads the list of names of those receiving degrees in geology, it is easy to assume that "Lou Henry" was just another one of the men in the graduating class.

Stanford's commencement ceremony was the culmination of a series of graduation activities, including a concert by the glee and mandolin club and a faculty-senior baseball game. Lou had escorts for many of the events, but she missed the senior dance for lack of a date. She wrote Evelyn Wight that she "felt like asking Johnnie what was the matter with the Betas," as the freshman and sophomore girls all had escorts, but the senior girls did not. "There were two or three girls whom no other men would think to take because everyone would suppose of course we would go with them."

Lou sat next to Stanford president David Starr Jordan at the alumni luncheon. Jordan took Lou's program and wrote her name at the top of it. "I am surprised you know it," Lou told him, as Jordan had not asked her name prior to writing it. She had been at various student-faculty events during her years at Stanford, and Jordan had never indicated that he could identify Lou by name.

"I have known it ever since you were a freshman," Jordan replied, and in a reference to his assumption that "Lou" was short for a longer name, he added, "And I have always wondered what the rest of the first part was." The program became a keepsake because in addition to writing Lou's name, Jordan drew several figures on it, including a chicken to represent the chicken salad served at the luncheon and "a beast" that Jordan named Gregory.

Two weeks following graduation, Lou was in despair. She opened her letter to Evelyn:

> [Y]ou have not yet had a letter from this A. B. (which unfortunately does not stand . . . for 'A Boy!')—ah, what wouldn't I give just about now to be one! They would not want me to stay meekly at home—I would not still have to face that old question still of how far obedience is dutiful and I would have something to work for.[20]

Lou tactfully blamed "an already overstocked market" as the reason for her unemployment, but the reality was much starker: She was a woman seeking to find success in the male-dominated world of field work.

Branner made efforts to find Lou the type of work she desired. Within a few weeks of her graduation from Stanford, he wrote:

> My dear Miss Henry:
>
> I have seen and spoken to Mr. Means about the place in the State Mining Bureau. He says that the position is just now being filled by Mr. Preston, but that Mr. Preston will give it up as soon as he finds other employment. The place will be offered to Means, but he will favor you as candidate, and he thinks you can get it. Both Means and I will do all we can for you.[21]

Unhappily for Lou, the unemployment situation put her back under her parents' roof and back into the role of an obedient daughter.

The United States declared war on Spain on April 25, 1898, following the sinking of the USS *Maine* in Havana, Cuba (then a protectorate of Spain). Although the event in Cuba served as the reason for declaring war, the first exchange of fire between the United States and Spain was the Battle of Manila Bay, The Philippines, on May 1. (The United States would not engage in battle in Cuba until June.) The war had a personal touch for Lou: She knew Stanford men who signed up to fight—enough to comprise half a company, roughly forty to fifty soldiers.

Florence Henry had put her sewing machine to good use to make bandages for the troops. "She pulled us both [Lou and Jean] right in," Lou wrote Evelyn, "and we have not been able to call our very breaths our own since. . . . We are so near the mobilization of the Manila troops and so many whom we know are leaving that I begin to feel that perhaps I will not have to envy the little maids of revolutionary days as I once did."[22]

Eight months later, on December 10, 1898, the United States and Spain signed a peace treaty in Paris. Cuba became an independent island. Guam and Puerto Rico became protectorates of the United States, and the United States purchased the Philippines from Spain for $20 million.[23]

Lou spent the duration of the war engaged in Red Cross work. The promised job with the State Mining Bureau never materialized. In the meantime, life had changed for Bert. Bewick, Moreing reassigned Bert to work with Chang Yen Mao, the director-general of the Kaiping Mining Company, considered to be the most valuable and the most potentially lucrative mine in all of China. Bert was to advise Chang on surveying China's gold mines. The salary increase to $12,500 annually and the improved living conditions opened the door for him to cable Lou: "Going to China via San Francisco. Will you go with me?"

The cable was transmitted through the post office. A new postmistress, who had yet to become familiar with all of the families in the community, thought the cable was from one man to another and posted it on the bulletin board. Family and friends who saw it—and who knew who Lou Hoover was—were amused.

Lou's response to the unconventional proposal was equally succinct. She wired Bert a one-word reply: "Yes."

CHAPTER 3

Newlywed in China

Lou Henry and Herbert Clark Hoover were married at noon on Friday, February 10, 1899, in the Henry home in Monterey. Florence stood next to the groom in front of the bay window in the dining room. Lou entered on her father's arm. Both bride and groom were attired in brown traveling suits. "They were a perfect match," Florence wrote to a friend. "Neither knew what the other would wear."[1] Members of both families and close friends who were living in California and could travel easily on short notice attended the wedding.

John Branner responded to the unexpected news with humor and a blessing:

> Here have I been all this time hunting high and low to find you a position to your liking, when you had one all the while, and the best one that could possibly have been found for you.
>
> Well, I'm done with you now! You may go; leave the country—with my blessing. And imagine me looking after you from the shore with a smile as broad as my face will admit of, and as happy as if you were my own children.
>
> Your loving professor-in-law.[2]

Father Ramon Mestres, the Catholic priest at the Spanish mission in Monterey, whom Lou had gotten to know during the year she taught at the Catholic school, performed the Hoovers' wedding. He agreed to officiate on short notice—the person Lou and Bert had hoped would marry them had died in December. Expediency had driven the choice of Father Mestres, but twenty-nine years later, Lou would answer charges that she was a secret Catholic who had led Bert astray of his Quaker upbringing.

After the ceremony, the wedding party posed on the steps leading up to the Henrys' home. Bert, lean and trim, was dressed in a three-piece suit with a watch chain visible in the pockets of his vest. He wore a high collar with a dark bow tie and a fedora. Lou, confident and self-assured, and flashing her distinctive gap-toothed grin, wore a dark, high-necked shirtwaist without ruffles or jewelry and a matching skirt. Her light-colored hat resembled a cross between a sombrero and a Stetson.

Bert had impressed his future in-laws. "We had made up our minds not to like him very well as he was going to take Lou so far away, but after he had been here a few days . . . I think we all liked him about as much as Lou did."[3]

The couple departed from the Monterey train station at 2 p.m. and set sail from San Francisco twenty-four hours later aboard the SS *Coptic*, bound for Shanghai, via Yokohama, Kyoto, and Nagasaki, Japan. "I have not been really seasick," Lou wrote to Evelyn Wight on the first letter she penned a week after setting sail from San Francisco and a few hours after the ship had departed from Honolulu. "Just a little squeamish sometimes, but always perfectly happy (physically) on deck."[4]

What Lou did not share with Evelyn was the unhappy surprise Lou received when she opened her diary for the first time since her wedding. Bert had discovered the small book, read Lou's private thoughts regarding her future, and destroyed the pages. "Once—long after [I] happened to open this little book and found all the pages now torn out—elaborately written in most fantastic, absurd, facetious imitation of my own supposed emotions—in Bert's handwriting!"[5] She makes no other mention of the event, but the lack of diary entries for the rest of the month suggests that Lou became more guarded about expressing her thoughts on paper.

Lou had journaled throughout her teenage years. While most of her entries were a simple recounting of her daily activities, there were times when she poured out on paper her anger and frustration at people or situations, including her resentment of the demands made by her mother. She had married a man who was uncomfortable expressing his emotions. Relatives had noted at the time of his mother's death that he had remained stoic, not crying once (at least not where he could be seen). Life with the Minthorns had reinforced that predisposition. Lou encouraged her new husband to record the couple's daily activities by sharing letter-writing duties to her parents. He typically scrawled a few lines at the end of each of Lou's letters, sometimes using the occasion to take a verbal jab at the time his wife spent jotting notes in her diary. Lou accepted her new husband's attitude with her characteristic uncomplaining good humor.

The *Coptic* anchored at the mouth of China's Yang-tee-Kiang River on a cold and windy Wednesday, March 8, 1899. The Hoovers boarded a launch that took them upriver to Shanghai. George Wilson, who had been with Bert in Australia, had expected the Hoovers to arrive on a different ship due to arrive a week later, so there was no familiar face to meet them. Bert waited at the dock for the delivery of his and Lou's luggage, while Lou proceeded to find them rooms at the Astor House.

Lou toured the city while Bert contacted his associates. She found it ostentatious, bizarre, and dirty, in contrast to the Oriental wonders described by Julian Ralph, a travelogue writer of the late nineteenth century who had traveled to China in 1893–94 at the request of *Harper's Magazine*. Ralph was a romantic, and he explained in the preface of his book, *Alone in China*: "If the book is not crowded with the reflections of gorgeous colors, strange scenes, and singular customs; . . . if it does not please the seekers after novelty and those who thirst for information, and if it fails to beget a kindly feeling for the people of the withering Flowery Kingdom, I have indeed performed my task badly."[6]

The Hoovers headed to Tianjin a week after their arrival in Shanghai. Located in northern China, the city would serve as Bert's base of operation.

Tianjin was home to over a million people and served as an important Chinese political and economic center. It comprised two cities at the confluence of the Peiho River and the Yuho (or Grand Canal). The original settlement was a walled city founded in 1405 and referred to as Tianjin City or Native City. Streets were narrow, buildings were close together, and there were limited public services. In 1858, the Chinese built an additional wall to keep out foreigners. Tianjin Foreign City, where the Hoovers would live, lay two miles south along the Peiho. The Foreign City housed the missionary settlement and the British, French, Japanese, and German concessions, of which the British had the largest concession of the four nations.[7]

The sole house Bert found available for rent looked charming from the outside, but was a "cheap, foreign affair" on closer inspection. He and Lou settled into a room at Tianjin's Astor House, and Bert left the following morning for Beijing. Lou encountered an old acquaintance from Iowa, Hal

Noble, in the hotel lobby, and the two explored Tianjin and shared meals together during the week of Bert's absence. When he returned from Beijing accompanied by George Wilson, the four dined together, establishing a practice of nightly dinner guests that would last through the Hoovers' White House years.

Lou was a delightful hostess and dinner companion, a fact that the newly married Bert had yet to fully appreciate. In one of the rare diary entries Bert penned, he wryly commented: "Dinner at the Detrings. Lou was at her best; and as usual, created her own atmosphere and so absorbed the interest of the party that I felt like a wet crow."[8]

Lou moved out of the Astor House in early April and into a room found for her by the local consul's wife, Mrs. James W. Ragsdale, while Bert embarked on an extensive trip throughout the region. Mrs. Stanley, a widowed missionary, was a "great motherly old soul," who provided Lou a comfortable room decorated with Mrs. Stanley's daughter's paintings and "nondescript fancy work."

The missionaries were kind and generous, but Lou chafed under the religious mindset of the community. "At a missionary's!" she had complained in her diary. Lou did not share the missionaries' passion for converting souls to Christianity. One day flowed into another, with little activity to distinguish among them, unhappily reminiscent of her months back home after she had graduated from Stanford. Her social life was defined by visits to others in the compound and sharing tea with the wives. After several weeks of her best effort to go along to get along, Lou committed what she considered to be a simple act of defiance: She did not attend church two weeks in a row, "and so shocked the dear missionaries."

To cope with some of the boredom, Lou studied Chinese—one of the most difficult languages in the world to master. Master it she did, gaining an impressive level of fluency that she retained throughout the rest of her life, along with mastery of Spanish, French, and other languages. Bert did not have the same gift for languages as his wife, but he maintained a limited vocabulary—sufficient so that when Lou wanted to discuss something privately in the presence of others, the couple could carry on a simple conversation in Chinese.

Bert returned to Tianjin at the end of May to a frustrated and angry wife. Lou assisted him in writing up his reports to be sent to Chinese officials and

Bewick Moreing, and she also made it clear to her husband that she did not wish to be left behind to languish in a widowed missionary's home. In fact, Lou had written to John Branner in early May that upon Bert's return at the end of the month, they would prepare for another expedition that "Mr. Hoover and I [will] command."

Word of Lou's educational background circulated through the mining community. The Hoovers traveled to Beijing to meet Chang Yen Mao in June. Chang was known to have nocturnal habits: His first meeting usually started at noon, dinner was served close to midnight, and he continued meetings until three or four a.m. before retiring to bed. The Chinese official paid the couple the high honor of visiting them in their hotel room during what we would consider "normal hours" simply to meet the "great American woman engineer," as the mining community now referred to Lou.

Fascination with the woman engineer had its limits. Mine workers feared her descending into the mines when she accompanied Bert on inspections. They believed she would bring a bad devil. On the occasions when she did go down a mine shaft, the miners performed an elaborate ceremony that included drums and firecrackers to chase away the evil spirits Lou might have left in the mine as a result of her visit.

At the end of June, the Hoovers moved into the eight-room Denly House. Lou described their lifestyle as "merely camping. . . . Very little furniture . . . and we do not want to buy much for three months." The Spartan lifestyle was short-lived. Bert's Chinese patrons protested the Hoovers' frugality. In China, a large staff represented a family's success and the goodwill of its Chinese hosts. Lou set up housekeeping with the requisite Chinese staff of a cook, a No. 1 Boy, and a No. 2 Boy.

Having servants did not necessarily make things easier. The first cook stayed out after a midnight curfew and received sixty lashings with bamboo from the authorities. Lou, in an apathetic tone, noted his late arrival at 10 a.m. and made no comment about the lacerations on his back. Instead, she noted that her favored servant, Kwoh, (the only servant she identifies by name), had prepared breakfast for her and Bert in the cook's absence. At the end of the same week, the Hoover's No. 2 Boy sipped a bottle of port throughout the evening while Lou and Bert entertained an associate of Bert's. No. 2 choked himself, causing a scene during the meal.

"Today decided to abolish the Cook and No. 2 boy," Bert wrote in the joint diary the couple kept through the month of July. The banishment of a cook lasted only two days, when a new one was hired to both Lou and Bert's combined relief. (Lou could not cook.)

The next day, Lou discovered that her Kappa Kappa Gamma key and gold nugget pin had been stolen. She was heartbroken. None of the servants admitted to the theft, and they spent a good bit of time pointing fingers and acting as if they were trying to identify the culprit.

Lou resisted adapting to Chinese customs. Even though she was a gifted conversationalist, Lou was impatient with the Chinese merchant's style of customer relationship-building, which involved a lengthy discussion of the merits of a piece of merchandise or a fabric and an equally lengthy bargaining session to determine a final price. She repeatedly complained in her diary about how long it took to buy just one item.

Lou clung to her belief in American exceptionalism throughout her life. Her sense of superiority in comparison to the many cultures she experienced stands in stark contrast to her scientific mind which reveled in exploring the wonders of nature and thrilled at new discoveries in the natural world. It is difficult to determine how much of Lou's beliefs were her own and how much were echoes of Bert's views. His memoirs describe local workers in the many countries where he worked in harsh and condescending language. He believed that the Chinese, native Australians, and other non-Europeans were less intelligent, less ambitious, and less hard-working than Americans. Lou's diaries and letters contain similar views.

In the case of China, ominous political winds informed the Hoovers' attitudes, and Bert was attuned to the potential impact on his work in China. "Li Hung-Chang accused by the Empress today," he wrote two days after a dust-up between consulate guards and rebels in front of the American consulate on July 4. "And things forbode [sic] another palace revolution in which changes of ministry may affect us."

The history of nineteenth century China is one of court intrigue and external tension between a nation intent on maintaining sovereignty over its people and its resources, and emerging powers that desired to exert influence in regions where there was potential for political influence and economic gain. The First Opium War (1839–1842) resulted when China prohibited the illegal importation of opium from its British colony neighbor, India, in an effort to end the widespread opium addiction. China closed the ports at

Shanghai and Canton and blockaded an estuary of the Pearl River at Hong Kong. Britain fought the closures and destroyed the blockade. Outnumbered and outmaneuvered by the British Army, the Chinese ceded control of the island of Hong Kong to Britain in the Treaty of Nanking, signed in 1842. China also increased from one to five the number of ports where Britons could reside and conduct trade.

In 1856, the British renewed hostilities with China, hoping to win additional port access and more freedom of movement within the country. This time, France joined in the fight, claiming the murder of a French missionary as its justification for war. Once again, the European forces prevailed. The Treaty of Tianjin, signed in 1859, gave Britain the right to establish British residents in Beijing, obtained more freedom of movement within the country for missionaries, and gained possession of the southern portion of the Kowloon Peninsula.[9]

In addition to Britain and France, Austria-Hungary, Germany, Italy, Japan, and Russia had interests in China. All wanted additional access to ports, and all sought opportunities to establish more residential enclaves within the country. The United States, newly recognized as a Pacific power, attempted to broker a solution. US Secretary of State John Hay proposed an "Open Door" policy in 1899 that would solidify the spheres of influence of those countries with interests in China.

Hay's "Open Door" proposal coincided with the emergence of a strong nationalist movement within China known as the Yihequan, Chinese for "Righteous and Harmonious Fists." Foreigners referred to the Yihequan as the Boxers, because of their practice of boxing and calisthenics which they believed made them invincible. The Boxers were especially hostile to Christian missionaries, whom they resented for their attempts to encourage the Chinese to abandon their traditional beliefs and customs in exchange for worshipping a foreign God. The Boxers accused Christians of demon worship, drinking blood, and mutilation of children. The Boxers had particular contempt for Chinese who converted to Christianity, and that contempt was heightened by the spread of the famine that had begun in northern China in 1899 and had impacted over a million people by 1900. The Boxers referred to Chinese converts as "rice Christians."[10]

Within the court, the Dowager Empress Tsu Hsi encouraged the Boxer uprisings. Her adoptive nephew, Emperor Kuang Hsu, had implemented a series of modernization reforms and taken steps to root out governmental corruption after China's disastrous defeat in the Sino-Japanese War (1894–95). Tsu opposed her nephew's reforms and viewed the Boxer movement as a way to prevent their success.[11]

By May 1900, hundreds of foreign missionaries and Chinese Christians flocked to Beijing for protection. On May 28 and 29, Boxers burned railroad stations between Beijing and outlying cities, including Paotingfu to the southwest, a city that was home to a large enclave of Presbyterian missionaries who were massacred by the Boxers. The railroad junction at Fengtai, located between Paotingfu and the Beijing's city center, was likewise burned.

In an unpublished memoir written in either 1917 or 1918, Lou wrote that she and Bert were warned to get out of China, but that Bert insisted on staying on out of a sense of duty to their loyal household servants and to his Chinese mine employees. (Bert was also likely staying to protect the financial interests of Bewick Moreing.) Conditions had deteriorated to the point where it was too dangerous to send Lou to safety alone. On June 1, 1900, she noted: "The Chinese Dragon Festival on which we were to be massacred by 8,000,000 [sic] heavenly soldiers—but the day passed quietly here." Four days later, she learned that on that same day, the Boxers had cut the railroad lines between Beijing and Tianjin. Nine hundred foreigners were trapped inside Beijing's Legation Quarter, which was next to the Forbidden Palace.[12]

Mary Bainbridge, wife of William E. Bainbridge, secretary of the US legation in Beijing, described the chaos in Beijing in a letter to Lou. "Things look a little dubious at the present. . . . We may have to have all the missionaries in our compound, d[octo]rs and all," Mary wrote. "The bridge on the electric railway was burned last night sometime," she reported to Lou. "How do you feel about all this? I do not imagine you are one of the nervous kind until some terrible calamity befalls us. Then there is not much use in fainting away."[13]

Lou was not "fainting away." On June 5, three thousand government Chinese and an international military force, including US Marines, arrived to protect Tianjin. "We present quite a military appearance—US, Brit., French, and Russian soldiers. Patrol at night. Also volunteers do noisy night duty." Lou helped to patrol the wall around the compound, assisted with nursing duties, and played hostess to American military.

Undaunted by the hostilities, she was

> [s]ent with a foraging party of 6 men to get mules and carts, shoot Boxers, and whip Chinese found in houses with . . . R.R. tools. Advanced thru two villages, inhabitants retreating to another . . . 1½ miles dir. In front of this village under a large cluster of trees were a line of men. When we reached within a ¼ of a mile of the trees we saw no Chinese whatsoever. We entered the wood with bayonets fixed and pieces loaded with empty chamber. We at once heard cheers of a large body of men armed with spears, long knives, and rifles. Their right was exposed, but their center and left were concealed except the heads by long grass. Their flags wave, swords and spears brandished, and the fight was opened by a rifle bullet which threw up the dirt 70 feet in front of the center of the squad. It was somewhat more than I had bargained for—fully 150–200 men, perhaps all armed with rifles, and full of fight. We were in line of skirmish when we opened fire point blank range distance about 100 yards. Frightening men (kowtowed) and the advance entered the road to charge.[14]

The Dowager Empress sent word on June 18 that war would soon be declared. She promised safe passage to the members of the Beijing legations as far as Tianjin. Diplomats were ordered to leave their legations in Beijing for their safety, and the Siege of Legations began on June 20. Sailors and marines of various nationalities who were stationed on ships anchored off the Chinese coast deployed to fight against the siege. The troops rebuilt the rail lines as they traveled from the coast toward Beijing, but they encountered strong Chinese Imperial artillery, now controlled by the empress, and were pushed back toward Tianjin.[15]

Two detachments of US Marines and four hundred Russian soldiers engaged the Boxers near Tianjin on June 20. Outnumbered, the Americans and Russians retreated. Two days later, a two-thousand-man force of British, Russian, German, Italian, and Japanese troops joined the Americans and Russians and engaged the Chinese. Bert, who had been out on patrol, dashed back to their home and told Lou to get in the cellar. Shells were coming at their house. "Lively till 4:30," Lou noted. She had been sitting calmly playing solitaire as bullets came through her door.

Bert remained with the men in the concession, building barriers and patrolling the area. Lou took her servants and provisions to the home of Mrs. Drew, where they cooked and provided shelter for thirty people, including customs officials and missionaries. Within twenty-four hours, hundreds of women and children had crowded into Gordon Hall, the city hall for the foreign concessions. Lou described the scene as bedlam. Phone lines had been cut, and shelling was constant. The men, including Bert, continued to patrol and attempt to protect the perimeter.

The concessions became a war zone. Provisions were tight. Wounded were starting to arrive, and Lou volunteered at the hospital. Ever the optimist, she observed that the soldiers' wounds were not as serious as she had expected, and that many of them complained because "they can't get in the scrap!"

An unsigned and undated memo on Directorate of General Mines letterhead described the war conditions in Tianjin:

> Been besieged British legation five weeks under continued fire Chinese troops since sixteenth by agreement been no firing fifty Marines all nationalities killed more wounded have provisions several weeks little ammunition If they continue shell or have done cannot hold long complete massacre follow hope relief can come soon glad hear victory Tientsin regret terrible cost all safe well.[16]

On July 6, the allied forces were reinforced by the arrival of the Ninth US Infantry, and an additional 318 marines arrived on July 10. The following day, the allies attacked Tianjin City to rout remaining Chinese and Boxer forces. The battle lasted all day and well into the night, ending when a night attack by Japanese forces broke through the Chinese defenses. The international forces entered the walled city of Tianjin, but instead of securing the city, widespread looting, especially by Russian troops, ensued.

On July 11, the Hoovers secured passage on a launch and had a quiet trip to Taku, where they disembarked. They moved into a well-furnished house and were able to secure fresh meats, vegetables, ice, and water. The military presence at Taku was sufficient to protect the residents from attacks, and Lou reported no assaults for the rest of the month.

On August 3, Lou and Bert packed their belongings to leave for Japan. China was still in a state of war, and the international military presence was strong. Lou wrote of seeing US Marines standing guard next to Sikhs. Scores of men-of-war and troop transports from France, Britain, Japan, Russia, and the United States were anchored in the waters near Taku.

The Hoovers were two of five passengers on a Japanese-owned boat. The days were warm, the water was calm, and the food was good. The quiet was a stark contrast to the life of mayhem that the Hoovers had experienced in the previous two months. In the peace and quiet of the journey, Lou gathered her thoughts in a letter to Evelyn Wight:

> Aug 8, 1900
>
> Well, Evelyn Wight-
>
> You missed one of the opportunities of your life by not coming to China in the summer of 1900. The very fact that the things have happened that have happened make it queer that your guardian star did not get you here in time for it.
>
> So many many many times I thought of you, and that you should have been here, at the most interesting siege and bombardment of the age. The men from Ladysmith—and we have them with us, "Terrible's" guns and all,—say the bombardment there could not compare with ours. The loss of life was greater than either Kimberly or Mafeking.[17]
>
> Only it was so short that we did not suffer from hunger, but neither did we have the chance of honorable or otherwise, surrender before us in case hunger ever should come. We simply had to stand by our guns until the end with one last bullet kept back for each one of ourselves. Our only hope was that the Chinese can't, won't, and don't charge, and they did not, to any alarming extent.
>
> So a good many hundred civilians and a couple of thousand troops sat still and repelled faint hearted charges while 10,000 or 15,000 Chinese troops and 20,000 Boxers plunked shells of all sizes into us for exactly one week, without a sound or word from the outside reaching us.
>
> Then the first relief cut their way in to us, 2,000 of them—enough to get in, but not to do anything more than we could when they got there.
>
> And for another two weeks we sat there while the relief came in from the south, at the rate of a thousand a day, more or less, while the Chinese gathered on the north more rapidly, and we gradually got to exchanging shells, instead of receiving them—and finally one day came when we

sent but did not receive, and at the same time, we who can, will, and do, charge,—charged.

And now the only question is the relief of Beijing. For more than a month we have had but two or three unreliable messages from there!

Do you realize it, that never have so many flags been in action together since our history began—Russian, Japanese, French, German, Australian, Italian, English, and American!

And such a motley array of troops—artillery, cavalry, infantry, marines, sailors, Cossacks, Sikh, Siamese, a couple of English Chinese regiments on our side. . .

But we are still living it—and just now they say "Kai fan" which means tiffin [lunch] is ready-and the ink is too bad to come back to it again-Goodbye-for the nonce, dear one-I think I will see you soon—

But oh, if you had been here!

Lou[18]

Lou was sad and angry about her Chinese experiences. Nearly all of the Hoovers' possessions had been destroyed. Lou's fledgling collection of antique porcelains and Bert's book collection were the only things that survived. In her unpublished memoir, Lou recounted, again, some of the details she had shared with Evelyn:

> In Tientsin there was real fighting—more than a month of it—, as intense fighting as there ever had been up to 1899. In our own little Tientsin alone we lost as many of our own white men as they lost at Ladysmith and Mafeking and Kimberly combined! Shells in our houses at any hour of the day or night, bullets swept up on the paths of a morning, not a word from any part of the outside for long weeks on end and the knowledge that we were not fighting for any honor or defense of small nations, or anything else but our own lives, and then when our ammunition or our strength gave out it was a question of a bullet for each of ourselves or a life of torture for as many hours or days as the mad fanatics who were loosed could keep us alive.[19]

When Lou initially arrived in China in March 1899, she had optimistically observed, "Bad beginning, good ending. China will be very good to us before we leave!" But after the birth of her first son, Herbert Junior, on August 4, 1903, she inserted a small note into her August 1900 diary on the same date:

> Aug. 4 (Little Herbert's future birthday) But I remember going down to Taku on barge! With Chang Yen Miu [sic], etc.! Or was that earlier? Why? And if so, why did we come back?[20]

Challenging Years

The Hoovers boarded the SS *Weimar* in Shanghai on Saturday, August 18, 1900, bound for London. The voyage was miserable. The Hoovers' first cabin, located below deck, was infested with crickets and cockroaches. A move to an upside cabin after the Shanghai passengers debarked in Hong Kong remedied the pest problem, but rough seas, poor food, and the absence of stimulating companionship to reduce the tedium of the six-week journey marked the passage to Europe. By the time the Hoovers arrived at London's Charing Cross Station at midnight on October 1, Lou had lost considerable weight, and she was fighting a bad cold.

Bert's employer, Charles Algernon Moreing, and his wife met the Hoovers at Charing Cross and hosted them at the Moreings' large country home in Esher, thirteen miles from London. Bert was immediately back in the city the next morning to meet with Bewick Moreing's management. Mrs. Moreing whisked Lou off to London to have a new wardrobe sewn. She "ordered the latest thing just over from Paris" from designers Arthur Phillips and the London shop of Redfern & Sons. The British couturier firm would later design the dress worn by Queen Alexandra at the coronation of her husband, King Edward VII. Gone were the days when Lou was indifferent to her appearance. She was now the fashion-conscious wife of an up-and-coming international mining engineer. To her mother's delight, Lou included orders for patterns, fabrics, and dresses in her letters home.

Bert met with Moreing and his senior partner, Thomas John Bewick, to discuss the terms of an agreement Bert had signed with Chang Yen Mao. In response to rumors of Chang's double-dealing with foreigners and Chinese, Chang had been arrested at the height of the rebellion, ostensibly for his protection, by a captain of the Royal Navy. His close association with both Bert and Gustav Detring added fuel to the suspicions.

Detring proposed to Chang that he grant Detring power of attorney over the Kaiping Mining Company to gain his freedom. Foreign ownership would protect the mine from being seized as war booty and prevent its coming under the control of one of the other European countries with interests in China. Chang agreed.

Detring, who had worked with Moreing to establish the initial contract between Moreing and Chang, wanted to exercise his power of attorney to convey the deed for the Kaiping Mining Company directly to Moreing. Bert insisted that Detring make out the deed to him as trustee. Now in London, Bert gave the deed to Moreing. Moreing created the Chinese Engineering and Mining Company and transferred the Kaiping Mining Company assets to the new entity, a clear violation of the terms of the agreement. In conjunction with the establishment of the firm, Moreing created a new stock issue which he sold to European shareholders. The net effect removed Chang's management authority and watered down the equity value for the Chinese owners.

While Bert engaged in his business machinations in London, Lou convalesced at the Moreings' home. Her cold had worsened, and the Moreings' doctor ordered her to bed. She canceled plans for a second fitting of her new wardrobe and spent her time reading, organizing her photographs of China in her albums, and working on her writing.

Lou wanted to write a marketable book about China and the dowager empress. Mansfield Allan, who was engaged to Lou's friend Evelyn Wight, was a literary agent with good connections in the New York publishing world. He talked with several publishers about their interest in a book about China. Each one offered various suggestions to Allan, but no one expressed enough interest to offer a contract. There were vague hints that a technical book about Chinese geography, geology, and topography related to trade would be welcome, especially if the book had John Branner's endorsement. Allan also suggested that Lou consider a book regarding Chinese manners and customs. Lou had been jotting down her observations and working to put together a solid manuscript. After she recovered from her cold, she traveled to London and spent her days researching in the British Library.

Lou had been an engaging and prolific writer since her teenage years. *St. Nicholas*, her favorite magazine as a teenager, had published some of her stories. Lou's high school and college compositions and her diaries reveal a keen observer of human nature and Mother Nature. She penned thoughtful insights into the political and social tenor of her times.

The desire for a successful writing career took on a new urgency after her marriage. Given their egalitarian relationship at Stanford, Lou reasonably anticipated that she would serve professionally alongside her husband in the minefields. However, Lou's successful navigation of the man's world of geology as the lone female student at Stanford was far different from the man's world that Lou encountered as the wife of a mining engineer in China. She found herself thrust into the very role she had hoped to avoid— that of the supportive wife who nurtured her husband's career. She stepped into that role out of love for Bert and a strong sense of duty, but she needed a way to define herself.

Success in the publishing world remained elusive. "What is the matter with that Mansfield Allan?" Lou wrote in frustration to Evelyn. "Has he changed his address, or has his heart grown cold toward me? He certainly isn't showing any encouragement toward striving genius.—I've written him at least a dozen epistles and documents in the past three months, but not one word has he deigned send London!"[1]

Unfortunately for Lou, nothing ever came of her connection to Mansfield Allan. After a brief marriage to Evelyn, he committed suicide at the age of twenty-nine. Nothing in Lou's and Evelyn's correspondence talks about possible causes. Evelyn never remarried, and she retained the last name of Allan for the rest of her life.

Bert wrapped up his business with Moreing, and the Hoovers left London for New York in late October. Lou stayed with Evelyn, who lived in Brooklyn, while Bert attended business meetings in Manhattan. (Brooklyn and Manhattan were considered two separate cities until they were consolidated in 1903. Although a train connected the two boroughs over the Brooklyn Bridge, travel between the two was slow and time-consuming.) Evelyn was delighted to reconnect with her friend from Stanford days. She took a week off from her teaching duties to spend time with Lou. The two women shopped, dined out, and caught up on each other's news. It was clear to Evelyn that Lou was not in robust health. After the Hoovers' departure from New York to travel west, Evelyn wrote to Florence Henry:

> After they have gone, I hope you will write me how Lou has stood all the railroading and what you think of her health generally. It seemed to me

> that she was suffering from a nervous reaction of all the excitement in China, and we wondered how she had even stood it all so well. Constant traveling is very hard on one's eating, and Bert says she lost steadily because she didn't eat enough on the journeys by water.[2]

After another brief stay in California, Bert and Lou were once again aboard ship, this time with Jean in tow. She wrote her parents that Lou still was unhealthily thin and had not regained her appetite. When the ship docked in Japan in January 1901, Lou and Jean remained in the country while Bert sailed to China. The two women rented an apartment in Tokyo's Shinjiku ward and sought medical attention for Lou.

Lou visited multiple doctors in the hopes of identifying the cause of her weight loss and the source of constant pain in her lower back. At the end of January, she and Jean traveled to Yokohama, the first city Lou had seen when she arrived in Japan in 1899. "People little, ugly, unkempt, unhappy looking," had been Lou's first impressions of Yokohama then, but now the city was a source of healing.

"We like Dr. Hall very much," wrote Jean, keeper of the diary in the early months of 1901, of a physician who figured out the reasons for Lou's malaise. "We have more confidence in him than Dr. McDonald."[3] Hall recommended "early rising and a long walk or ride" every morning before breakfast as a means of stimulating Lou's appetite. He also prescribed the daily administration of electrical treatment.

Hall prescribed an electric "bath," a popular treatment of the era which exposed a patient to ultraviolet light. One exposure method was a simple bed on which a patient lay with her or his face covered to protect the eyes from UV rays. Another popular form of the bath was a box in which a patient sat on a stool in an enclosed cabinet with the head exposed through a hole in the top. The box then aimed UV rays at the body. The belief was that light exposure cured a range of ills from eczema to unexplained weight loss, as in Lou's case.

Hall identified Lou's back pain as a broken coccyx and advised surgery to have it removed. (The coccyx, or tailbone, is the vestigial portion of the lower spine.) A year earlier, Lou's foot had slipped off the pedal as she was climbing onto her bicycle seat, and she slid to the ground. The bicycle rolled forward fast enough for the front of the metal seat to hit her sharply at the end of her spine. She ignored the pain at the time and continued with her ride. However, Lou experienced constant pain in her lower back from that day forward.

In the weeks leading up to the operation, Lou went about her usual routine—a morning walk or ride, visits with friends, and shopping for porcelains. Her years in the Far East kindled a lifelong love for antique Chinese porcelain, and Lou's understanding of geology and the composition of the clay made her a knowledgeable and avid collector. She focused her collection on pieces from the Ming (1368–1662 C.E.) and K'ang Hse (1662–1720 C.E.) periods—the blue and white porcelains. Lou's collection would survive the family's around-the-world travel before finding a permanent home with her in Palo Alto.

Hall and two other physicians oversaw Lou's surgery. An English nurse and Yoshi, a nineteen-year-old Japanese woman, hired as a housekeeper and companion for Lou and Jean, were attendants.

Lou convalesced in a Yokohama hotel. Throughout March, she expected Bert to travel to see her, but he cabled that he could not leave China. He and Detring were embroiled in an argument with Chang over his acceptance of the changes Moreing had made in the agreement negotiated the previous August. Moreing had added the financial inducement of fifty thousand additional shares each for Detring and Chang to buy the men's agreement. Detring was delighted with the offer. He and Bert backdated the original agreement to avoid calling attention to Moreing's alteration of the terms, but Chang saw through the deception. He protested the new terms, arguing that they stripped him of his management authority and gave Bert the final say in the mines' operations. Bert attempted to assuage Chang by saying that a memorandum of understanding would govern relations among the partners, not the written agreement. Again, Chang saw through the ruse. Only when diplomats and a Moreing attorney pressured Chang to agree to the terms did he acquiesce.

Lou returned to Tientsin in April, accompanied by Jean. She chronicled the sisters' activities, which consisted of making rounds of visits to families in the concession, caring for the sick, and attending dinners. Jean played her violin as entertainment for dinner guests and participated in musicales. Once the Hoovers confirmed they were leaving China for good, August and September were spent packing in preparation for their final departure. Lou had her "last glimpse of 'dear old China'" aboard the SS *Kashing* on September 26, 1901, bound for San Francisco.

The Hoovers' California stay was brief. Bert was anxious to get to London to discuss his employment with Bewick Moreing. He and Lou arrived in the city in early November 1901. Bewick, who owned forty percent of the firm, was retiring. Bert accepted the offer of a partnership and twenty percent in the company. Bewick divided the remaining twenty percent evenly between A. Stanley Rowe, who served as financial secretary, and Thomas W. Wellstead, a mechanical engineer. Moreing retained the sixty percent controlling interest.[4] Of the four partners, Bert had the strongest desire to travel to inspect mines and oversee operations, and he and Lou continued their travels on behalf of the firm.

They left London on December 19, 1901, and arrived in Perth, Australia, in mid-January, nearly a month into the Southern Hemisphere's summer. Perth "is rather an attractive city," but "the people one sees about the streets are decidedly 'common,'" Lou wrote her father a week after her arrival.

Kalgoorlie, Western Australia, three hundred miles east of Perth, was the base for Bert's operations, as it had been when he had worked in Australia before his marriage. The town typified the rough and tumble Australian outback. Prostitution was legal. Residents and visitors had a choice of saloons, and violence was common. When Lou accompanied Bert on mine inspections, she was often the first woman miners had seen in as many as four years.

She loved the life and cheerfully described the lengthy trips the couple made in an open wagon in the Australian heat and dust. Together, Lou and Bert traveled a circuit to visit the mines that Bert oversaw—from Kalgoorlie north to Menzies and then further north to Leonora and other mines in that part of the country.

"Tomorrow we start at 5 a.m. on a long trip," Lou wrote her family in early February from Leonora. "Go to Lawless by tomorrow night, changing horses three times. Make a couple of short trips of a couple of days out from there, and one of a week or more over to Lake May, and then here again. After a few more days here then back to Kalgoorlie."[5]

Lou described her first experience with termites as "white-winged flies that liked to bore into wood." A canvas bag that used evaporative cooling to keep water cool when carried by a pack animal so fascinated her that she drew pictures of it in separate letters to her father and Jean and encouraged them to make one for their day trips on horseback.

Lou was not as cheerful when she wrote Jean in response to an article about Bert in the San Francisco *Chronicle* that Florence had sent. While in California, Bert had met with a Stanford classmate who had become a reporter for the paper. During the interview, Bert let on how much money he had earned in China. The reporter dubbed Bert the "highest salaried man of his years in the world" at $33,000. Lou's reaction to the article is an early indication of her perception that people were jealous of Bert's success and growing wealth. It is one of the first examples of the role she would assume as the keeper and curator of her husband's reputation.

> It does make us feel insignificant though to realize that our money achievements so far outweigh anything else we have done in the eyes of our California acquaintances. Still, I suppose that a good many of our old "student friends" like Archie Rice . . . envy us that more than they would anything else we have or might do, so it's what they have to talk about. Too bad they can't stop talking altogether. I'm so sorry Bert's in the firm now, and that apparently everybody knows it. It would be so interesting to see just how far they would let that salary pile up before they were satisfied.[6]

Bert finished his work in Australia by the end of February. Australians were "going home" for the coronation of King Edward VII, and the couple did not depart for London until early April. Their voyage on the German-owned SS *Barbarossa* was a good trip filled with interesting fellow travelers, including many mining people that the couple knew. Lou found the journey tremendously enjoyable, thanks to excellent table companions and great friends. "And we have more good things to eat each meal than we can manage!! Altogether I think you would enjoy sea travelling more than you did in your experiences on the Pacific," Lou wrote Jean.

Life in Australia had restored Lou's natural optimism, and she looked forward to a time in England and visits back home. At a distance of over seven thousand nautical miles, and in the absence of instant communication, neither she nor Bert could have suspected the unwelcome surprises they would find upon their return to London.

CHAPTER 5

Power Couple

Lou spent a quiet summer in England in a rented cottage on Walton-on-Thames while Bert attended to business in the States. She worked on her book about China, and she took some courses at the London School of Mines to strengthen her operational knowledge of mining. Bert had begun to write articles on mine management for professional journals that Lou copyedited prior to submission. She also edited his regular reports to Bewick Moreing. Her own writing projects stalled.

London was the business hub of the world's mining industry in the early part of the twentieth century. As manager of Bewick Moreing's overseas operations, Bert oversaw mines in Australia, New Zealand, Egypt, India, the Malay States, and Burma. From 1901 to 1907, he and Lou traveled to an average of five or six countries annually.

Travel would always be a necessary part of the Hoovers' lives, but they hoped to curtail their peripatetic lifestyle and establish a home base. In the fall, Lou leased 39 Hyde Park Gate, in London's Kensington section. Both Hoover sons were born here: Herbert Clark Junior, on August 4, 1903, and Allan Henry, on July 19, 1907.

The home that evoked the strongest memories, though, was the Red House. Lou leased the property shortly after Allan's birth, and Bert remembered it as "a delightful old but small house with a garden in Campden Hill, London . . . so old that we were required to prevent our cows from wandering in High Street or hanging our laundry in view of the neighbors."[1]

The Hoovers' tenancy at Red House continued a legacy of adventuresome world travelers. The immediate previous family to live in it had been William Martin Conway, later known as Baron Conway of Allington Castle, his wife Katrina, and their daughter Agnes. Conway had explored the Himalayas, Kashmir, the Alps, South America, and the Arctic. He became director general of Britain's Imperial War Museum in 1917 and served in that capacity until his death in 1937.[2]

The Hoovers added to the home's legacy. In the years before World War I, the dinner table was surrounded nightly by an eclectic mix of engineers, ex-pat Americans, and artists. Lou was especially drawn to writers and musicians. The Hoovers maintained an informal friendship with Joseph Conrad, author of notable works, including *Lord Jim* and *Nostromo*, that reflected his years as a mariner and his life-changing trip to Congo. Mary Austin, a writer and playwright whose themes varied from southwestern Native American culture to observations of her travels throughout Europe, received financial help from Bert to produce her plays. Her autobiography, *A Woman of Genius*, published in 1912, was dedicated to: "Lou Henry Hoover and some pleasant memories of the Red House in Hornton Street." In later years, Lou would become good friends with Ignacy Jan Paderewski, the pianist who also served a short tenure as Poland's prime minister following World War I.

By the end of 1902, Bert was dissatisfied with his partnership with Moreing. Bert's long absences from Bewick Moreing's headquarters removed him from day-to-day decision making and from the details of deal structuring. As the man in the field negotiating directly with mine owners and governments, Bert expected Moreing to pay him the same percentage that the senior partner took from the deal. Moreing disagreed. Bert received considerably less than he believed was his due considering he had consummated the transaction and was key to Bewick Moreing's international success. And while Moreing was attentive to the details of mining contracts, he was not as meticulous when it came to the firm's routine, day-to-day financial transactions. These he entrusted to Stanley Rowe, the firm's financial secretary.

The day after Christmas, Lou and Bert joined Rowe and his wife for an enjoyable evening at the theater. During the evening, Rowe made what seemed an odd request of Bert: If anything happened to him, would Bert care for Rowe's family? Bert said that he would.

Bert walked into his London office the following morning. He found a note from Rowe on his desk. The financial secretary confessed to embezzling from Bewick Moreing. By the time Bert discovered the confession, Rowe had fled. Not even his wife knew his whereabouts.

Rowe had paid for a series of stock speculations with Bewick Moreing funds. When the speculations failed, Rowe covered his losses by issuing forged shares of stock in the names of the companies represented by Bewick Moreing. Rowe also used the power of attorney granted him by Bert for use when Bert was overseas and appropriated Bert's personal savings of £4,000 (the equivalent of over £600,000 today). The total theft was valued at £1 million.

The severity of Rowe's theft demanded immediate action. Moreing was in China, where he was trying to salvage Bert's arrangements with Chang Yen Mao and the Chinese Engineering and Mining Company. In Moreing's absence, Bert and Wellstead met with Bewick Moreing's bankers and attorneys. Their advisors told the two that they, along with Moreing, were jointly and individually liable for Rowe's perfidy. Bert agreed that the firm would cover the losses and released a statement to that effect to the press before getting Moreing's approval. Moreing, angry at Bert's public acknowledgment of the firm's responsibility, had no choice but to agree.

Rowe's theft dashed Bert's intentions of talking Moreing into cashing him out of the partnership upon the senior partner's return from China. Now, Bert's personal savings were gone, and he had a legal responsibility to reimburse shareholders. Tensions in the London office ran high. A decade later, Lou described the relationship between Bert and Moreing as a "constant and unending fight . . . —real fighting to the knife."

The British newspapers initially applauded Bewick Moreing's honorable handling of the matter, and the move elevated the firm's profile in mining circles. Bert's announcement deflected criticism of the firm that had come from a recent investigation into the Great Fingall Mine in Australia, one of Bewick Moreing's most profitable mines. The *Times of London* reported: "The original suggestion was that a committee should be appointed to strengthen the hands of the board [of the Great Fingall], but in view of the honorable intention of Messrs. Bewick, Moreing, and Co., recently made public, which made it clear that they undertook to make themselves responsible for the defalcations of Mr. Rowe, the late secretary, the aspect has quite changed."[3]

Within a matter of months after the dust from the Rowe scandal settled, two new lawsuits were filed. Either one alone threatened to derail Bert's career; the two together could destroy it.

A broker named Edgar Storey accused Bert and Rowe of backing out of a deal to buy $100,000 in stock from Storey on a joint account. Bert, who had emerged as a hero from his handling of Rowe's embezzlement, now stood to have his reputation ruined. There is no evidence that Bert ever had dealings with Storey or that Bert knew about Rowe's relationship with Storey, but a jury found for Storey and awarded him £30,000. If required to pay, this debt, added to Bert's other indebtedness, could bring an end to his mining career and force him to declare bankruptcy. Bert appealed the verdict.

Chang Yen Mao filed the other lawsuit on May 7, 1903, against Bewick Moreing. He accused the firm of defrauding him and the Chinese shareholders that Chang represented. Bert was not officially a defendant in the suit, but as Moreing's principal negotiator in the deal, Bert's conduct in the affair was placed under a microscope.

Coming on the heels of the Rowe debacle, the timing of Storey's and Chang's lawsuits could not have been worse for Bert. The newspapers were critical of Bewick Moreing's negotiations with Chang. Editorials suggested that Bewick Moreing's conduct reflected poorly on all European firms seeking to do business in the East. Bert was singled out. The British Foreign Office viewed him as Bewick Moreing's straw man and concluded that he had fleeced Chinese shareholders. It was "a case of rogues falling out."[4]

The "knife point" took its toll on Bert. Exhausted and feverish at the end of the day, he spent evenings with his head in Lou's lap. She applied ice to his forehead and did her best to distract him from the day's pressures. Lou submitted her writings about China to various publishers in the hope of selling an article or two to generate some income. She had no success, in part because Lou had lost her connection with the New York publishing world.

Lou poured her energies into devising ways to amuse and distract Bert, a practice she would maintain for the next three decades. She invited people for meals who would simultaneously engage, entertain, and intellectually satisfy her husband, with the hope that they would deflect Bert's constant attention to the demands of his working life.

"He is so active, mentally, that it keeps me more than busy thinking of something new to give him entertainment for a few hours," Lou wrote her mother. "And, of course, if he realized it was done for that special purpose he would cease to be 'entertained' at once."[5]

What Lou did not write her mother was that Lou was expecting the couple's first child; news she kept secret from her family until late in her pregnancy. In early June, she wrote her family: "For I felt Mama would only worry so much about us all if she staid [sic] there. Or else she would come on over here,—and I would really rather she came at any other time." There was a hint at the end of the letter of the tension that Lou and Bert were experiencing. "It is too bad that so many things had to come together—all Bert's troubles—, the fact that he could not go to America now,—that I could not possibly think of leaving him.—that we will probably have to go away somewhere in the autumn, so for economical [sic] reasons could not suggest your coming over for such a few weeks before then."[6] She assured her parents that she and Bert were well and happy.

It was an admirable bluff. Bert was more forthright with his brother, Theodore. The doctor ordered Bert to drop everything and get away from London. In late June, he and Lou departed for the French Riviera. "I was ordered away by the doctor as the late jar had rather smashed my nerves but I am allright [sic] again and though we are compelled to draw in our horns a little we have hopes of getting on our feet again someday."[7]

The couple returned to London in time for Herbert's birth on August 4. Jean had traveled to Europe to be with her sister. "Well, I've seen it—and it really is wonderful," Jean wrote her parents. "Nothing like it. . . . Lou says that it takes after me, as it insists on keeping its finger in its mouth and punching up its nose all the time. . . . I see that I have used 'its' all the time, but it seems so ludicrous to call such a mite of a thing 'he.'"[8] The "mite" weighed in at a sturdy seven pounds, fifteen ounces.

Even Lou's close friend Evelyn did not know that a baby was on the way. "Your most surprising good news reached Van Buren St[reet] after I had left home for a little trip up the Hudson with Mother Allan," Evelyn wrote to Florence Henry after receiving a letter from the new grandmother. "—[A]nd just now we have returned to find it here. . . .I never was more surprised in my life, and when I catch my breath, I think I shall be as greatly delighted."[9]

Herbert's birth marked a positive turn in his parents' fortunes. The appeals court reviewed the Storey trial in the fall, found that he had failed to establish a connection between Bert and Rowe, and reversed the lower court's verdict. Storey then took the case to the House of Lords, which confirmed the appeals court's ruling. The news brought tremendous relief to the Hoovers, even as the Chang case dragged through the British courts.

Following the announcement of the Storey verdicts, Bert resumed his traveling on behalf of Bewick Moreing in mid-September. The three Hoovers, together with a nurse, boarded a ship bound for Australia. Lou carried five-week-old Herbert in a wicker laundry basket through which she had threaded a rope around the top to serve as handles. (Allan, too, would make his maiden voyage at the age of five weeks. By then, his older brother was a seasoned traveler: Herbert circumnavigated the globe twice by his first birthday.)

Bert's handling of the Rowe embezzlement burnished his reputation, and the final outcome of the Storey trial worked in Bert's favor. Bert had become an acknowledged expert in the world's mineral market through a combination of word-of-mouth and his well-placed articles in professional publications. His elevated professional status opened doors for Lou in social circles. She was introduced to Australia's governor general, Hallam, Lord Tennyson and his wife. Hallam was the son of Alfred, Lord Tennyson, the renowned poet. Lou was also invited to an "at home" held by the prime minister's wife, Mrs. Alfred Deakin. As a polite guest, Lou returned the invitations, and she organized dinner parties that not only helped Bert relax but also strengthened his career prospects. As Lou noted in a diary entry, Bert had become a valuable advisor sought out by "so many people whom we never heard of before—and a string of people always to see Bert."[10]

Lou's social life in Australia was as active as her life had been as a new bride in China. She deftly juggled her maternal responsibilities even as she built relationships that would enhance Bert's career. "Haunting curio shops and doing necessary shopping," reads one diary entry from those months. "Took the boy to fit him for a new bonnet, and he howled lustily—is always exhibiting his father's dislike for clothing.—Otherwise charming." She marked the "firsts": Boy put into short frocks. Baby turned over. Boy turned five months old and got his first tooth!"

World travel was routine for the Hoover family. In 1907, they traveled to Burma, Malaysia (then known as the Malay States), and Sri Lanka (formerly Ceylon), as well as to Australia and New Zealand. Burma made such an impression on Lou that she scribbled a lament to the country some thirty years later when she read of the bombing it was experiencing during World War II. "Bombs over Burma. That beautiful peaceful country utterly unconnected with the fundamental or superficial. . . . And there are bombs hailing upon the Burmese—those simple, charming, cheerful people, living their lives, innocent of complication, in the problems activating the fighting forces."[11]

Five years after the Rowe disaster, Bert realized his goal of selling his share of the Bewick Moreing partnership. He convinced Moreing that his continuous overwork on behalf of the company brought about ill health. For a man with Hoover's robust physical constitution, it is likely that Moreing saw through Bert's ruse. Bert had been hinting about an interest in selling out for several years, and he eventually wore down the senior partner. Bert sold his share to William J. Loring, his long-time associate from Stanford days. Then, in a brazen violation of the non-compete agreement he had just signed with Loring, Bert opened a mining consultancy in London in the same office building that housed his former employer.

The new freedom allowed Bert and Lou to spend more time on a joint project that she had devised in 1905. She was interested in translating an important Latin treatise on mining, *De Re Metallica.* Published in 1556, *De Re Metallica* was the work of the German scientist Georg Bauer, whose name was Latinized to Georgius Agricola ('Bauer' is German for farmer; 'Agricola' is Latin for the same). Agricola's treatise contained his observations on assaying and smelting ores, mine construction, and the refinement of metals. His understanding of mining was still relevant in the twentieth century—for those who could read his book.

One of the challenges associated with *De Re Metallica,* even for Latin scholars, was Agricola's use of technical terms that had never found their way into modern languages. There were also portions of the text where, in the absence of an appropriate Latin term, Agricola coined his own.

Lou and Bert were best equipped to bring the insights of *De Re Metallica* into the twentieth century, and they made an ideal team. Lou's gift for languages, her proficiency in Latin and German, and the skill she had honed over the years as Bert's editor, combined with Bert's extensive knowledge of mining operations, allowed the two to work through the difficult and sometimes obscure text to produce a manuscript that was recognized as a masterful translation; one still consulted in the twenty-first century.

The couple worked on the project for seven years. It strengthened their intimacy and made a valuable contribution to the world of mining and metallurgy. Their joint efforts evoked poignant memories for Bert when he paid a visit to Red House during a visit to England in 1938. At the time, he and Lou spent most of the year apart—she at her home in Palo Alto; he in a suite of apartments in the Waldorf Astoria Hotel in New York. The recollection of their togetherness during the collaboration was strong. Bert wrote Lou:

> I imagined again, sitting on the opposite side of the desk from you, with the manuscripts and the reference books of Agricola, piled between us, as we worked over the translation of De Re Metallica. Again I saw "Pete" [Herbert Jr.] at the little table in the corner, making marks and announcing that he was writing a book, too; and "Bub" [Allan] clambering into his mother's lap and demanding to know what the book said.[12]

The Hoovers self-published the work in 1912 with assistance of their friend, Edgar Rickard, publisher of the London-based *Mining Magazine*. The 1912 work emulated the book design of the original document. Three thousand copies were printed on heavy linen paper, and the edition contained the woodcuts found in the original edition. Each copy was bound in a vellum cover. Over half of the printed copies were given away to mining engineers and students. The Hoovers spent over $20,000 of their own money on the endeavor.[13]

One review lauded the translation as "a noteworthy monument of patient and intelligent scholarship and generous private expenditure, and is worthily dedicated to Professor John Caspar Branner, of Stanford University, under the inspiration of whose teaching it was conceived and executed."[14]

The Hoovers' English translation of the treatise caught the attention of the Mining and Metallurgical Society of America, which awarded its first gold medal to both Lou and Bert at its meeting in New York on March 9, 1914. Lou's acceptance speech is a delightful poke at the conventions of after-dinner speech-making. It contains a sly dig at Bert, whom, she said, "was the most unhappy and distracted-looking man" at the dinner of the Royal Geographical Gold Medal dinner, where he was recognized for the publication of a pamphlet on Agricola. "This man," Lou noted, "said he would rather go farthest north than face the audience" at the dinner. "Well, we [sic] said the Society of Mining and Metallurgy are not such taskmasters as that, they have seen fit in their folly to award us that wonderful medal."

One could hear vestiges of the young Lou at the end of her speech, her indefatigable joy, and her delicious, self-deprecating humor:

> I want to thank you personally for this beautiful thing and for all it means. And it means far more to me in one way than you can guess. It will rehabilitate me in the eyes of my family. I have a small boy who a few years ago began to measure the world in terms of cups and medals. And when at the

> age of six he won his gymnasium class's silver medal for the running high jump—at 2'7"—he came home with pleasant curiosity respecting the medals possessed by other members of the family. And father's and Mother's [sic] position has not been as assured as it should have been. This will help most materially in adjusting the desired balance in the family.
>
> So, in [Agricola's] name, and ours, and that of the small boy's in California, I thank you for this—and for all the untrue, but delightful things you have said about us this evening.[15]

De Re Metallica was the high point of Lou's brief career as a published author. Her highly descriptive observations of China never made it to publication as a book, falling victim to the couple's extensive travels and early-century lawsuits against Bewick Moreing for Bert's handling of matters with Chang Yen Mao and for accepting kickbacks in a scheme in Australia. Lou's research and writing about Cixi, the Dowager Empress of China who had been behind the Boxer Rebellion atrocities, appeared in the British periodical, the *Contemporary Review*, in 1909. Lou's biographical sketch of the seismologist John Milne appeared in the journal of The Seismological Society of America in 1912. Lou met Milne after the scientist had retired to the Isle of Wight, located on the southern coast of England. She wrote about his travels in Japan, where he pioneered work in seismometry and earthquake monitoring. John C. Branner had nominated Lou for membership in the society in 1911. She was elected two days later, and her membership made her eligible to submit articles to the society. Lou was the first woman to publish in the organization's professional journal.

Bert wrote a book that boosted his reputation in mining circles. *Principles of Mining: Valuation, Organization, and Administration—Copper, Gold, Lead, Silver, Tin, and Zinc* was published in 1909. Lou had been his copy editor, although Bert does not acknowledge her contribution in the work.

Lou became more active with women's organizations as the Hoovers' lifestyle change allowed them to spend extended periods of time in London. In 1908, she was nominated for membership in the Society of American Women in London (SAWL). Founded in 1899, SAWL's mission was to "lead to useful service, a center of our own, in the land of our sojourn." Like its American counterparts, the clubs that formed the General Federation of Women's Clubs, SAWL offered its expertise and advice on educational, social, philanthropic, economic, artistic, and literary subjects.[16] Members included Jennie Jerome, the wife of Lord Randolph Churchill and the mother of future prime minister, Winston Churchill; Consuelo Vanderbilt, wife of the Duke of Marlborough; and Alyssa Pearsall Smith, the first wife of philosopher Bertrand Russell, who was the daughter of a successful Philadelphia businessman.

Lou was immediately tapped to join the Education and Philanthropic Committee, which encompassed the heart of SAWL's mission. The philanthropic arm provided scholarships for study to needy students and offered financial help to widows and to those facing hardship, including those living in the Browning Settlement, a home for the poor. The committee provided an Easter Sunday dinner for East London's poor and held an annual tea to raise funds and collect toys for residents of Browning Settlement and children attending the Notting Hill Day Nursery.

The educational side of the committee arranged regular Salon Lectures and brought in notable names and debated some of the important topics of the times. The French-born Hilaire Belloc, who was a prolific English-speaking author, poet, and historian, spoke on the French Revolution. The committee heard speakers on China, a report on conditions in the Balkans, and the fight for women's suffrage in the United States.

Lou eventually became chair of the committee, and she hosted salon gatherings at the Red House. The organizational talents that had led her to form an Agassiz club in high school and the leadership skills that had made her popular among her friends at LA Normal and Stanford asserted themselves once more. SAWL gave Lou a space of her own. She did not have to think about how to entertain Bert or meet his demands, and she did not need to concern herself with sustaining relationships that could help Bert with his career. SAWL was the first time since her marriage where Lou could be simply Lou Henry Hoover.

SAWL leadership acknowledged Lou's organizational talents. In 1910, SAWL's president urged Lou to run for the office of first vice president. Lou agreed and was elected. She was re-elected in 1912. The position carried with it a seat on SAWL's executive committee, which set the organization's agenda, and it put Lou in line to assume the presidency of the club.

Lou reluctantly agreed to run for a third term as vice president in 1914.

On May 24, 1914, Lou received a cable that the society's president, Mrs. William Righter Comings, had resigned due to the death of her husband. Lou was now president of SAWL. Unforeseen world events would prove to make the presidency of SAWL more important than it had been since its founding. And it would also set the stage for the next quarter century of Lou's life.

CHAPTER 6

A World and a Marriage Transformed

By the end of March 1914, the Hoovers had returned to the Red House with the plan to remain in Britain through most of the summer and return to the United States in time to enroll the boys in school in California. Both Allan and Herbert had picked up British habits and traces of a British accent, and Lou and Bert decided it was time to have their sons immersed in American life. Cataclysmic world events upended those plans.

Europe was a political tinder box in 1914. Britain and Germany were locked in a fierce naval rivalry. France viewed Germany with distrust following its invasion and occupation during the Franco-Prussian War (1870–71). Russia eyed Germany as an untrustworthy neighbor on its eastern border. In short, three major powers viewed Germany as a menace to peace on the continent.

At the same time, the Hapsburg Empire of Austria-Hungary that dominated south-central Europe sought to expand its sphere of influence. In 1908, it annexed the Balkan nation of Bosnia and Herzegovina from the Ottoman Empire. The move angered citizens of the Balkan country, who had been anxious for home rule. Meanwhile, neighboring Serbia, which had ties with the Bosnian Slavic population, desired to draw Bosnia and Herzegovina into the Serbian sphere of influence.

On June 28, 1914, the Austro-Hungarian Archduke Franz Ferdinand, and his wife Sophie, Duchess of Hohenberg, traveled to the Bosnia-Herzegovina capital Sarajevo to inspect imperial troops. A large parade, which included the royal couple's unprotected car, wove its way through the city streets. Among the people lining those streets was a group of Bosnian Serb young men committed to the assassination of the heir to the imperial throne. One threw a bomb at the archduke's vehicle, which bounced off the car, leaving its occupants unharmed.

At a reception and luncheon in the Town Hall following the parade, the archduke brushed off the failed assassination attempt. After the festivities, the royal couple climbed back into their open vehicle to leave the city. The driver made a wrong turn and stopped to turn around. Gavrilo Princip, a nineteen-year-old member of the anarchic group seeking to assassinate Franz Ferdinand, seized the opportunity and murdered the archduke and his wife.

The assassination inflamed the tensions rippling throughout Europe. On July 24, the Austro-Hungarian government delivered a note to Serbia. It accused the Balkan nation of "abetting propaganda against the Monarchy, with tolerating apology for crime, and with . . . indirect responsibility for the assassination of Archduke Francis Ferdinand and the Duchess of Hohenberg." The note further alleged that Serbian officers and officials had provided the weapons used by the assassins and permitted the passage of the assassins from Serbia into Bosnia. The letter demanded that the Serbian government provide assurances to Austria-Hungary that it would no longer encourage and support anti-Austria-Hungary rhetoric. The Empire demanded the right to hold tribunals in Serbia to hold accountable those responsible for the assassination.[1]

The Serbian response was measured. Serbia desired to maintain cordial relations with Austria-Hungary but asserted that a foreign government could not hold tribunals on Serbian soil. Austria-Hungary replied that the Serbian response was unsatisfactory. The German and Russian governments attempted to mediate the dispute. Instead of seeking to work through a diplomatic solution, Austria-Hungary declared war on Serbia on July 28. Russia supported Serbia, and the tsar ordered his armies to mobilize. Hoping to stave off an invasion and war, British Foreign Secretary Sir Edwin Grey sent peace proposals to Germany and Russia on July 29, who forwarded them to Austria-Hungary. France and Italy supported the proposals, recommending a peaceful solution without an invasion.

On July 30, Germany began to mobilize for war. It ordered Russia to cease its mobilization, giving the tsar a twelve-hour time limit. Austria-Hungary invaded Serbia, and it declared war on Russia. On August 1, French President Raymond Poincaré ordered a mobilization of troops which he described as a precautionary measure. Although officially allied with Germany, Italy declared its neutrality.

On August 2, Germany ordered Russia and France to cease mobilization.

Without any formal declaration of war, Germany invaded France, Belgium, Luxembourg, and Switzerland. On August 3, Belgium and Luxembourg appealed to Britain, asking it to help preserve the smaller countries' neutrality. England gave Germany six hours to get out of Belgium and provide assurances to respect Belgian neutrality. Germany replied that it would not honor the request, and at seven p.m. on August 4, Britain declared war on Germany. The European continent plunged into what would become a brutal, four-year conflict that wiped out nearly an entire generation of men and re-made the map of Europe.

In response to the start of war, Britain extended a bank holiday, initially declared for August 1 through 3, until August 5 to forestall a run on cash reserves and to create policies related to foreign exchange practices, including how to honor notes drawn on banks in what were now enemy countries. With the banks closed, no one could access accounts or cash travelers' checks.

Shipping lines were in turmoil. One of the principal steamship lines that transported Americans across the Atlantic, the German-flag Hamburg Amerika line, ceased passenger operation. Middle—and upper-class Americans who traveled to Europe for the summer found themselves frantically attempting to locate other ways to return to the United States. American businessmen formed a Citizens' Committee and set up shop in the White Banqueting Room in the Savoy Hotel to assist their countrymen. The committee included Alfred Vanderbilt, a scion of the Vanderbilt family, and George T. Oliver, a US senator from Pennsylvania.

Word of their efforts reached Lou, and "[h]earing on Tuesday [two days after Britain entered the war] that this was one of the sights of London, I went to see it, and was surprised to find large numbers of distracted women among the inquirers. It was evident that many of them were in real distress. There was only one organization in London competent to deal with the emergency, so I asked the Executive Committee of the Society for American Women in London to hold a meeting at the Savoy first thing Wednesday morning."[2]

The executive committee agreed that SAWL had the resources to assist stranded women, and Lou set up shop in a corner of the Savoy's large ballroom with "one small table, the usual writing-desk supply of Savoy stationery, and the pleasant gold-backed chairs of the Savoy ballroom."[3]

American embassies across the continent directed US citizens to Great Britain, as it was the only available European port not controlled by Germany or its allies. London rapidly became a terminus for an estimated 125,000 Americans stranded across Europe. The changes wrought by the war's outbreak stretched the financial resources of teachers and students on holiday beyond their budgets. Americans employed by European firms had some of the direst needs, as their incomes had been terminated. "I gathered such cash as could be found amongst my business associates," Lou wrote in a report to US ambassador to Great Britain Walter Hines Page, "and securing some volunteers, opened an office at the [American] consulate, where small advances [from personal funds] were made with or without security, to tide people over until the banks were open four days later. I may mention here that pending more effective arrangements we advanced about $4,500 in small sums and that we have since received repayment of all this except about $250."[4]

In his memoirs, Bert writes that there was antagonism between the Citizens' Committee created by Oliver and Vanderbilt and the Committee of American Residents in London, a relief group that Bert formed. Once he had organized his own relief committee, Bert demanded that the Citizens' Committee merge with his group, which Vanderbilt and Oliver refused to do. Lou described SAWL's working relationship with the Vanderbilt-Oliver committee as complementary. In its roughly two months of operation, the Citizens' Committee acquired sufficient funding to assist Americans with purchasing return tickets. When Vanderbilt and Oliver were able to secure their passage to the United States, they ended their relief efforts and turned their remaining monies over to SAWL.

Lou and her committee members engaged in the day-to-day work of finding space on steamers and comforting distraught, stranded countrymen and—women. Those efforts included securing lodging, procuring railway tickets, and helping to cover living expenses for destitute Americans. Bert used his chairmanship of the Residents' Committee to establish connections that would open a door for him to aid the larger war effort.

Bert began to express his interest in moving into public service around 1910 in a conversation with Stanford president David Starr Jordan. Bert's career had made him a wealthy man. With economic security came the drive to do something more than earn money. Though he may have long since abandoned any formal association with his Friends upbringing, the lessons stuck. Bert desired to do something good for humankind. The war handed him that opportunity.

The Hoovers had been booked to sail for the United States on a German-flag ship, *Vaterland*, scheduled to depart on August 13. That ship was removed from service, as was the next one on which the Hoovers bought tickets, the *Aquitania*. They were finally able to secure berths aboard the *Lusitania*, a British-flagged ship, and Lou and the boys departed for California on October 3. Bert remained at the Red House to oversee his considerable business interests. He had ownership stakes in mines in Russia, South Africa, Australia, and Burma, all of which would be impacted by the war. The Russian mine alone was larger than the size of Belgium.[5]

Bert's decision to remain in Britain provided him with the public service opportunity he sought. That opportunity would alter the fabric of the Hoovers' marriage for the remainder of their days together.

Millard Shaler was a Kansas native and engineer based in Brussels as an employee of the Guggenheim Mining Company. When war broke out, Britain embargoed food shipments to enemy countries, including Belgium. A small country with limited farmland, Belgium imported nearly eighty-five percent of its total food supply. German troops had immediately confiscated available foodstuffs upon its invasion, leaving the Belgian population to fend for itself. In a few short weeks, the entire Belgian population faced starvation. By the end of the first month of the war, nearly thirty percent of the population lived on a diet of soup, bread, and potatoes.

The Germans had brutally invaded the tiny country. German troops killed the entire population, some 383 citizens, of the town of Tamines. In the university town of Louvain, the Germans shot the mayor, the university rector, and hundreds of civilians. Then, it ordered the remaining population of forty-two thousand to evacuate. The university library, which housed Gothic and Renaissance manuscripts, was torched. In all, some 1,100 buildings were destroyed in the one town alone. The Germans' atrocities suggested they would have no compunction about starving an entire nation.

A group of Brussels-based businessmen formed the Comité Central de Secours et d'Alimentation (Central Relief and Food Committee) and chose Shaler to travel to London to purchase food. Amazingly, the German occupiers permitted him to go.

The Belgian government in exile made £20,000 available for the first food purchases, and Shaler secured a commitment from the British government for an additional £100,000 worth of food, but Shaler hit a roadblock when he sought a way to export the food to Belgium. London would not guarantee that a ship would make it through the British blockade. A British official suggested that Shaler seek American authorization to designate the shipment with US provenance to ensure the ship's safe passage. (The United States, in the early years of the war, had declared neutrality.)

Shaler sought US Ambassador Page's assistance in securing the necessary paperwork from the United States. Page, unwilling to act unilaterally, wired the State Department, which responded that it wanted German approval to release the shipment. A ship laden with foodstuffs languished in a British port as the bureaucratic delays lengthened.

Although both his parents were Americans, Edgar Rickard had been born and reared in Belgium, where his father worked as an engineer. Edgar maintained close contacts with the expatriate engineering community in the small nation, and he was good friends with Shaler. Shaler turned to Edgar for help, and he, in turn, introduced Shaler to Bert. Upon hearing the details of Shaler's efforts, Bert contacted a friend at the London bureau of the Associated Press and launched a public relations campaign to motivate a response from the State Department. Washington remained unmoved.

In assessing the situation, Bert recognized that approaching the problem on a shipment-by-shipment basis was inefficient and ineffective. He created a proposal, which he presented to Ambassador Page, calling for an organized effort to feed Belgium's starving populace. At the same time, the members of the Comité Central met and decided to extend their operations throughout Belgium. It sought and received German agreement that they would not confiscate the food shipments designated for the Belgian population to feed the occupiers. The American ambassador to Belgium, Brand Whitlock, was dispatched to London to see what he could do to organize a comprehensive food relief effort.

Whitlock arrived to find that Page, Shaler, and Hoover already engaged in a similar conversation regarding relief. The men finalized the details of an organization known as the Commission for Relief in Belgium, or CRB, for short. With the necessary approvals in hand, Bert commenced ordering the first of many shipments of wheat through a broker connection in Chicago. He arranged shipping through an agent based in Rotterdam. British secretary of war Lord Horatio Kitchener assured that the blockade would be waived for food shipments to Belgium. The enormity of the project energized Bert. Lou would soon find herself immersed in the public relations and fundraising essential to the CRB's success.

The future of the CRB hinged on an outpouring of financial support from Americans who were, to date, not impacted by the war. In Bert's mind, the most effective tool to solicit that support was to generate massive publicity. He immediately enlisted Lou in the effort. She had barely gotten herself, Herbert, and Allan settled in a rented home in Palo Alto when Bert cabled:

> Over one million people on bread line in Belgium at present moment with supplies estimated to last from one to three weeks. While we are securing some supplies here for emergency purposes real situation cannot be met without direct exports from States and we shall require upwards of twenty thousand tons foodstuffs monthly. Can you interest . . . prominent San Franciscans to present shipload food from California . . . I can think of no greater contribution to this occasion of world's stress than a food ship from California and if possible one from Oregon and another from Washington. It might be pointed out that our Commission is largely Californian and that we should have support of our own state. Could also make some claim as to Oregon in my connection.[6]

Bert wanted Lou to return to London as quickly as possible. "It is the greatest work to which we could be devoted," he impressed upon her in another message.[7]

Lou successfully raised enough funds within a few short weeks from her contacts in California to fund a boatload of food designated for Belgium. Her letter to the Kansas governor requesting assistance with securing wheat shipments drew a quick response and resulted in a second shipload.[8]

Bert, however, was not satisfied with Lou's presence stateside, and he sent her a series of telegrams asking her to return and join him in London. She was angry at how Bert seemed to discount the value of her work regarding the CRB, and she was displeased at the thought of leaving her sons in California.

> You may think I am not busy building fences over here, but I just am. I believe it has been worth my coming, even if there were no boys in the

> problem. And the more this war goes on and the more I see the boys in California—the more glad I am I brought them over.
>
> I should have been worried beyond endurance if I had stayed in England with them—but I am sorry you think I am foolish![9]

Undaunted by his wife's anger, Bert, ignoring the dangers of trans-Atlantic crossings, continued to ask Lou to rejoin him in London. German submarines, the notorious *Untersee* Boats, or U-Boats, had begun to attack ships bringing food supplies to Britain in retaliation to the British blockade. (The Germans would eventually start a systematic series of attacks on civilian transport and war matériel shipping in international waters beginning in 1915.)

Lou prepared herself emotionally for the voyage. Scheduled to sail for Europe on the morning of November 25, she spent a sleepless night at the Gotham Hotel in New York writing letters that reflected her anguish at the forthcoming voyage.

Lou penned a heartfelt plea to Jackson E. Reynolds, in which she asked him to raise Herbert and Allan if she and Bert became casualties of the war. Reynolds had graduated with Bert in Stanford's Pioneer Class of 1896. He went on to get a law degree from Columbia University and took a position on its law faculty upon graduation. He was the general counsel for the Central Railroad of New Jersey when Lou asked him to become the guardian of her sons.[10]

"Dear Mr. Reynolds," Lou opened her letter, written on Stanford University letterhead. "I am doing the very inconsiderate thing of leaving you a present of my boys, if anything should 'happen' to Bert and me, that we could not go on assuming responsibility for them ourselves,—and of doing it without first asking your permission."

Lou's letter is one of rare frankness. She initially assures him that she is not asking him to provide a home and full-time parenting for Herbert and Allan. But as she moves through the letter, revealing the details of her thought process, it is clear that is exactly what she hopes Reynolds will agree to do. Reynolds, Lou explains, has the "right balance to make good men out of my boys, physically, intellectually, and in the yet higher things." She requests that he "direct their education and let them see enough of you to get your ideals of the world."

Lou explains why she thinks available relatives and friends, who might express an interest in assuming guardianship of her sons, are unsuitable. She would entrust the boys to her father, but he has not kept up with changes in education and would be too old to assume responsibility for two young boys. Bert's brother Theodore "is too much of a dreamer in some ways, and I disagree with his ideals in others." Lou does not want the boys to live with her mother or sister, Jean, who was now married. "The influence of those women, over long periods, I think would have a lot of negative tendencies I don't want the boys to acquire."

She saw her long-time friend Evelyn Wight Allan as impractical and observed she would give the boys "too much of the pampering some women give boys." Katherine Everts Jewett, a friend of Lou's and an educator like Evelyn, would be a good choice, but she had a strong interest in theater and was too busy with her many projects to take responsibility for rearing someone else's children.

After detailing her reasoning, Lou comes right out and makes her complete request: "I have not tried to lead up to suggesting you taking the boys yourself,—I have not tried to guard against it. If it happens that they could belong somewhat to you and your lovely wife, my soul would rest somewhere above you, in contentment."[11]

Lou then wrote a letter addressed to "kith or kin of Herbert Clark Hoover and of Lou Henry Hoover." In more diplomatic language than she had used in her letter to Reynolds, Lou outlined her rationale for asking Reynolds to serve as her sons' guardian and trustee. Stating that she was speaking for both herself and Bert, she wrote that the two of them "feel it would be better to have someone other than a relative undertake the task. And both from ability, education, ideals, and apparent lack of conflicting duties, [Reynolds] seems the most suitable of our many friends." She asked her family to honor her request, even if the letter itself was not a legally binding document. "And the boys themselves, our dear Herbert and Allan, will undertake with the direction of Mr. Reynolds, and the assistance of the many beloved relatives and friends, to become as brave, true honest boys and men as they were trying to be with their own father and mother."[12]

It was four o'clock on the morning of November 25, 1914, when Lou wrote her final letter, "[t]o be given to Herbert Hoover Jr. if his mother should die. And to Allan, when he is old enough."

The poignant letter opens with her sadness at leaving Herbert at the train station and her concerns that she may not return to him from this trip. She assures him that she expects to return to him and Allan. Without going into details about the possibility of a German attack on her ship, she acknowledges the possibility that she will never see him again.

Lou describes what can best be defined as her theology. "There is a great power beyond us; that controls and guides us and all the affairs about us." But God, she tells Herbert, also gives us strength and power to do things. And, sometimes, when we do not feel strong enough, we can ask God to give us more strength. This, Lou told her son, is prayer. "And we can just ask God suddenly at any time—in school or out in the street or anywhere, for some extra strength to come and help us do something—and it is just as much a prayer as what we ask at night when we go to bed."

There is a part that "lives inside us now that we call the 'soul,'—so some people call the 'spirit'—the force or power part of us," Lou wrote Herbert Junior. "And that's what I want you to be perfectly sure about me. I know that if I should die, I can pray my soul to go over to my two dear little boys and to help and comfort their souls. Of course, you can't see it or hear it. But sometimes you will know I am there."

Lou ends her letter as if she is seeking her own reassurance that she will return to California to care for her sons. "And I will ask God not to have me go up in that place he has called Heaven until it is time for you to come, too." She finishes by telling Herbert how much she loves him and how she believes that her love and desire to be back to care for him will happen because of how strongly she wants that for herself and her sons.[13]

Taken together, the three letters written in the midnight hours for November 24–25 are one of the only instances where Lou expresses fear bordering on despair. When she acknowledged the possibility of being killed during the Boxer Rebellion, she recounted the details with a cool reserve and a touch of humor. She never described being fearful when she traveled the Australian outback. Even when she experienced rough seas during her innumerable voyages, she wrote about the inconvenience, but she never suggested that she had reason to fear the ship going down.

The war generated a different set of emotions. One wonders if Bert considered the possibility that Lou's life could be lost at sea, even as he sent her telegram after telegram imploring her to return to London to assist him with the launch of the CRB. He had lost both of his parents by the time he was the age of his son Herbert. Yet, ambition and drive overrode Bert's paternal instincts, and he insisted that his wife override her maternal ones.

Lou's belief that she was abandoning her sons shifted the dynamic between her and Bert. When the boys were younger, Lou frequently left them in the care of a hired nurse or nanny while she traveled with Bert to inspect mines or attended dinners and events that could promote his career. What is clear from Lou's letters on the night before she sailed is that she had begun to bond with her sons now that they were older and were less "children" and more "young people." Bert had asked her to choose between him and them. It was not a fair request.

Lou resumed her role as the support pillar for Bert's work. She kept the doors of the Red House open for people day and night and always had a meal to offer or a spare bed if needed. She juggled the demands of the relief effort while trying to manage affairs and care for the boys while they were across the ocean in California. Bert eventually acknowledged Lou's sacrifice on behalf of the Belgian relief effort in a short, hand-written paragraph penned in 1960, sixteen years after her death and four years before his own. Lou, Bert acknowledged, was an integral part of an intense effort to save an entire nation. One wonders if he had voiced those thoughts to his wife at any point in their years together.

The CRB established a US-based office at 71 Broadway in New York City and organized state chapters across the United States. State executive committees and depots where donors could bring food existed in all forty-eight states (Alaska and Hawaii did not enter the Union until 1959). The CRB's Women's Division connected with the American Women's Club chapters and the Women's Section of the National Conference on Catholic Charities. Society women found it fashionable to engage with assisting in the Belgian relief effort. Such notable women as the author and New York hostess Edith Wharton and San Francisco socialite Alma Spreckels became involved in raising funds. Bert's name is listed as the chairman of the CRB. Lou, who worked assiduously behind the scenes, is not listed in the masthead for the Women's Division.

Lou crisscrossed the dangerous Atlantic as a one-woman PR machine for the CRB. Her gift of observation and her flair for colorful descriptions made her ideal to go out on the stump to generate financial support for the organization. In a talk delivered in 1915, she carefully explained how the Belgians had come to suffer their plight. She graphically outlined the brutality of the German occupation and detailed how the economy was devastated because the Germans had taken over the rail system and confiscated manufacturing that would assist their war effort. Except for teachers and a handful of small business owners, the entire country was at an industrial standstill.

Lou evoked compassion and empathy in her talks as she shared the details of the food served to the Belgians: "One liter of soup, of a thick, rich consistency much appreciated by the people and very nutritious. It usually contains a large percentage of green vegetables, most useful in maintaining the health of a community, and a good quantity of potatoes." The ration also included 300 grams of "excellent bread per day" and a weekly allotment of potatoes, coffee, tea, or cocoa, salt, and

> a small assortment of the different luxuries which America has sent over. The fact that these brave people were getting a sufficient supply of wholesome, clean food, instead of disease and machine-gun ammunition, and getting it without wounding their self-respect, through the ordinary paths of personal benevolence, filled me with a joyous thankfulness. Queerly enough, I find the effect on American men quite the reverse. They are frightfully depressed by it. My own husband will not visit a bread line unless compelled to, and—like most other men—has his eyes near full of tears before he leaves.[14]

Lou gave a talk in New York City shortly after the United States entered the war in April 1917. "See yourself in their place," Lou opened her address as she laid out the experiences of the Belgian people. "See Belgium as this country, as New York and the country immediately surrounding, see her stores and streets as your stores and streets, her people as yourselves, your family and your neighbors—the distances as your friends in Brooklyn, on Long Island, in the towns and on the farms upstate."

There is no commerce; there is no work. "Time hangs heavy on our hands. No cooking to do. . . . No sewing to do but to mend and to do over and over and over the same material we have worked on for years. Gardening in the spring and summer if we have or are near some little land. There is no music or theater which we will attend as the only ones permitted are those under German direction and patronized by them, and we would not be under the same roof with them, nor listen to what they have planned for us."

Lou's talks evoked not only sympathy but also donations. Although roughly three-fourths of its funds came through governments, the CRB pursued an active fundraising effort throughout the war. By the November 1918 Armistice, the Commission for the Relief in Belgium had handled nearly one billion dollars, with an overhead rate, according to the final accounting report, of less than one percent. Following the war's end, the CRB was rolled into the American Relief Administration (ARA), which continued to assist Belgium and other war-torn nations in a postwar recovery.[15]

The CRB was Bert's organization, and it bore all the imprints of his management style. The official history of the CRB described the organization as a "piratical state organized for benevolence." It operated with a high level of fiscal independence, even though national governments were the source of over seventy-five percent of its monies. (After the United States' entry into the war and Bert's appointment as Food Administrator in the Wilson Administration, the bulk of the funding came as a direct appropriation from Congress.) The CRB arranged for pricing, negotiated its own treaties, and secured special passports to travel behind enemy lines.[16] Bert's vision and his efforts saved an entire nation. Nine million Belgian and French citizens behind enemy lines received two nutritious meals daily during the conflict.

At the same time she was raising funds for the CRB, Lou continued to serve as the president of SAWL and as a board member of the newly created American Women's War Relief Fund (AWWRF), where she was honorary secretary and treasurer of the Economic Committee. The War Relief Fund was an adjunct to SAWL. Members of the executive board were Americans who had married into royalty or were married to or were the daughters of famous men. The Fund's president was Lady Paget, née Minnie Stevens, who was the heiress of New York hotelier Paran Stevens and married to Sir Arthur Paget. The Duchess of Marlborough was the Chairman. Lady Randolph Churchill was a member of the Executive Committee. Mrs. John Jacob Astor was vice president. Lou served alongside Ruth Bryan Owen on the Economic Committee. Owen was the daughter of William Jennings Bryan and married to Reginald Owen, an officer in the Royal British Engineers. She would serve in Congress for two terms, from 1929 to 1933, when Franklin

Delano Roosevelt named her the first woman ambassador and appointed her to Denmark.

The AWWRF focused on three areas. It founded a hospital to treat wounded soldiers, purchased an ambulance ship to transport wounded soldiers across the English Channel, and engaged in economic relief work by employing the wives and mothers of the men fighting the war.

Lou astutely analyzed the employment conditions in Great Britain as a result of the war. While there was virtually no unemployment in male-dominated industries, Lou estimated that unemployment for women was more than one hundred percent greater than the year before the war began. It was expected that the unemployment rate for women would continue to increase since most of them were engaged in trades not critical to the war effort. However, most of these women were the sole breadwinners for their families, and they needed employment.

The Economic Relief Committee sought to fill the gap created by the war. "I belong to two committees who are relieving distress in England by running establishments that we call factories for the employment of women who have been thrown out of their work by the war," Lou explained in a speech to an unidentified group. "One employs nearly one hundred of them, making sewn garments; at first, garments for the equipment of the American Women's Red Cross Hospital [another arm of the AWWRF]; after that, the factory took orders from any of the friends of the members of its committee for garments for charitable distribution whether for the Red Cross hospitals or for destitute women and children. The support for this has been adequate to keep these hundred women engaged for the next three months on these orders."[17]

The motivation behind the effort was to maintain a woman's dignity by providing her an opportunity to earn a living. The trade union set the wage of ten shillings for forty hours of work a week. It was considered a living wage for one woman with one child. The Economic Committee supplemented the wage of women with more than one child. The workers received dinner (the largest meal was served at noon) and tea daily.

The Economic Committee also set up a knitting factory, which employed thirty women at the time of Lou's address. The goal was to double the number of employees as more support was received for the enterprise.

The Committee eventually opened three factories in Woolwich, St. Pancras, and Bethnal Green. All were well-lit, warm, and well-ventilated—a significant departure from the typically dark, dirty, cold, damp, and dangerous factories of the era. What also made the Committee's work remarkable was Lou's acknowledgment of the need for childcare. Lou noted that the employees' children were either enrolled in school or a crèche (daycare). The Committee planned to establish its own crèches for its employees.

Lou believed in the dignity of work versus the ignominy of a handout. Earning an income, however small, boosted a person's morale and sense of self-worth. This view summed up the driving philosophy behind the factories: "[The women] will work for a wage which gives them a bare living and, economically, it is much better to give them this sum as a wage which they can earn than it would be to put the same amount of money into gratuitous distribution of food, fuel, and clothing for them."[18] Lou would never waver from her belief in the dignity of work over a handout, even as Americans struggled to find employment following the onset of what became the Great Depression.

Lou resigned her position as honorary treasurer of the AWWRF in May 1915 when she returned to California to tend to her sons. "I find that it is quite necessary for me to go to California to be absent some weeks," she wrote to "My dear Duchess [of Marlborough]. . . . The length of the time really depends on the course of the War and the movements of my husband." She assured the duchess that work was proceeding well in the factory workrooms and that SAWL's special committees "seem to be doing excellent work." Lou shared the details of SAWL's intention of establishing a maternity home in Belgium once the shelling there had abated. She planned to ask Mrs. Walter Burns to chair the committee overseeing the home's establishment. "I thought this choice would meet with your approval. She seems very practical and has had quite a little experience with the Paignton Hospital."[19]

At the same time that Lou worked on relief efforts in and around London, she became involved in the CRB's efforts to find markets for Belgian lace. Flanders is traditionally considered the region where Belgian lace-making began as a fine art and an enterprise in the sixteenth century. Flemish lace was bobbin lace, a technique that could use up to 1,200 different threads wound on spools, or bobbins, woven into delicate patterns. Women were traditionally the lace makers, and as is typical of female-dominated industries, the pay was lower than for men engaged in equally demanding work. In 1911, before the start of the war, Queen Elizabeth of Belgium recognized the value of her nation's lace makers. She approved the work of a group of royal women who expressed a desire to protect lace craftswomen and their livelihoods. *Amies de la Dentelle*, the Friends of Lace, was formed, and the organization assumed responsibility for improving Belgium's lace schools, their method of teaching, and their rate of pay. The Friends' leverage was their patronage: Schools that improved their teaching methods and working conditions could count on members of Friends of Lace to buy their work and refer other customers.

When Germany invaded Belgium in 1914, the Friends of Lace created an emergency committee, the Brussels Lace Committee, and named the wife of the American ambassador, Ella Brainerd Whitlock, as the honorary chairman. Many of the lace dealers initially refused to work with the committee, but after the committee was recognized by the CRB, together with a gift of $25,000 from the United States, the dealers cooperated.

The four Belgian women who directed the relief work were a countess who was a lady-in-waiting to the Belgian queen; an American-born woman who had married a Belgian noble; and two other prominent, untitled Belgian women.[20] The Germans imposed restrictions across the lace-making regions in efforts to shut down the industry, but the women who headed the Lace Committee were undeterred. Through the auspices of the CRB, Bert negotiated an agreement that allowed the CRB to import the thread to Belgium and take out an equivalent amount of finished product to be sold among the Allied nations. Charlotte Kellogg, a friend of Lou's from Stanford days who chronicled the history of the lace-makers during the war, wrote that 45,000 women lace makers' names were on the Lace Committee's list.[21]

Lou wrote to her sister-in-law, Mildred: "I terribly wanted to see you before I went away on business. I am not seeing anybody for pleasure, so I must deny myself that, but I find the only time I've got are these unexpected minutes over an unexpected tea, so I am dictating to Miss Edwards, and making Abbie [Rickard] listen intelligently while I speak between bites of Miss Warren's round walnut cookies!!"

Lou asked Mildred to consider being a "chief advisor to a philanthropic lace business." She went on to explain: "There are 50,000 Belgian lace workers out of work. If any part of these women had work, their wages would buy just that much more food and make the charitable contributions of America and other countries go just so much further."

Five thousand [British] pounds worth of lace had already been purchased, with another ten thousand pounds approved on credit. The Lace Committee had secured dealers willing to handle the lace, and there was already inventory on hand in Belgium to be sold. The arrangement released the available lace in portions to prevent flooding the market at any one time. The dealers had agreed to handle the sales with no middlemen's profit, allowing all proceeds to go to the workers themselves. "Now," Lou urged Mildred, "the point is, how to get this sold in America!"[22]

Although Mildred agreed to the role of "chief advisor," Lou actively marketed the lace. She discussed with the Duchess of Marlborough the possibility of British women assisting in lace-making in the War Committee's factories. She explained to Millard Shaler that she was not going into the lace business herself, but she was keeping track of who was engaged in the work of selling the Belgian lace. As she told him, "Really, I fancy my chief function will be to act as forwarding agent by aid of the Commission!"[23]

The San Francisco *Bulletin* printed Lou's letter to Charlotte Kellogg about the project's success: "We are also supporting a Belgian lace movement. The well-to-do people in Belgium, who are doing so much to save their own situation, are taking up this cause of the lace workers. . . .So we are taking charge of a great quantity of lace to be sold in the United States by the commission [the CRB], or, rather, through a commission appointed by them. Every penny of the proceeds will go to the workers."[24]

Lou departed Great Britain at the end of May 1915 aboard the *St. Louis,* three weeks after the sinking of the *Lusitania* on May 7, 1915. The lost ship was the one that had taken Lou and her sons home following the outbreak of the war the previous year. The sunken ship carried personal loss. Lindon Bates Jr. had been aboard. He was the son of the director of the New York office for the CRB, Lindon Bates Sr., and the chair of the Women's Division, Josephine Bates. Like his parents, Lindon Junior was involved with the work of the CRB, and he was traveling on its behalf when the Germans torpedoed the liner.

Lindon Bates Sr. had an impressive career as an engineer. His work included designing the plan for the American building of the Panama Canal, which began in 1904, and he completed it shortly after the war began on August 15, 1914. He was also instrumental in raising the grade of the city of Galveston, Texas, after a devastating hurricane had destroyed it in 1900.

Lindon Bates Jr., a graduate of Yale University, was involved with his father in their company, the Bates Engineering Company. He was also an author of several books that reflected the years of travel he had experienced during his upbringing and in pursuit of his career.

When news of the *Lusitania*'s fate reached England, Bert reached out to his network of contacts to learn whether or not the younger Bates had survived. Reports were that he had given his life-saving belt to a woman passenger and, as a result of his selflessness, had lost his life. Bates's body eventually washed ashore in Ireland at the end of July.[25]

Lou's hasty departure from England, as noted in her resignation letter to the Duchess of Marlborough, may have been, in part, connected to young Bates's death. His memorial service was held on June 10, at New York's Fifth Avenue Presbyterian Church, three days after Lou had arrived in the United States, where she delivered a eulogy.

The New York *Tribune* described Lou's tribute to Lindon Bates Jr., as the "most impressive" of those delivered. In her remarks, Lou movingly described her pain at the loss of a young man who was looked up to as an older brother by her sons. Her eulogy captures a sense of the anxiety that Lou lived with over the dangers of transatlantic travel in wartime. And it reveals a hidden spirituality that is not generally attributed to her.

> Young Lindon I first knew as a schoolboy. . . . This boy was wonderfully blessed in the possession of that sunny, dauntless, tireless self—and of a Father and Mother who surrounded him, supplied him with encouragement, with the highest point of view into the larger things of life together with the fullest sympathies in the hearty, healthy, joyous round of lusty boyhood. . . .
>
> For women and for children he laid down his life and over his sacrifice we reach the sacred hands of maternity in benediction. Such death is not death; it is resurrection. Such bed is not a grave; it is immortality. On the altar of our adoption, we lay for him the Cross and Crown, the united symbol of Immortal Manhood: Greater love hath no man than this, that a man lay down his life for his friends.[26]

Prior to the death of Lindon Junior, the relationship between the senior Bates and Bert had grown tense. The CRB had secured permanent financing by mid-1915, and Bates believed that all appeals for donations should stop.

Bert disagreed because the CRB's work had expanded from feeding Belgium to providing aid for those impoverished by the war. Bert wanted to modify the CRB's PR to promote its work of saving the destitute—a departure from the original message that the purpose of the CRB was to save a nation. The revised statement, as Bert saw it, legitimized the CRB's continued fundraising. Bates, who believed the CRB's fundraising apparatus was no longer necessary, refused to modify the PR, as requested by Bert.

In August, an article appeared in an issue of the *Saturday Evening Post,* which reported that the CRB had rapidly grown to become "one of the most efficient business machines of the world . . . due primarily to the genius of Lindon W. Bates."[27]

In response to the *Post* article, an anonymous piece appeared in the *Bellman,* a literary magazine published in Minneapolis. The content suggests Bert's influence, if not outright authorship. "Mr. Bates may be and doubtless is 'eminent among the civil engineers of the world,' " the article noted, "but it was the genius of his superior in the commission, who gave him his appointment, Herbert C. Hoover, that made the Commission for Relief in Belgium what it is, and Mr. Bates's part in it was both subordinate and comparatively insignificant."[28]

Bates, angered by the article and propelled by his disagreement with Bert over the CRB's mission, traveled to Washington with a file of personal correspondence and CRB documents related to Bert's oversight of the organization. Bates notified the US State Department and the US Department of Justice that Bert violated the Logan Act. The act forbids a United States citizen from dealing directly with a foreign government without appropriate authority. Bert had, in fact, violated the act.

CRB committee members in the New York office urged Bert to do something about Bates. Bert boarded the *St. Paul* and arrived in New York on October 24. Just three days before he departed England, Bert had cabled Lou that he had no plans to come to America. Now, she received a telegram that read: "Developments make it absolutely necessary for me proceed New York. Expect leave here Sixteenth . . . Do not wish anyone to know of journey as do not wish to be bothered exterior interest. Expect remain one week."[29]

Lou ignored Bert's wish "not . . . to be bothered." The boys had not seen their father in over a year. She boarded a train to New York with them in the hope of spending time together as an intact family. Lou arrived to find Bert involved in day-and-night negotiations regarding his reputation, the work of the CRB, and his iron-clad grip on its management. He then traveled to Washington to meet with members of Congress and with Colonel Edward House, an advisor to President Wilson.

For Lou and the boys, the trip was a domestic failure. "New York was such a jumble. [Bert] spent his entire time on Belgium Commission business. I scarcely saw him, and never had time for a word or any other subject. The hotel sitting-room always had 3 or 4 men there discussing that."[30] Lou was careful to keep any knowledge she had about Bert's fight to retain his position in the CRB out of her written correspondence.

Senator Henry Cabot Lodge, an influential member of the Senate Foreign Relations Committee, wrote the State Department that he believed that Bert had violated the Logan Act. Word circulated in Washington that he should consider stepping down from the CRB. Bert met with State Department officials, members of Congress, and the House. The State Department requested that Bert write a defense of his activities. He described the work of the CRB as similar to that of other non-combatant organizations, such as the Red Cross. The CRB was a "bright spot in the war, a bright spot that counterbalanced the criticisms that America was only interested in profiting from the war."[31]

Bert's explanation satisfied Washington officials, but there were suggestions that it would be best if he stepped down from his leadership role. He returned to New York, determined to solidify support for his position. He reorganized the operations of the New York office. At the same time, he circulated the idea that the grief-stricken Bates had become unhinged and had levied the charges at Bert because he was unable to think clearly. It was a cruel and ruthless jab at a man who had been not only a friend and supporter of the CRB's work but who had suffered the loss of his namesake in the execution of that work.

The Bates incident was one of the rare times when Lou did not jump to Bert's defense and rationalize his behavior. Years later, when Lou wrote a quasi-memoir to her sons, she described the change that the war and work on the CRB had wrought in their father: "Can you remember that as a fun-making, fun-enjoying person he completely changed? Not that he became altogether solemn and serious, not that a quaint whimsicality does not persist and is highly entertaining,—but the old sparkling spontaneity is now only occasionally glimpsed far below the surface."[32]

The "fun-making, fun-enjoying person" had become single-minded. Bert drove himself hard in the world he now occupied—a world that mixed public service and philanthropy cloaked in the horrors of war. He shared that world primarily with men who, like Bert, had been successful professionally and financially and felt obligated to do more. They responded with alacrity to Bert's leadership, called him "Chief," and ceded command to him. The close partnership that had been the underlying dynamic in the Hoovers' marriage before the war faded away.

"For many years after the spring of 1899 I was so very intimately associated with him that I can say almost without exception he carried on no mining or business enterprises or negotiations that I did not know practically all the details of," Lou told her sons in that same set of recollections.[33] With the onset of war, Lou and Bert's relationship shifted. The partnership that had produced *De Re Metallica* was a thing of the past.

CHAPTER 7

A New Life's Purpose

During Lou's six months in Europe, eight-year-old Allan lived with his grandparents in Monterey, while twelve-year-old Herbert lived with Birge and Grace Clark in Palo Alto. Birge was an art and architecture professor at Stanford who would eventually work with Lou on designing and constructing her house on San Juan Hill in Palo Alto.

"Herbert often wishes, (as the rest of us do), that you were here," Grace wrote Lou in late April 1915. "He keeps himself so busy that he is happy. . . . Herbert and I had a good visit here by ourselves Tuesday, and he knows you want to see him just as bad as he wants to see you. He is a splendid, brave boy, and we love him and are proud of him."[1]

Unwilling to be separated, again, from her children, Lou brought them along when she sailed to London in December 1915. She returned to the Red House to nurse an ailing Bert, who was suffering from severe headaches and experiencing chronic ear infections. Consumed by the work of the CRB, he was aloof and distant. The toll of the responsibility was best expressed by a sign on the mantle of the CRB's London offices: "THIS CANNOT GO ON FOREVER."[2] Lou brought a lightness of spirit and an underlying optimism to what had been a gloomy home in her absence.

Red House served as a combination of Hoover residence and hotel for CRB associates. Abbie and Edgar Rickard and their two girls had a permanent suite of rooms there. Advisors and businessmen came through the door day and night. Lou welcomed each one warmly, fed them, and provided a place to sleep when needed. She trained the boys to welcome every stranger who knocked on the door. The family lived through the Zeppelin bombing of London, including the night Herbert and Allan climbed a ladder to a trap door in the attic leading to the roof—and sat there watching the bombing. It was only after frantically searching the house that Lou and Bert thought to check the roof. There, they found their sons and sat atop the house with them through the air raid.

Neither Bert nor Lou was adventurous enough to continue watching bombs over London with the boys. They decided that it was safer if Lou returned to the States with them. The three departed London in January 1917, with no immediate plans to return to Britain. Four months later, the United States entered the war, and Washington would become Bert's new base of operation.

Woodrow Wilson had taken the oath of office for his second term on March 4, 1917. Wilson had campaigned on the slogan, "He kept us out of war," but by the time of his inauguration, it was all but given in private circles that the United States would enter the European conflict.

The British had intercepted a telegram on January 19, 1917, sent from the German Secretary of State for Foreign Affairs Arthur Zimmermann to the German ambassador to Mexico, Heinrich von Eckardt. To prevent the Germans from discovering that their codes had been broken, the British delayed sharing the decrypted message with the United States until the end of February. Zimmermann's telegram revealed Germany's intention to resume unrestricted submarine warfare (i.e., attack unarmed vessels) while seeking to maintain US neutrality. However, if the Germans were unsuccessful in keeping America out of the war, they asked the Mexican government to ally with it. Germany would help Mexico reclaim territories ceded to the United States. "[M]ake war together, make peace together," was part of the message the German ambassador was to convey to the Mexican government.[3]

Attacks on unarmed vessels violated the *Sussex* Pledge, so-called because it was issued after the Germans had attacked the passenger ferry HMS *Sussex* that ran between Folkestone, England, and Dieppe, France. Following vigorous protests by the United States, the Kaiser's government promised in May 1916 that the German navy would stop torpedoing passenger ships. It would allow the crews of merchant ships that carried war matérial to exit their vessels before the Germans sunk them. The intercepted telegram revealed Germany's plans to reverse that commitment.

Wilson made the case for the United States to enter the war to a joint session of Congress, held on April 2, 1917. Congress voted for the declaration of war on April 6. The United States mobilized immediately.

The war footing affected every part of the American economy. The United

States had supplied its European allies with food, weapons, medical supplies, and vehicles from the conflict's start. Now, the nation further ramped up production in all sectors to clothe, feed, and arm its own military personnel, house them on foreign soil, and care for its wounded. The challenge was to continue to supply the Allied war effort while maintaining the standard of living at home.

Sufficient food for soldiers abroad and people at home became an immediate concern. The rich farmlands of France were significant battlefields. England had limited arable land. Spain and Italy were officially neutral, but it was an open secret that they were feeding both sides of the war. Once known as the breadbasket of Europe, the Ukrainian heartland was trapped inside the crumbling tsarist dynasty that would lead to the Bolshevik Revolution of October 1917.

Bert had talked with Edward House about his interest in a government position when he had been in Washington to resolve the Bates controversy. With the United States' entry into the war, Bert reached out to his government contacts. His initial opportunity to join the Wilson Administration was a limited one. The government asked Bert to chair the committee on food supply and prices of a newly established Council of National Defense. "We are all tremendously delighted here that Bert has had official recognition from Washington," Edgar Rickard cabled Lou, but Edgar had reservations about the importance of the assignment:

> I am afraid that I do not join with . . . others in thinking that Bert was wise in accepting the Chairmanship of food control. I was in Washington two weeks ago and saw [Hugh] Gibson and Secretary Lane, and I got the impression definitely in my mind that this food control business would not carry the authority with it that it should, and I cabled personally to Bert to this effect, but evidently he had more specific advice and thought that the warning was unnecessary, and it is quite on the cards that I am entirely mistaken in my views.[4]

What Edgar saw as a mere crack in the door, Bert interpreted as a sizeable gap. He assembled a team of men who would help him turn his bit part in the war drama into a major role. And, in Bert's preoccupation with his new position in Washington, it fell to Edgar to inform Lou of her husband's movements.

"My dear Lou Henry," Edgar wrote Lou:

> I returned on Wednesday morning from a six-day trip into Canada and found that no word had been sent you in regard to Bert's plans, as it was the general assumption here that he would probably be communicating with you direct. I have no doubt that this is the case, but fearing that you may not have full advice, I telegraphed you on Thursday. . . .
>
> I am telegraphing you to the effect that he is sailing on the *Philadelphia*, [Bert was still in London at the time] although we have no confirmation from him direct, this being taken from a telegram from [Vernon] Kellogg to his wife.[5]

Over the next few months, Edgar became the conduit by which Lou and Bert communicated. When Bert arrived in the United States on May 3, Edgar cabled Lou: "Bert arrived this morning safe and well." Lou corresponded with Edgar about the disposition of the furniture in the Red House, negotiations on a lease for a home in Washington, and the work Bert was doing to build the office of Food Administrator.

Edgar, and his wife Abbie, had become intimate friends with the Hoovers following the Rickards' arrival in London in 1910 when Edgar assumed ownership of *Mining Magazine*. In the small world of mining engineers, the Hoovers and Rickards had known of each other, and after the Rickards relocated to Great Britain, the four became inseparable friends.

They traveled together throughout Europe and Northern Africa in the years leading up to the war. (They had left their children at home with their nannies.) A combined pot of money called the "Seeing Cairo" fund, created by windfalls that came either to Bert or Edgar, paid for their trips. These were carefree excursions, free of the usual mix of sightseeing and Bert's business meetings that characterized Lou and Bert's journeys over the years. The four agreed on a general destination and avoided commitment to a specific itinerary. Instead, they randomly chose places to explore until it was time to return to London.

Edgar and Bert became joint owners in multiple businesses that included the Intercontinental Development Company, a holding company for a cotton farm in the San Joaquin Valley, the Penobscot Paper Company, and a rug company. They had an ownership interest in a realty firm in Duluth,

Minnesota, and in the publishing company of the Washington *Herald*. Edgar served as the financial secretary for the West Branch Corporation, a holding company that managed the Hoovers' assets.

Edgar was more than Lou's friend and the family's financial manager. He was her link in the communication chain to Bert and a rock of strength to Lou. It was from Edgar that Lou learned Bert's plans, details of back-office politics, and even, sometimes, Bert's thoughts. The correspondence between Lou and Edgar in the years between the CRB and the presidency reveals Edgar's respect and compassion for Lou. The steady flow of information Edgar provided about Bert's activities demonstrates Bert's ongoing failure to inform his wife of his plans. Lou, for her part, came to rely on Edgar as an emotionally steadying presence. Underneath Lou's extraordinary administrative competence and self-assurance lay the vestiges of the college student who lost a coat or tore a pocket or became forgetful when she was under stress. Edgar understood this, and he ably soothed Lou by stepping in when she was overwhelmed to help her find the lost article (once it was a fur coat) or to make the transition from one location to another under a tight schedule.

In his new role as chair of the food committee, Bert directed the CRB's massive public relations machine to create the perception in the public's mind that the food supply needed to be managed at the national level to ensure that no one went hungry. Within weeks, he convinced Wilson's key advisors that a cabinet-level office was essential for the task. Wilson agreed and asked Congress to establish the office of Food Administration and approve Bert as its administrator. It was, Wilson insisted, "absolutely necessary that unquestionable powers should be placed in [Hoover's] hands."[6] Congress agreed.

Critics labeled Bert a "food dictator," and he waged a successful public relations campaign to dispel that perception, even as he nationalized his food plan. "This administration [of food distribution] can largely be carried out through coordination and regulation of the existing legitimate distributive agencies supplemented by certain emergency bodies composed of representatives of the producers, distributors, and consumers," Bert assured a nervous public.[7] He emphasized volunteerism and cooperation without rationing. He urged homemakers to sign a pledge testifying to their food conservation. His call to action was so compelling that the Milwaukee *Journal*

Sentinel reported that 100 percent of the homes in Green Lake County and 80 percent of the homes in Milwaukee signed the pledge that read: "At table I'll not leave a scrap of food upon my plate. And I'll not eat between meals, but for supper time I'll wait."[8]

"Food Will Win the War" was the slogan cranked out by the public relations arm of Bert's new agency. At his urging, the nation signed on to wheatless Mondays, meatless Tuesdays, and porkless Saturdays.

Lou remained in California as Bert assumed his new duties as Food Administrator and assembled his staff, which included naming Edgar as his Assistant Administrator. Bert had agreed to give up his leadership of the CRB upon assuming his food administration duties, but, in fact, he continued to hold the reins of both organizations. The ever-faithful and equally energetic Edgar helped Bert juggle both roles.

Bert and his team of associates took up residence in a suite of rooms in Washington's Willard Hotel. Lou asked Edgar to see if he could lease the Charles Francis Adams house at a reasonable rent, and Bert signed the lease for the house in August. By early September, the Hoovers were still waiting for Adams's signature on the document. The uncertainty kept Lou in California with the boys, even as the new school year started.

Bert had taken the position of Food Administrator at no salary, but political life in Washington was costly. "We have had two delegations here of State Administrators," Edgar informed Lou in September, "and in each case, they have been entertained for lunch and dinner at the Chevy Chase Club, amounting to several hundred dollars. Besides this, the whole of the cost of operating the three jitneys is now charged personally to the house account, and I am trying to dig out bills to form an estimate, but you need not feel at all uncomfortable in regard to this matter."[9]

Despite the Hoovers' now considerable wealth, Lou was careful about how she spent money and conscientious about maintaining her personal and household accounts. One of her priorities was to build a family home on her property on San Juan Hill on the Stanford campus. Construction costs were estimated to be $50,000–$60,000, a considerable sum for an era when the average price of a home was $3,000. Lou hired Louis C. Mullgardt, a local architect, to draw up plans. Mullgardt, in a breach of confidence, leaked word of the commission and its projected cost.

Mullgardt failed to understand that his client's husband was in the middle of telling the nation to cut back and economize. Public backlash was swift, and Lou was angry that her privacy had been violated. In a scathing letter to the Stanford *Daily Palo Alto* editor, Lou demonstrated her efforts to manage Bert's public image. She responded to charges of unpatriotic behavior leveled at her husband and detailed her role in the planned house:

> Referring to your paper of April 4, I am inclined to take exception to the implied declaration credited to me as there has never been any such "denial brought about by the attacks made on my husband." Numerous friends have asked me about the rumored house on the campus, and they all get some version of the same story so that your representative must have taken his statement second or third hand from one of them.
>
> I do not think it makes the least difference to the patriotism of anyone in California, or any other part of the world, as to what kind of residence any official lives in, or what his manner of life is, as long as it is decent and honorable. And I should feel no necessity of making a public defense of my husband if he were building a two million dollar house, nor should I feel that that would in any way influence what was any soul's abstract idea of right and wrong patriotism.
>
> Just in answer to the question of many neighboring friends, I may say that Mr. Hoover has never considered building a house on campus; that I [sic] was going to build a cottage on my lot on San Juan Hill in the autumn of 1914, and as all of my friends know, was on my way back for that purpose when the war broke out. The many all-occupying events since that have prevented my giving more than an occasional passing thought to the subject when I have been on the campus, and the matter waits until one has time and inclination for such peaceful contemplation.[10]

Lou fired Mullgardt. She told people she did not like his proposed design, and she shelved the project. Rather than pursue construction on the lot, Lou purchased an existing home on the campus to serve as her California residence. She installed Carrie Goodhue, a sorority sister from Stanford who had served as a sometimes nanny to the boys in England, to serve as caretaker in exchange for room and board.

Lou and the boys settled into the Adams home at 1701 Massachusetts Avenue in the fall of 1917. She enrolled Herbert and Allan in Sidwell Friends

School, a Quaker institution noted for its superior educational program and favored by Washington's upper class. Lou organized home life around Bert's round-the-clock schedule while looking for opportunities to engage in meaningful organizational work.

The time had come for the Hoovers to say goodbye to the Red House. Lou's friend, Alice Dickson, who was working on behalf of the Women's Division of The American Committee (a part of the CRB network of organizations), was tasked with the unenviable job of sorting, packing, and shipping fifteen years of accumulated possessions from the Hoovers' life in London. Dickson quickly discovered that Lou and Bert went their separate ways without communication, even in matters that concerned them both.

"You have asked me in a letter just received if I know Mr. Agnew [Bert's agent in London]," Dickson wrote Lou, "and evidently you do not know the financial arrangements which HCH made in true typical fashion. In about 20 words, he made the arrangements [by] saying, 'Will you do it? See Agnew, get money from him.' I don't think he actually said, 'don't bother me,' but I knew he meant it, so I scurried around to find who and where Mr. Agnew might be."[11]

Under separate instructions from Lou and Bert, Dickson meticulously packed and cataloged Lou's copies of the Hoovers' edition of *De Re Metallica,* Bert's engineering books, Lou's voluminous files of photos and newspaper articles, and a collection of old books. "According to Mr. Hoover's wishes, all the old books in his study are being very carefully packed in specially made cases, zinc lined and to be sealed. They are being wrapped according to British Museum methods. These cases are to be stored at Harrods." Dickson made a point of assuring Lou that she was taking special care of the picture albums and collections of clippings that Lou had accumulated.[12] Lou had a fondness for collecting and organizing newspaper clippings and political cartoons. Edgar Rickard saved and arranged in chronological order a year's worth of political cartoons about Bert and the Food Administration at Lou's request.[13]

Before long, Dickson found herself unwittingly caught between the conflicting wishes of the two Hoovers. Her unenviable situation became difficult because she was responsible for overseeing the Hoovers' funds to maintain the house and prepare it to be let, but Dickson had to go through Bert's men, Agnew and Poland, to have checks written.

"Dear Ladye of the Perfect Silence," Dickson wrote in a combination teasing and plaintive greeting, "I have just heard from Mrs. Allen that you are (or were) in Washington. That means busier than ever. Nevertheless, I do want about five monosyllabic words from you in reply to questions on a separate sheet. You know I never report anything to Mr. Hoover. I presume Mr. Agnew does as I report everything to him."[14]

In the absence of clear direction from Lou, Dickson "used 'my best judgment'. I fear you will be suggesting I use someone else's if my own best is so bad." Lou apparently had no qualms about Dickson's judgment. During the remainder of the year, Dickson oversaw the sale of unwanted furniture and kitchen equipment, the leasing of the property, the termination of many of Lou's club memberships, the renewal of appropriate insurance policies, and the careful packing and insuring of Lou's collection of Chinese porcelain, which included vases, plates, and ginger jars. In a letter dated December 1, 1917, Dickson notified Lou that she had let the Red House. The furniture and belongings had been placed in storage.

World War I changed the face of the nation's capital. Before the war, Washington catered to the male legislators, their male aides, and the men who served as clerks and secretaries in the cabinet departments. Now, women flocked to Washington to fill administrative positions vacated by men who had gone to war. Boarding houses had been designed to accommodate men, and there were few places where women could socialize in a safe, wholesome environment.

Lou saw a need for a club, similar in concept to the Society for American Women in London, where single women could socialize and relax in comfort and safety. In November, she asked Edgar to advance her funds to rent a house at 1710 I Street to serve as the Food Administration clubhouse for women working in that and other federal agencies. Abbie Rickard, Ethel Bagg, and another good friend from SAWL, Mrs. Ben Allen, agreed to serve on the club's board. By December, the club was in full swing. Six months later, Lou had rented two adjoining houses to serve as dining and residence halls. The club hosted musicales and lectures, as well as a weekly dance. Soldiers posted nearby were invited to attend.

The club's organization and operation reflected Lou's administrative style. She assumed fiduciary responsibility for the club's expenses, and she used her network of friends and associates to staff and oversee the day-to-day operation. Abbie, and another of Lou's friends, Adeline Fuller, managed the club's administrative functions and monitored its finances. Gladys McDougal, an instructor at Cornell University's Department of Home Economics, who Bert had hired, handled the dining room operation. Alida Henriques, a Rhode Island native and society fixture, became a trusted friend of Lou's over the years and organized the social activities. Following the Armistice signing on November 11, 1918, the Food Administration Club transformed into the Woman's City Club of Washington, with a new location on Jackson Place, near the White House. The club's tearoom was furnished from the contents of the Food Administration Club's dining room.[15]

Another opportunity for Lou resulted from a request by Juliette Gordon Low, founder of the Girl Scouts of America. She asked Lou to serve as acting District Commissioner in Washington. In 1915, the then–three-year-old organization was incorporated under the laws of its District of Columbia headquarters. The following year, to accommodate the women contributing the majority of the money to fund the Scouts, the organization moved its national headquarters from Washington to New York. Much of Washington's local leadership decamped with the move, and Low sought to replace those women.

Juliette Gordon Low, "Daisy" to her family, was born into a well-to-do family in Savannah, Georgia, in October 1860, six months before the start of the Civil War. Her mother descended from one of the founding families of Chicago, and her father was the son of the first president of the Central Railroad and Banking Company, which built the first railroad to connect the cotton fields in Georgia's interior with the port at Savannah.

There was little in Low's well-to-do upbringing to suggest that she would one day found an organization dedicated to girls' physical and emotional development. She enjoyed music and art and continued to paint and sculpt as an adult. She was a skilled sharpshooter who shot a tiger during a stay in India. In her late teens, Low sustained two consecutive injuries to her ears that led to deafness, which became complete as she aged.

In 1886, Daisy married William Mackay Low, the brother of a boarding school classmate. The couple divided their time between London and Savannah. The marriage was an unhappy one, and William Low abandoned Daisy in 1902 to live with his mistress. He died suddenly in 1905, while he and Daisy were in the middle of divorce proceedings. Low had bequeathed his estate to his mistress and provided a small allowance to Juliette. She challenged the will in court and won. Now a wealthy woman, Juliette Low continued to divide her time between her Savannah home and her estate in England.

In 1911, Juliette Gordon Low met Lord Robert Baden-Powell at a luncheon. Baden-Powell had been a career officer who served in the British Army from 1876 to 1910, with postings in India and Africa. He had written a military training manual called "Aids to Scouting," and the book had become popular with teachers. It was used by Sir William Smith, founder of the Boys' Brigade, as a training manual, and Smith recommended that Baden-Powell rewrite his book to appeal to a younger readership.

Baden-Powell took up Smith's suggestion, and he revised the text. In 1907, Baden-Powell held a camp for twenty-two boys from mixed backgrounds to test out his ideas on youths. The camp's success led to the publication of the revised book in 1908 as a six-installment article series. Boys gravitated to the ideas in the book and spontaneously formed groups to implement Baden-Powell's ideas. Boy Scouts grew from this grassroots beginning. At the urging of King Edward VII, Baden-Powell resigned his Army commission in 1910 and devoted his time to promoting Scouting.

The idea of scouting energized Daisy Low. "I've got something for the girls of Savannah, and all of America, and all the world, and we're going to start it tonight!" she told a cousin.[16]

Daisy organized her first troop in Savannah in March 1912. As with the one Baden-Powell had founded in England, she was determined that her organization would offer leadership skills and opportunities for personal development to all girls.

Until her encounter with Baden-Powell, Daisy had a history of enthusiastically embracing new projects, then losing interest rapidly and dropping them. Girl Scouts was different; Low had discovered her life's work. As well, of all the organizations that Lou Henry Hoover led through her life, Girl Scouts would represent her life's work in many respects.

Although their upbringing could not have been more different, Lou Henry Hoover and Juliette Gordon Low shared remarkably similar temperaments. Both were natural-born leaders and gifted organizers. They had a way of charming people into doing things for them. Both were raised in an era when women built networks of friends and acquaintances, whom they would later call upon to support their causes. Neither allowed conventional expectations of women to limit their vision, even though they spent their lifetimes struggling against those very expectations.

The ethos of the Girl Scouts reflected that struggle. In its early existence, the Girl Scouts straddled the line between promoting domesticity and encouraging independence and self-sufficiency. It was the same dualism that Lou managed in her own life.

When Daisy first approached her, Lou felt that she was too busy with her work for the CRB to take on responsibility as commissioner for the District, so she turned to a friend she had met by accident—literally. Lou and Washington socialite Henrietta Bates Brooke became acquainted when their vehicles collided in a minor wreck in Washington. Brooke's name came to mind as the perfect person to serve as the new commissioner. Lou went to visit Brooke at her home, where she was suffering from an attack of appendicitis. Lou was at her most persuasive self. "Being in no physical condition to deny any request, [Mrs. Hoover] quickly persuaded me to build a council, so when I got well, I had that to do," Brooke wrote in her memoir.[17]

Brooke served as commissioner through 1917, when Daisy once again approached Lou about taking the position. This time, Lou accepted. She hired Ruth Sampson, a recent Stanford graduate, to help her reorganize the Washington Scouting organization. Under Lou's guidance, Sampson recruited women to serve on the local board of directors and troop leaders. Sampson's employment would be the start in a steady stream of recently graduated Stanford women whom Lou hired to assist her in Washington. In addition to a salary, Lou covered room and board. Many of the women stayed at the Hoover home. Today we would call Lou's efforts "mentoring": The women gained employment experience, a chance to start a career, and access to a list of valuable and influential contacts.

Shortly after Lou agreed to become involved with the Girl Scouts, Daisy asked Lou if she would be willing to serve as a vice president of the national organization. Lou accepted the invitation, with the understanding that she would be dividing her time between Washington and California. "We all wanted you so very much," Daisy wrote Lou, thanking her for agreeing to join the Girl Scouts' board, "and it will encourage us to have your name and your sympathy. . . .It don't [sic] matter when you return to California. You see, the vice presidents represent the four corners of the country, but they do not represent in work [sic] any district or locality because they are national officers and their connection is with National Headquarters."[18] Lou was elected second vice president of the national organization at its December meeting. First Lady Edith Wilson agreed to serve as honorary president, creating a tradition that continues through today.

The Girl Scouts attracted college-educated women into all levels of leadership. The donors and executive board represented some of America's wealthier women who saw an opportunity to promote independence in young women. Many early local troop leaders were young women graduates from elite women's colleges such as Wellesley and Vassar. If still unmarried and unemployed, parents expected their daughters to move back home, just as Lou had done upon her graduation from Stanford. Involvement in Scouting gave these women an acceptable outlet to build relationships and hone organizational skills.

The United States' involvement in the war helped fuel Scouting's rising popularity. Reports from Army training camps lamented the poor physical condition of many of the draftees, spurring a move to encourage better fitness. With its focus on self-reliance and outdoor activities, Scouting offered a way for girls to be a part of the war effort. Membership nearly tripled between 1917 to 1918, jumping from 12,812 girls to 34,081.[19]

Lou promoted Bert's agenda as Food Administrator through her work with the scouts. She spoke at local meetings and encouraged girls to plant war gardens in their backyards. Scouts from other parts of the country were asked to stop by the District's headquarters when they traveled to Washington to register and to get information to help them establish war gardens at home. A story in the Washington *Star,* titled "Mr. Hoover's Own War Garden," included a photo of Lou supervising the scouts as they cultivated the rows and examined the Hoovers' backyard corn crop.

Lou once again took to the stump on behalf of Bert's work. She traveled the country to promote "Hooverizing," a new verb in Americans' lexicon that symbolized modifying diets to reduce the danger of food shortages and reducing food waste. "Hoover Domestic Menage is thoroughly Hooverized," read an article title in the Washington *Evening Star*.

> In all the land, no housewife follows more closely the rulings of the United States Food Administration than does Mrs. Hoover, wife of the food ad-

> ministrator, with the cooperation of her famous colored cook. This cook, who is well known to the most exclusive circles of Washington, was one of the first converts to the conservation of food and one of the most ardent.[20]

The public was assured that Bert had given up his morning bacon, soups were vegetarian only, sugar rarely if ever, used, and vegetable oil replaced lard and butter. Giving up sugar was "Mrs. Hoover's greatest self-denial." She later told an interviewer, "I was the trial goat. . . .They tried everything on me first. Then, if I bore up under the experiment, they tried it on the rest of America."[21]

Lou's social activities merited mention on the society pages. She hosted Victor Horta, a Belgian architect and designer and one of the founders of the Art Nouveau movement, at her home as a benefit for Belgian refugee children. She organized a campaign among her society friends to sell forget-me-nots on the streets of Washington, DC, on behalf of Belgian children. "Mrs. Vanderbilt Sells Flowers on Avenue," announced the headline of the March 18, Washington *Times*. This Mrs. Vanderbilt, the widow of George Vanderbilt, the builder of Biltmore House, in Asheville, North Carolina, was part of the brigade of "cabinet wives and society women" organized by Lou.[22]

The wedding of Lou's long-time friend Ethel Bagg to State Department diplomat Arthur Bullard was an occasion for a profile on Lou in the Washington *Herald*, the paper in which Bert held an ownership interest. Lou hosted the wedding in August at her summer residence, "Into-the-Woods," located in a suburban section of Washington. "That is the sort of thing Mrs. Hoover is always doing," noted the *Herald*'s society reporter, E. C. Drum-Hunt. "[T]here is not likely to be any entertaining of 'the smart set,' . . . but I fancy there will be a good many pleasant little parties for the young women whom war work has brought to Washington from all parts of the country, especially those who are employed in the Food Administration, whom Mrs. Hoover regards as her particular charge." The Girl Scouts, noted Drum-Hunt, had been entertained at "Into-the-Woods" the previous week.[23]

Lou was portrayed as an attentive wife and mother rather than emphasizing her prodigious organizational skills and financial acumen. "When Mr. Hoover is at home, she devotes herself to making home as restful a place for him as possible—shielding and sheltering him from outsiders and making 'home' veritably a haven or refuge for an overworked man who is carrying a very heavy burden of responsibility." When he is not a home, Lou's attention is turned to her sons and to "the lonely young people whom the Kaiser's vaulting ambition has brought to Washington."[24]

In truth, the couple led separate, parallel lives. "I was not with him [Bert] very much," Lou told a newspaper reporter in a 1921 interview. "I commuted between California, where we lived, and Washington, where he was stationed, and I could have done exactly as I pleased."[25]

CHAPTER 8

Time of Transition

By the end of August 1918, German U-boat attacks in the Atlantic shipping lanes had all but ceased. The United States Army decided that it was safe enough to begin sending its wounded soldiers home. An official with the Washington office of the American Red Cross contacted Lou and asked her if she would create a temporary organization that would arrange for the soldiers to be accompanied from the ships to their hometowns.

The Red Cross created the position of Associate Director of the Bureau of Canteen Service for Lou in August 1918. She oversaw the recruitment of the volunteers, and she drafted and edited the manuals that they and troop commanders were to use. The volunteers did their best to make the men comfortable as they traveled home by train. They served meals and snacks and distributed "books, magazines, games, postcards, flowers, and such available luxuries in the way of fruit, sweets, etc., as is wise for the patients."[1]

Every organization that Lou worked with depended upon the commitment and skill of its volunteers. Lou had experience working with a variety of personalities, and her innate diplomacy enabled her to soothe egos and calm troubled workers. The Red Cross presented a new challenge. It was difficult to find qualified volunteers to accompany the soldiers. Transporting the most serious hospital cases on trains that made multiple stops along their routes posed health risks. Lou's biggest problem was dealing with inexperienced officers who had risen rapidly through the ranks due to the war, but who had no true leadership abilities.

Most of the difficulties, Lou wrote to the Red Cross, were "due to the faulty functioning of . . . young men of mediocre ability and no experience in the problems they suddenly have to face, and with a lack of imagination."[2]

Lou resigned, at the end of November, shortly after the Armistice had been signed. "Perhaps it will be best for me to submit in writing my idea of a practical scheme of cooperation of the Red Cross with your Department in helping to care for the wounded and invalids in transit," she wrote with her typical graciousness in her resignation letter to Surgeon General Winford H. Smith.[3] In reality, Lou had lost patience with people who thought they knew all the answers when they, in fact, did not even know the right questions.

On October 3, 1918, the German imperial chancellor notified President Wilson of a desire to open negotiations to end the war. The backchannel diplomacy was so secretive that days before the end of the war, the Allied Forces' chief purchasing agent, Charles Gates Dawes, informed General John Pershing that food, war materiel, and hay for the livestock would run out in a few short weeks unless a new source of supplies could be found. The war raged until the last minutes before the Allies and Central Powers signed the Armistice on November 11, 1918, at 8:00 a.m. Paris time.

The absence of gunfire brought home the horrible devastation wrought on agriculture by the fighting. Europe had struggled for four years to feed its people, and winter would soon set in. Now, faced with surpluses, Dawes sold flour to Italy and arranged for the sale of $3 million worth of food to Belgium. His plans to sell additional surplus foodstuffs were stopped when Dawes received a cable from Washington: Herbert Hoover would oversee the distribution of food in the army's possession.

President Wilson designated Bert as a special representative charged with the responsibility for relief and economic rehabilitation and appointed him to the United States' peace delegation. Bert interpreted his loosely configured role as providing him with wide latitude to define the job as he saw fit. In his customary fashion, Bert inserted himself into a vast array of decisions related to food distribution across the continent. In a letter to Dawes, dated December 24, 1918, Bert wrote: "I am of course more primarily interested in this [Peace] Conference than anyone else, as its largest purpose from an American point of view will be to determine the method by which foodstuffs sold to Germany are to be financed."[4]

Bert's interests went beyond the financing of food sales to Germany and its allies. He sought to leverage his position into new responsibilities and greater political influence. "Next to President Wilson, [Bert] is the outstanding figure in Paris," Edgar wrote Lou, exaggerating the level of Bert's influence in what were highly contentious peace negotiations among the Allied nations. "He is called on for advice in all matters in addition to FOOD [sic]."

At the mention of Hoover's name at a subcommittee meeting, one of the members exploded that "he was damned tired of having all decisions held in abeyance until this man Hoover's opinion could be ascertained."[5]

With Bert in Europe, Lou decamped to California in the hope of escaping the influenza pandemic that had begun to spread worldwide in 1917 and would not disappear, as mysteriously as it had appeared, until 1919. The previous winter, Lou had withdrawn both her sons from school. Allan had suffered from ear and throat infections, as had his brother Herbert, whose health had never been robust. (These were the days before the discovery of antibiotics.) Lou believed the boys would be safer away from Washington.

Edgar and others in Bert's inner circle updated Lou on her husband's wishes and whereabouts. "I had any number of inquiries for you; and Bert says that anytime you feel so inclined, to bring Allen [sic] over and join him," Edgar wrote Lou. "[Bert] does not know when he can come home, but I have been trying to persuade him that he should come over [return to the United States] while the President is in Washington as the activity of the Peace Conference died as soon as the President left. If you should decide to go [to Europe], be sure to cable first to avoid a possible passing at sea."[6]

"I don't feel that I can leave the boys just at this minute," Lou replied to Edgar in a telegram that illustrated how removed Bert was from his family's lives. "Herbert has just had his tonsils out and has to be watched for a few weeks. Allan, at the moment, is in Monterey, but exceedingly well."[7] Lou had also begun drafting the plans for her dream home in Palo Alto. Birge Clark and his father, Arthur, who chaired Stanford's art and architecture department, were the architects. She advised Bert of her intentions, and he sent a cable to Edgar to be forwarded to her:

> My dear Lou Henry:
>
> I am quoting below in full cable received from Bert for transmission to you.
>
> 'Food 665 April twenty-second for Rickard. Please transmit following to Mrs. Hoover QUOTE Build your house as you planned it yourself. Probably won't use it much for fifteen years but want it right then. . . . Could you not bring boys here in June returning with me July or August? Love ENDQUOTE'[8]

Lou did not respond directly to Bert's question. Instead, she wrote Edgar: "Charlotte Kellogg tells me that she hears from the New York office that Bert will not leave Europe before September?"[9]

While Bert remained in Europe, Lou served as his unofficial ambassador. She wrote Edgar that she "entertained in [Bert's] name" a steady stream of visitors from the East Coast and Europe. She asked Edgar to see what he could do to hang onto the lease on the Adams's house in Washington. "If heaps of these Europeans are coming over whom Bert will have to be nice to, it is much the most appropriate appearing house I know there—and very convenient. Entertaining in it arranges itself, picturesquely—and fairly easily."[10]

Members of Congress contacted Lou for information from Bert rather than get in touch with staff at the Food Administration. Congressman Oscar Bland asked her to find out how much sugar was sold to Europe since the US declaration of war, prompting a hasty night telegram to Edgar: "For Bert, please wire me immediately sugar sold in Europe by you or your agencies since our declaration of war and to whom and when if you do not have this information where can I get it at once?" She added: "When will you be over here?"[11]

Lou continued her own rigorous schedule of activities, dividing her time between Washington and Palo Alto. In addition to serving as one of the national vice presidents for the Girl Scouts, she stayed in touch with Charlotte Kellogg to ensure that the remaining orders for Belgian lace were fulfilled. Lou joined the boards of organizations that supported women's education and addressed the needs of working women. After the CRB's reorganization into the American Relief Administration, funding was redirected to aiding children orphaned by the war. Lou became involved in work to assist with finding homes for orphans of American citizens and providing aid and relief to orphaned children in France and Belgium. She undertook projects to build children's libraries in both those countries.

The Hoovers' furniture was still in England in early 1919. With her home under construction, Lou had arranged, through Edgar, to have the furniture shipped to California. Bert, back in Europe, overruled her plans. "Our furniture has arrived in New York, and we have had no trouble in passing it through customs," Edgar wrote Lou on April 2 regarding his belongings. "I do not understand why Bert changed his mind about [your] furniture as he was quite positive in agreeing to your plan to have it shipped to California. It is possible that he preferred to wait until he could get a ship to take it direct rather than having it come to New York for transshipment."[12]

The furniture had not arrived by mid-May, and Lou was becoming frantic. Construction on the new home on San Juan Hill was progressing well. She wrote Edgar:

> Do you know what is happening to my furniture? If it is coming through pretty soon I will wait for it instead of getting some things here which I will really have to get if it is not coming soon. . . .Also, there are measures of certain important articles which I need before the house gets very far along.

Lou considered writing Agnew to have the pictures and pieces of furniture measured, but she heard conflicting reports about the whereabouts of her belongings.

> Now, from different people, I have heard rumors that they [the furniture] are remaining indefinitely in England, they are on the sea on their way to California, that they are on the sea on their way to New York, that they are coming through a van uncrated, that they have been crated! Have you any idea what has happened to them, or where I can get in touch with anybody who will be able to get at them for an hour?[13]

The furniture eventually arrived with breakage and water damage. Lou settled the claim on the water damage for $4,250 (nearly a thousand dollars more than an American's average annual salary at the time) and an additional claim for the breakage. But she could now move forward with the next phase of construction on her home.

Lou had designed an asymmetrical, three-story home that nestled into the hillside of the Hoovers' Palo Alto property. Generally considered to be constructed in the pueblo style, the main floor contained a master suite, Bert's library, and the main entrance to the home. The upper story featured bedrooms for Herbert and Allan and Lou's study. Servants' quarters and guest rooms were located on the third floor. The building construction was reinforced concrete, per Bert's instructions that the home be fireproof. The façade varied among brick, tile, and stucco. The walkways were brick paving over a concrete slab. The flat roofs and the sleeping porches were distinctive Lou touches.

While the home's exterior has a southwestern, Native American look, the interior design reflected an eclectic collection of architectural elements reminiscent of some of the places Lou had lived in Europe and Asia. Leaded glass and asymmetrical Tudor-style windows provided a British touch. Arches and pergolas in the main rooms reflected a Mediterranean influence.

"Mrs. Hoover was to make decisions about architecture," Birge Clark recalled. "[She] came over to look at drawings frequently and came unannounced." Lou worked with clay models of the structure and climbed the tall construction platforms to see the view from each of the rooms.

She was determined to have the house built according to her vision and was diplomatic in conveying her desires. "She always started with praise," Clark recalled. "Then she would suggest changes if she did not like [something we were doing]. She made her own sketches of the elevations, specs, and details. She had carefully thought about what she wanted. . . . . She was the main creative force behind the house."[14]

Lou consulted Bert as she moved forward with the project. He had definite ideas about what he thought the house should look like, but his indirect communication style through telegrams left the decisions open to Lou's discretion. He is alleged to have told Clark at some point during the design phase: "I don't care what it looks like, as long as it does not look like the insane asylum of [Ray Lyman] Wilbur's over there."[15] (Ray Lyman Wilbur was president of Stanford University.)

Lou decided that construction progress on her house was moving along smoothly enough that she could join Bert in Europe. She and Allan departed New York on the SS *Imperator* in late July and met Bert in Paris. On August 4, Lou, along with Allan and Adaline Fuller, who inspected orphanages in Warsaw on behalf of the ARA, journeyed from Paris through northern France and into Belgium. Mr. White, who had been a stretcher-bearer during the war, accompanied them. "[He] had many exciting times in the war, being severely gassed in October, from which he has hardly recovered yet," Lou reported in a letter to Herbert. "While carrying stretchers, he had four different assistants shot at the other end of the stretcher, and once, after twelve days work, or seven days real work and five days supposed rest, he only had eleven men left of his corps of thirty-nine. So, you can see stretcher bearing is not a very enviable job."

Lou surveyed first-hand the massive destruction wrought by the war. Every house in the sixty communes that the CRB had kept fed through the war was demolished. The French and Americans found fifty people who had been living in cellars. "We found the city hall where Daddy had the wonderful unexpected meeting with the mayors of the sixty communes, about which you remember. It is on a square, and out in front two old women and a younger one had opened little stores—one had fruit and various poor little things to eat, and the other one had threads and needles, shoestrings, very poor cloth, and other necessities of that sort."

They visited St. Quentin, which had served as the headquarters for the CRB. Lou likened it to San Francisco after the earthquake. The whole country near Cambrai "had been dug up by the war operations. Now it is very largely covered over with woods and wildflowers, but until this summer it had looked very much like the country all about the geyser district in New Zealand, which perhaps you can no longer remember, or the district of the Yellowstone. Allan said, 'It certainly looked like a big mess.' "[16]

Lou, Bert, and Allan returned to the United States at the end of August. Bert stayed in New York. Lou and Allan proceeded to California, where she once again juggled Bert's demands, the needs of her children, and concerns about her mother.

Florence Henry was suffering from colon cancer, and Lou felt obligated to be near her family in California. In November, she cabled Edgar: "Urgent. Please have Wilbur wire me soonest possible moment what doctor at Lane Hospital to put in charge of examination of Mother immediately regarding threatened malignant trouble in colon. Also tell Bert I could not start east until satisfactory outcome of same examination. Otherwise all well here."[17]

Ray Lyman Wilbur immediately responded with a recommendation, and Lou's mother underwent surgery for colon cancer. Florence Henry recovered from the operation, but it was clear that her health was declining.

During the months of separation, communication between Lou and Bert consisted of a hodgepodge of telegrams containing requests or tersely worded statements and information about the other's activities. Lou's communiqués were signed by one of her assistants; Bert's were signed by either his assistants or the faithful go-between Edgar. The couple operated on different trajectories much of the time, but Lou would adjust her course to align with Bert's when he needed her. Her notes to co-members and fellow officers of the various organizations on which Lou served often contained some version of the phrase, "I am sorry, but Bert has asked me to." His indifference and self-centeredness frustrated her, but Lou remained fiercely loyal to her husband.

That loyalty was demonstrated as Republicans looked to the presidential election in 1920. The White House was considered up for grabs by both parties. Woodrow Wilson was a Democrat, but that party label had a different connotation in the second decade of the twentieth century than it does in the first decades of the twenty-first. The Democratic Party dominated the former states of the confederacy, a direct result of Lincoln, who had issued the Emancipation Proclamation to free enslaved peoples, being a Republican. Wilson was only the third Democrat to win the presidency since the founding of the Republican Party in 1856 (James Buchanan and Grover Cleveland were the other two). Many political observers considered Wilson's election an aberration—more the result of Theodore Roosevelt's Bull Moose Party splitting off Republican voters from the incumbent president, William Howard Taft in the 1912 election, than a national movement toward the Democratic Party.

Less than twelve months after the Armistice, the patriotic fervor that had gripped the United States had given way to labor unrest and a weakened economy. Soldiers returned to their hometowns to find that immigrants had taken their jobs. Europe was getting its industrial base back on its feet, slashing demand for American products. American industry was in the middle of retooling from war to consumer products manufacturing. Factory owners reduced wages to stay profitable, a move that enraged unions and led to strikes. Farmers were feeling the pain of reduced demand, as they no longer fed two continents. There were surpluses, and commodity prices were at rock bottom. Economic pain outweighed diplomatic gain. The Republicans had a good chance to win the presidency.

Bert's name was first floated as a potential presidential candidate at a dinner of the American Mining and Metallurgical Engineers at New York's Waldorf Hotel on September 16, 1919. Toastmaster Henry L. Sanders introduced Bert as "fit to guide the ship of state." The New York *Sun* reported: "Each one of the 1,200 diners immediately joined in a spontaneous demonstration over the obvious suggestion. Within half a minute, they were chanting in unison: 'One, two, three, four. Who are we for? Herbert Hoover!'"[18]

Bert acknowledged the crowd's enthusiasm but kept his remarks focused on the conclusions he had drawn from his experiences with the CRB and as Food Administrator. "My first conviction is that this whole philosophy of Socialism is bankrupting itself," Bert asserted. He made a case for American economic superiority and exceptionalism. America had grown away from Europe and had assumed a position of moral leadership in the world. The nation could lead the world because of the idealism and hope that were woven into the fabric of American life. "Our sister civilization in Europe is today recovering from a great illness," Bert concluded. "The many new democracies that we have inspired are striving for our ideals. We alone have the economic and moral reserve with which to carry our neighbor back to strength. To do this is also true Americanism."[19]

Publicly, Bert indicated no strong interest in running for president, while privately he explored the idea with his closest advisors. He spent the autumn of 1919 working with former President Taft and prominent Republicans Charles Evans Hughes and Elihu Root to gather enough Senate support for Senate ratification of the Treaty of Versailles.

The treaty was doomed to fail in the Senate. Senate Democrats, in line with President Wilson, supported the treaty. The Republicans were divided. Wilson's advisors, including Colonel House and Bert, had urged the President to invite Henry Cabot Lodge, the Republican chair of the Senate Foreign Relations Committee, to accompany Wilson to the Paris peace talks. The president, who despised Lodge, ignored the recommendation.

Lodge responded to the slight by leading a group of Republican senators called the "Reservationists"—those who had reservations about the Treaty. They were willing to consider a vote for ratification if their concerns were addressed. Wilson did not extend his diplomacy to Lodge and his Reservationists. The president angrily instructed the Democrats to reject Lodge's plan. When the final ratification vote was taken on November 19, enough Democrats had joined the Republicans opposed to the treaty to defeat it. The United States never ratified the Treaty of Versailles.

Bert's recent biographers indicate that, in the aftermath of the defeat of the Versailles treaty, he saw no future in political office and hoped to make a success of newspaper ownership. In addition to his ownership share in the Washington *Herald*, Bert partnered with friend Ben Allen for the purchase of the Sacramento *Union*. Bert attempted, unsuccessfully, to purchase the Baltimore *Sun*. But his heart was still in relief work, and he continued to travel the country to raise funds to feed, clothe, shelter, and educate European children whose lives were forever altered by the war.

Lou wanted to settle down in California and spend more time with her sons. Herbert would soon go off to college, and Allan was about to become a teenager. In addition to concerns about her ailing mother, her sister Jean's marriage was falling apart. Jean and her husband Guthrie Large had purchased a ranch with money she had brought to the marriage. Guthrie made a series of bad business decisions and argued with Jean over management of the farm. Charles Henry had given money to his son-in-law in the hope that he would find a way to make something work, but Large never found a path to business success. He had served in Europe during the war and returned home harsher and more difficult to live with than he had been before he had deployed. California was a joint property state, and Guthrie was entitled to a fifty percent share of anything Jean owned. Florence Henry held the deed to the property on which she and Charles lived, and she had originally planned to will joint ownership to her daughters. Fearful of enriching her ne'er-do-well son-in-law, Florence deeded the entire property to Lou to prevent Guthrie from having a claim to Jean's portion upon Florence's death. The move was as much a statement about Herbert Hoover as it was about Guthrie Large.

When Bert determined to run for president, Lou set aside her disappointments about Bert's unwillingness to settle down in California. She set to work promoting his candidacy.

People in Lou's circle urged Bert to run. The chair of the Department of Home Economics of the General Federation of Women's Clubs, Flora Hartley Greene, wrote Lou in February 1919: "I should like to see Mr. Hoover become a candidate for President on the platform that stood for right, truth, and justice to everybody."

Greene also wanted to see Lou as First Lady: "As for yourself, you could do much in setting standards in the White House. You and I have had enough experience with the so-called Society Set in the United States to know that the college woman of the right type has much to give Washington Society in the way of social standards. I can foresee your drawing room as an intellectual center, one of real culture where right standards of thought, of action, and of right living shall be established for the whole United States."[20]

Bert's long absences from the United States posed a hurdle. Rumors circulated that he had become a British citizen. Edgar sought a photograph of Bert's birthplace in West Branch as proof of his American birth. Lou oversaw the construction of a yearly itinerary to show Bert had returned to the United States every year following his graduation from Stanford. She also worked with a fellow Stanford alumnus and magazine publisher Charles Field on Bert's campaign biographies.

Lou and Field had a playful relationship. She Latinized his name in their correspondence, referring to him as Carolus Ager. He, in turn, put a French spin on her name. "My dear L'Houvre," he opened one letter to Lou. "(Doesn't that look fascinating in print?)" he teased. He would later settle on "Louvre," a play on Lou's name and a nod to the venerable French art museum.

Field took credit for starting a "Me and Hoover" boom in October shortly after Bert's New York speech and circulated the itinerary showing Bert's annual return visits to the United States. "I have had a lovely time going after this story [Bert's travel itinerary from 1899 until 1919]," Field wrote Lou. "[E]ver since you approved my going after Theodore [Hoover] for such records as he has, and everybody has been more than cordial and helpful, but, believe me, I have not used your name more than to say you were aware of the business."[21]

Field oversaw the writing of campaign biographies about Bert by two different authors. One was the Hoovers' friend, Vernon Kellogg; the other was Rose Lane Wilder, a former newspaper reporter for Hearst's San Francisco *Union*.

> I hope that you will not be pained by the story as it developed. Certainly no one could try to be more delicate in the thing than I. I met a man last evening who is abroad in the land gathering material for a similar work, for the Boston Post. So, of course, you are in for it. But wait till you see the sweetness we are putting into our story. The first chapter is about ready, and I am positive that our sketch of the ancestry of the Honorable Bert is a distinct contribution to the nation's desirable information at this time.[22]

Charlotte and Vernon Kellogg had worked with Bert and Lou in the CRB, and the Kelloggs continued to remain active in the ARA. They both sought to boost Bert's candidacy with their writings. In 1917, Charlotte had published the book *Women of Belgium: Turning Tragedy to Triumph*. Her book *Bobbins of Belgium: A Book of Belgian Lace, Lace-Workers, Lace-Schools and Lace-Villages*, published in February 1920, detailed the life-saving exchange of Belgian lace for food overseen by the CRB.

Vernon, a trained scientist who directed CRB efforts on the ground in Belgium before joining Bert at the Food Administration, penned *Herbert Hoover: The Man and His Work*. Field serialized it in his publication, *Everybody's Magazine*. The initial installment under Kellogg's byline depicted Bert's childhood as harsh and unforgiving. The article suggested that Jesse and Hulda Hoover abused and neglected their young son. The piece cast Bert's uncle, John Minthorn, in a negative light. The article gave no credit to the Oregon family who provided Bert with a home, educated him, and gave their blessing for him to leave to attend Stanford.

Minthorn, who had not communicated regularly with his adopted nephew since Bert had departed for California, expressed to Theodore Hoover his unhappiness with the article. Minthorn placed much of the blame on Kellogg, although he suggested that Bert was ultimately behind the story. A comment in a letter from Field to Lou suggests that the publisher had a hand in the tone of the article, while attempting to place the blame squarely on Kellogg.

> I feel quite helpless. Vernon Kellogg has had the benefit of direct consultation. I have felt in honor bound not to make you or Bert in the slightest degree "responsible" and by "authentic" I have not meant to include either of you.[23]

Kellogg's article failed to generate the empathy for Bert it had intended to arouse. Shortly after his article appeared in *Everybody's Magazine*, sections of Rose Wilder Lane's biography of Bert were printed in Field's other publication, *Sunset Magazine*. Lane was the daughter of Laura Ingalls Wilder, the author of the children's series, *Little House on the Prairie*. Lane had become a successful freelance writer, and her articles appeared in *Country Gentleman*, *Saturday Evening Post*, *Cosmopolitan* (a literary magazine at the time), and *McCall's*. She secretly edited her mother's *Little House* books, and she would later become associated with Ayn Rand and other founders of Libertarianism.

Lane honed her craft at the *Union* under the tutelage of a friend of William Randolph Hearst and had adopted some of his methods of "yellow journalism," which emphasized sensationalism over fact. Lane never dealt directly with Bert or Lou, which she acknowledged to the couple when she tried to make amends for her book years later, after Bert had become president. Lane's contacts were Theodore Hoover and other Hoover relatives with whom Field put her in touch. Lane explained her approach to the biography, *The Making of Herbert Hoover,* in the Introduction:

> The method used in handling this biographical material is so unusual that a word of explanation is necessary. The facts on which the story is based I do not believe to be open to dispute. Every detail of them has been collected with meticulous care from sources of unquestionable authority. The interpretation of them is my own. I have endeavored to present as a living human being the man whose life has been made by these facts, to show the influences of heredity and environment that went toward the making of his character as I believe it to be.[24]

Field's letter to Lou following publication of Lane's biography suggests that he knew Lou would be displeased with the book. He feared the loss of a good friendship.

> [Lane's] biography has been a strange experience! I have put a vast amount of affectionate loyalty into it. It is possible that because of it I may lose some precious friendship.
>
> Please believe in the sincerity behind the spirit of the work. Perhaps I cannot ask more. If I have rushed in roughshod where angels fear to tread, I shall have to take my medicine.
>
> Hoping for something better than going through the bankruptcy court of friendship.[25]

Lou was clearly unhappy with Lane's work. Ever diplomatic, she asked her assistant, Dare Stark, to convey her displeasure in a carefully worded noted:

> Dear Mr. Field:
>
> Mrs. Hoover said didn't you think it would be a very nice idea if you wrote a little introduction for your and Miss Lane's book? It would serve

> two purposes, be a matter of real interest and also be an obvious means of explaining any of the many inaccuracies which a reader might notice.[26]

Kellogg's and Lane's books did little to boost Bert's candidacy. Additional damage came from assaults by Hiram Johnson on Bert as an uncaring husband and a man of questionable morals. Johnson was a liberal senator from California and had been Theodore Roosevelt's vice-presidential running mate on the 1912 Bull Moose Party ticket. In 1920, Johnson succeeded in winning the primary vote of his home state as its favorite son over Bert. Lou angrily vented her frustrations at Johnson's attacks in a letter she titled, "An article written in 1920 by a friend of 'the Hoovers' and sent to Mrs. Hoover." The personal details, tone, and intimate knowledge of family life make it clear that the "friend" was Lou herself.

She attacked Johnson's integrity and responded to the multiple allegations about Bert's heritage and character. Bert was accused of being a Catholic (a reference to his marriage having been officiated by a Catholic priest), and when confronted with the fact that he was a Quaker, the response was, "Ah, yes, by birth, but Mrs. Hoover is a Catholic and her influence over him is so great that he is practically one himself." If people did believe that Bert was born in the United States, they were then told that he was "pro-British" and had filled out the papers to become a British citizen.

The "friend's" letter went on to describe Bert's relationship with his family:

> The story is bruited [rumored] abroad that the Hoovers are notoriously unhappy in their family life, and he a hard, impossible, overbearing man to live with. The fact that his wife and family have accompanied him into what are considered the most impossible places for families to go, when they could have very comfortably remained in civilization, is known, of course, to hundreds of their friends, and especially to the very circles which the San Francisco Johnson Committees could most easily reach if looking for confirmation of its stories.[27]

But the most telling aspect of the letter's authorship was the intimate detail of Lou's role in her marriage.

> Like many other American men, much occupied with business, and with capable wives, the homemaking was considered the wife's business. She always found the house she thought they would like to live in (usually in-

> deed, took him around for final approval, although not always even that), furnished it, (if it were unfurnished), engaged the servants, ordered the menu and paid the bills. Therefore, it never occurred to either of them that she should worry him by taking around any of the little papers that had to be taken out, rents, leases, insurance, all such she took out in her own name as a matter of course. And so, in England, in China, in New York, as in California, the home was in her name and run by her.[28]

It is unclear to whom, if anyone, Lou sent her "letter." As is the case with other of Lou's writings where she poured out her frustrations on paper, it was likely sent to a select group of friends and family as a discreet way of discrediting someone she disagreed with and promoting her recollections and point of view.

The Republican National Convention was held during four sweltering days in June at the Blackstone Hotel in Chicago. The nomination was hotly contested. Illinois governor Frank O. Lowden was favored to win. Johnson, Bert, Army Chief of Staff Leonard Wood, Pennsylvania senator Philander Knox, Massachusetts governor Calvin Coolidge, and former Supreme Court Justice Charles Evans Hughes, were all in the running. No one expected the outcome: Ohio Senator Warren Harding was nominated as the party's presidential candidate; Coolidge was the vice-presidential candidate.

Bert and Lou waited out the convention in an apartment she had leased for him at 876 Park Avenue, in New York. The results disappointed, but Bert analyzed his campaign's mistakes and determined he would lay the groundwork for a serious run for the presidency in the next cycle. That meant building a stronger base in California so that he could rightfully call it his home state. He considered ways in which to establish his bona fides. If Lou argued for Bert to return to California with her and find something that would keep him at home, it is unrecorded. She returned to Palo Alto to be near her parents and to monitor construction on San Juan Hill. Bert continued his relief work in New York and cultivated a relationship with the newly anointed Republican presidential nominee.

CHAPTER 9

The Wearer of Many Hats

"A lot of [Bert's] friends and admirers, as you probably heard, tried to make him President last autumn, much against his own advice and desire," Lou wrote in a post-election letter to a long-time friend living in Ceylon. Lou's description of Bert's would-be candidacy was a masterful piece of political artifice. It denied how actively Bert had pursued, with her help, the nomination, and it contained a hint of her relief at the outcome. "Consequently, we were quite pleased when their efforts were beaten by the regular old politicians." Of president-elect Warren G. Harding, Lou opined: "Now everyone is wondering what kind of President this new man is going to make,—and no one at all sure, as he is one of the sort who promises everything to everybody. So, one cannot judge what he will really prove to be in actual operation."[1]

Lou would get to observe close-up what Harding would "really prove . . . in actual operation." The president-elect named Bert Secretary of Commerce, one of the last cabinet positions filled.

Lou was the most prominent of the cabinet wives. She had been active in Washington social circles for three-and-a-half years by the time of Harding's inauguration on March 4, 1921. The society pages of the Washington newspapers routinely reported on her activities, and she had been photographed for *Vogue*, a new magazine that had quickly acquired a reputation as an authoritative source on fashion trends and influential people. Lou's establishment of the women's clubhouse for female Food Administration employees, her organizational work on behalf of the Red Cross, and her ongoing work with the Girl Scouts made her a well-respected figure. She was a member of the American Association of University Women (AAUW), active in the Women's Division of the Mining and Metallurgical Society of America, and a member of and financial contributor to the League of Women Voters. Lou had received international recognition for her work to aid the Belgian people: Queen Elisabeth of Belgium had awarded Lou the *Médaille de la Reine* (Queen's Medal) in June 1919, and King Albert bestowed the *Croix de Chevalier de l'Ordre de Léopold* (Knight's Cross of the Order of Leopold) on Lou and Bert that September.

The new first lady, Florence Kling Harding, nicknamed "The Duchess," had helped Warren Harding manage his newspaper business and shepherded his rise to political power. She projected the image of a devoted wife whose primary interests were meal preparation and homemaking when, in fact, she attended her husband's cabinet meetings and proved to be an astute political observer and advisor. Like Lou, Florence believed in woman suffrage. Florence and Lou bonded over a shared interest in promoting girls' physical activity. The first lady supported the Camp Fire Girls (former first lady Frances Cleveland Preston was a member of the board), which offered a program similar to the Girl Scouts, and Florence took seriously her role as honorary president of the Scouts.

The first lady was expected to be the leader of social Washington, and there was potential for a rivalry between Lou and Florence. Lou was too busy to care about social leadership, and she respectfully deferred to Florence Harding. When she was in Washington, Lou attended teas and gatherings that included cabinet wives. However, there were also a number of occasions where Lou's Scout responsibilities and family demands in California made for legitimate reasons to skip some of the first lady's get-togethers.

With Bert's cabinet appointment, Lou decided to buy a home in Washington. She purchased a three-story, twenty-one room house at 2300 S Street. The Hoovers' neighbors included former president Wilson, who lived in seclusion as a result of his stroke, and journalist Mark Sullivan. Sullivan was a Republican who had gained widespread respect for his work as a muckraker who reported on corruption in government. He and his family became good friends with the Hoovers during their years at 2300.

Lou was nationally recognized for her contributions to engineering and science, and young women seeking careers in those fields sought her out. In spring 1921, she received a questionnaire from Zelma Boeshar, an architectural engineering student at Ohio State University researching a report on "Facts about Women Engineers." Lou's responses reflect a combination of her interest in encouraging young women to pursue their dreams and her frustration with how they accepted society's restrictions on their abilities:

ZELMA: What kinds of Engineering do you consider appropriate for a woman?

LOU: Any that she feels capable of and interested in attempting.

ZELMA: Why?

LOU: Why not?

ZELMA: Does a man's idea of a woman's sphere have a direct bearing on her career as an engineer?

LOU: As much as it does in law, medicine, and other professions.

ZELMA: Do you consider a woman's physical weakness a great disadvantage?

LOU: A woman who has taken correct care of herself all of her life should have no so-called '**physical weakness**.' (Lou underlined and typed over the response a second time so that it appeared bold-faced.)

ZELMA: Is the engineering profession a test of her womanliness?

LOU: Question incomprehensible to me.

ZELMA: Does it tend to make her masculine?

LOU: Just what do you mean by that? How? Why?

ZELMA: Does it tend to make her unconventional?

LOU: If by 'unconventional' you mean unusual, it would, wouldn't it?

ZELMA: Do you think intuition helps a woman in engineering?

LOU: Certainly, and imagination and many other useful characteristics of either man or woman.

ZELMA: Have you any suggestions not noted here?

LOU: No.[2]

Lou forwarded Boeshar's questionnaire to two female friends Lou thought could offer additional insights. May Bradford Shockley, a practicing civil engineer in Nevada, had served as a deputy United States land surveyor. Dr. Clelia Duel Mosher headed Women's Physical Education at Stanford. Shockley responded in much the same vein as Lou, informing Boeshar that she did not divide subjects into areas of "masculine intelligence" and "feminine intelligence." Mosher summed up the women's dismay at the questionnaire in a letter to Lou: "The set of questions enclosed in your note are both amusing and discouraging. I could write a small volume on the subject, but I will refrain." She enclosed a copy of the proceedings on a conference on women's physical strength and recommended that Boeshar read it.[3]

The United States' entry into World War I ignited a re-examination of women's roles. They stepped into jobs that had traditionally been the purview of men, including positions now considered traditional female employment, such as administrative assistants. Fashions took on a radical change, with women abandoning corsets and long, full skirts in favor of slimmed down, boyish looking shifts that came to the knee or slightly below—a scandalous look in the eyes of some, but an opportunity for new freedom embraced by the majority of women. An increasing number of women enrolled in college, and, as Lou had felt when she graduated from Stanford, these educated women looked for more than a return ticket home to await a marriage proposal. "It is very possible to have both a home and career as we are released from so many of the burdens of our mothers and grandmothers," Lou told delegates in a speech to the National League of Women Voters. She was also an advocate of women becoming fully engaged in civic life.

> I am very interested in the principles and progress of the League of Women Voters, and I am always interested in the work women are doing in California. California women are pioneers, here developing the Civic Center and forum as means to train citizens . . . on child labor, the primacy of education, moral underpinning of civil society, party protocols and fundamentals. We must always defend the League against criticism that it is only a woman's party.[4]

Lou raised the first flag over her completed Palo Alto home on July 4, 1921, with only her groundskeeper present. The residence, complete with swimming pool, encompassed 12,480 square feet. The home became the hub for family and friends and housed the Hoovers' menagerie, which included Allan's collection of turtles and a pet alligator, and the Hoovers' dogs. Both Lou and Bert loved dogs. In the early 1920s, they owned an Irish terrier named Rags and kept his son from a litter of puppies he sired. They eventually acquired a Belgian shepherd, named Tut, who would accompany them to the White House. Weegie, a Norwegian elkhound, would replace Tut, who died in 1929 (and would merit an obituary in the *New York Times*).

Lou spent the early part of July unpacking boxes and arranging furniture and decorative items. She divided her time between her domestic chores and keeping a close watch on her mother, whose health was failing. Bert had wired on July 7 to ask Lou to meet him in Chicago on the 15th, and she consulted Florence's physician before agreeing to the trip. The doctor encouraged her to go.

With no real change in her mother's condition, Lou felt comfortable joining her family in New England for rare vacation time together in August. On August 17, she received word that her mother was quickly fading. Lou took the first available train out of Boston, but she arrived too late to say her final good-bye. Florence Henry died on August 18 while Lou was en route to California. "Mother had started her long journey the evening before I finished my short one," Lou wrote to her friend Alida Henriques, who, together with Philippi Harding, was managing the household at 2300 for Lou.[5]

Charles Henry met Lou at the train station on the afternoon of August 19. She found her mother "asleep on a sofa near the window which does not look toward the swimming pool," Lou wrote Herbert and Allan. "She looked so calm and peaceful, as she did a number of years ago, before she began having so much pain."[6] Bert had not accompanied his wife to California.

Florence Weed Henry's funeral was held at the University Chapel on the Stanford University campus. She was cremated, in accordance with her wishes. Cremation was only available in San Francisco, and Lou had anticipated that the immediate family would make the trip alone. To her surprise and pleasure, a car with other Stanford professors and another car filled with women neighbors accompanied the Henry family to San Francisco.

"You must always remember that there are just the sweetest people living on this hill and campus [than] there are anywhere in the world!" Lou told her sons. "And they all loved Grandma so much."[7]

Allan had expected his mother to return immediately after his grandmother's funeral, but Lou remained in California to await Herbert's arrival for the start of his freshman year at Stanford. "The people in Washington think I had better stay here until Herbert gets out [to California]," Lou wrote her younger son. "I think they are quite right about it myself,—for there would be absolutely none of the family here to see him if I did not,—and there are a good many things I can do in a few days to help him along."[8]

It was a spur-of-the-moment decision, and Lou did not consider that Henriques had other plans. She wanted to return to her home in Rhode Island to escape Washington's miserable August weather. Her regular updates on activities in the Washington house included a request for Lou's planned return. Lou ignored Henriques's entreaties.

Allan, too, bombarded his mother with letters. Lou intended to enroll Allan in the D.C. Public Schools and she needed to choose between Central High School and Western. Lou preferred Central, based on its layout, but Allan knew more of the boys at Western, located in tony Georgetown. Friends urged Lou to choose Western. "Now from just a snobbish social point of view," Lou wrote Henriques, with whom she was discussing the merits of each school via letter, "I don't believe in being influenced by such arguments, but there is no doubt there is a great deal more interest in knowing the same boys well in and out of school."

The route to Western from the Hoover home provided Lou with some peace of mind. "[A]s Allan will doubtless go over on a bicycle, the ride to Western is so much more soothing to Mother's nerves than the one to Central!"[9] Decision made, Lou asked Henriques to follow up with Philippi Harding to ensure that arrangements had been made for Allan's enrollment at Western. The forbearing Henriques followed through, as requested.

There were times when Lou tuned out the needs of others to concentrate on what she needed for herself. She was not one to articulate that she needed time alone. She became, as Alice Dickson had once defined her, "the Ladye of the Perfect Silence." The death of her mother, the milestone of her elder son starting at Stanford, and seeing her father's grief combined to propel Lou to carve out a space in which she could process all that was taking place in her life in such a short period of time. Bert did not provide his wife with emotional support, and Lou counted on her close circle of friends to understand and accommodate her.

After Herbert arrived in California, Lou embarked in her Cadillac on a father-daughter cross-country camping trip from California to 2300. "We have wanted the California Cadillac in Washington," Lou wrote Allan by way of explanation for her decision not to return more quickly by train, "and I have always longed to drive across, so I told Grandpa I was going to do that now, at the opportune time, and, of course, he is coming along, so that I won't have to be alone!" Lou, Charles Henry, her nephew Del (who would live with the Hoovers for the school year), and Charles Henry's houseman, Matias, headed east.

Lou did her best to assuage her upset son about her extended absence. "It seems that you will have to be fearfully brave again — and do something that you will not at all want to. And that is to start school without your dear old Mum being on hand to see you off, or to hear all the stories there are to tell when you get back! However, I think it is much harder on me than on you."[10]

She recommended he ask either Philippi Harding or Alida Henriques to accompany him on the first day to make sure his enrollment was smooth. "Do you want to go over and get the lay of the land with someone?" Lou asked her son. "Or, perhaps Daddy can spare Mr. Herter or Mr. Emmett, if you desire a man." Lou's final suggestion was for Allan to solicit the help of an upperclassman of his acquaintance who will "be very good to tell you what to do,—what kinds of things to take, in the way of pencils, notebooks, etc., and even what kind of clothes to wear."

In the end, Lou depended on Allan to trust in her love and commitment to him. "I do love you so! I want to do everything for you myself—I can't bear to leave interesting things like starting to new schools to other people to do for you! Do love me a little bit sometime!"[11]

The trip from Palo Alto to Washington took thirty-five days. Despite Charles's advanced years (he would have been close to seventy years old at the time of the trip), travel arrangements were spartan. The four erected tents and slept on tent cots wherever they could find a suitable camping area. In Coble, Nevada, where, Lou reported to Allan, there was "absolutely no place to camp near this barren little [train] station," Lou, Del, and Charles set up their cots in the train station waiting room and gave Matias the sole empty room in "the shack that calls itself a hotel."[12]

In the higher altitudes, around Lovelock, Nevada; and Fort Collins, Colorado; it was cold enough for their water buckets to freeze. Charles' descriptions of the scenery that he recorded in a small diary echoed Lou's writing style. He described their campsite along the North Platte River, in Nebraska as "[b]eautiful flat in the mountains. Small canyons with stream flowing through them to the No[rth] Platte River. Would like to camp here for months."[13]

In Iowa, they visited Bert's uncle Allan Hoover, and then proceeded to reconnect with old acquaintances in Waterloo. In West Branch, Lou met some of Bert's relatives, who conducted a tour of the town, including Bert's birthplace.

After departing West Branch, Lou covered roughly two hundred miles daily. They experienced flat tires and needed some minor repairs along the way, arriving in Washington on Sunday, October 16. The journey was sufficiently noteworthy that the *Washington Times* highlighted it eighteen months later as part of an article about the "fads and foibles of cabinet wives":

> [Mrs. Hoover] had hardly had a chance to collect any fads, for she has been since her marriage traveling about in most of the countries of the world. Yet she is fond of outdoor life, so much so that on a recent journey from California to Washington she came all the way in her car, driving herself and camping out along the road. To drive a car twenty-five hundred miles, across mountains and plains, was some feat. So, it is evident that Mrs. Hoover is capable of qualifying as an expert chauffeur.[14]

Lou managed her household by letter and telegram as she crossed the country. (Alida Henriques had finally departed to Rhode Island.) Lou instructed Philippi, who was running the house, on how to take care of Allan's school needs, tennis lessons, and doctors' appointments. Lou reminded her to invite visitors to join Bert for breakfast and dinner so that he would be surrounded by people who would stimulate him and engage him in conversation.

Lou had long ago accepted that Bert was indifferent to what it took to run a household, and she handled its day-to-day operation without engaging his input. She believed that changing women's roles outside of the home necessitated changes inside. But Lou had accepted that the kind of changes in domestic arrangements that she envisioned would not occur in her own household. On occasion, Lou expressed her unhappiness to Jean and to a select group of friends with the way her marriage had evolved.

Lou undertook a study of other people's marriages, prompted by a comment made to her by a woman when Lou was age twelve: "Whatever you do in life, don't get married." She kept a file of her observations of other couples, hoping one day to publish her findings. "I have been quite interested in this subject of marriage since I was quite a little girl," Lou explained to Philippi when Lou gave her the folder of notes for safekeeping.

> It never seemed to me that it was quite a fair proposition the way it was worked now. We have preserved too many of the customs that went with the age when it was reasonable for mother to stay home and do all the work, and father to settle the affairs outside where he knew the circumstances.
>
> Now that father himself has changed the economic order, it is silly for us to hold many of the trivial-seeming, yet vital, social customs." Women, Lou observed, worked just as hard as men. "I . . . wonder . . . why certain customs prevailed or why it was so terrible for some people to break them, in ways that seemed quite reasonable to me."[15]

Alice Dickson summed up the dynamic of the Hoovers' marriage in a letter to Lou:

> [I have] an impression of you that is always so strong in my mind and which was renewed when I was with you this time. Whenever I see the Chief and get, as it were, a recharge of faith that there are men in public service with the mental attitude of a universal mind which is so much needed in our public life, I like to hear him and have him heard; but there never fails to be in my mind the strong reaction of the cost to you, or rather do I mean, the wonderful contribution you make in holding in reserve the potential power that is in you to create separately. I don't suppose most men could understand that in reality you are doing a more difficult work and to that extent bigger.[16]

Not all of Lou's circle agreed with Alice Dickson. Mary Austin considered Lou to be a doormat. Austin took public aim at the Hoovers' marriage in a chapter in her book on Washington wives, *Boudoir Mirrors of Washington*. The book portrayed sixteen politically and socially prominent Washington wives. It included stories about Alice Roosevelt Longworth, Florence Kling Harding, and Grace Coolidge. A chapter on cabinet wives profiled four women as a group, but Lou merited a chapter of her own. An advertisement for the book in the Washington *Evening Star* read "Catty? No! All the tales that keep feminine tongues wagging in Washington are set forth."[17]

Although it was published as an anonymous work, it was an open secret that Austin authored *Boudoir Mirrors*. Her take on Lou, (and Bert, too, for that matter), was a reversal of the laudatory dedication Austin had included in her book, *A Woman of Genius*. "I want to be a background for Bertie!" opens the chapter on Lou, which is followed by the rhetorical question: "How is that for wifely ambition in these progressive days? That is Mrs. Herbert Hoover's avowed job in life. I wonder how many other women want to be 'a background for Bertie'?"[18]

Austin wielded her verbal rapier against both Hoovers, but she was especially critical of Lou. Ignoring the accolades others had bestowed on Lou, Austin paints Lou as a woman of achievement who has "too much ability to be submerged." What angered Austin was that although Lou shared her views about women's independence, she was not "in-your-face" about them. Being in the public eye had done little to change Lou's attitudes: She remained modest, publicity averse, and frugal. Lou preferred to work behind the scenes, drawing only as much public attention as needed to help her with her cause. Austin, who had once asked Bert to bail her out of jail after being arrested for participating in a suffrage demonstration in London, thought Lou should be more outspoken—abrasively so, if necessary. Austin had once told Lou that a woman who was "tactful and femininely helpful . . . is more than likely to be third rate."[19]

In her most pointed criticism of Lou, Austin questions why someone who has the courage to travel the world, stand up in the face of war, and trek the outdoors could not transfer that same courage to "social explorations." Remarking on how modestly the Hoovers lived, in spite of their wealth, Austin wryly, and somewhat cruelly, observed: "There has always been Hooverizing in the Hoover home, and it wasn't a war-time innovation. They all did it, Bertie, the Background, and the Boys."[20]

The Hoovers and Austin had parted company before *Boudoir Mirrors* was published. For Hoover friends, the book was considered nothing more than Austin's revenge for the rejection. Bert had grown tired of Austin's persistent efforts to push her way into his inner circle, especially after he became Food Administrator and she asked to be put in charge of publicity. He had left it to Lou to terminate the relationship. After eating breakfast with the Hoovers one morning in Washington and making her case to be his publicist, Bert and Lou walked Austin to the door. When she was gone, Bert said: "Well, Mother! We simply can't take time to put up with such women now. Do find some way of keeping her away after this."

"It was difficult to do," Lou wrote her family years after the fact, "and doubtless I was rude before I succeeded in having her cease her suggestions of further conferences with one or the other of us."[21]

Lou never forgot Austin's harsh assessment of her relationship to Bert. Nearly ten years after the book's publication, (and long after it had been forgotten by the public), Lou defended herself to her sons: "And she published anonymously, but unmistakably, an utterly inaccurate article about me in a collection of descriptions of Washington women."[22]

Austin's observation's aside, Lou's intimate circle—Edgar and Abbie Rickard, Alida Henriques, Alice Dickson, Philippi Harding, and Dare Stark—understood Lou's struggles to create a life that reflected her own gifts, while taking a back seat to the life Bert's ambition had crafted for her. These friends loved and admired her. Many of them unselfishly sacrificed their time to allow Lou to pursue her interests. Some, such as Abbie and Edgar Rickard, joined Lou in serving the organizations in which she had become active.

Abbie's dedication to Lou deepened after the executive board of the Girl Scouts of America elected her national president at its annual meeting in Savannah in January 1922. She assumed leadership of an organization that had grown in ten years from a single troop in Savannah, Georgia, to a nationwide network of troops in 47 of America's 48 states. Membership was close to 50,000 and would more than quintuple by the end of the decade to 275,000 girls.

The Girl Scouts' finances were shaky. Juliette Low was an excellent recruiter, but she lacked the skills or experience to establish a strong fund-raising base. A good portion of the money needed to run the Scout organization came from the wealthy benefactresses who were board members. Operating expenses for 1922 alone were put at $122,000.

Lou was an exceptional fund-raiser, thanks to her years of work on behalf of the Society for American Women in London, the CRB, and the Belgian laceworkers. Her objective was not simply to raise the necessary funds to keep the Girl Scouts in business, but to build a positive image of the organization in the public's mind.

Lou organized a parade of 7,500 scouts to march up New York's Fifth Avenue in October as a kickoff to National Girl Scout Week. In honor of the Scout pledge to "do a good turn daily," girl scouts distributed dolls, fruits, and flowers to area hospitals. The diversity of the organization was on display. "Practically every race and creed was represented in the ranks of the Girl Scouts, including ten little Chinese girls," one newspaper reported. A troop of blind girls gave an exhibition of their ability to complete basic household tasks, including sewing, knitting, bandaging, and first aid. As part of the fundraising efforts, adults were "recruited" to join the organization and asked to pay one dollar in dues.[23]

At the time Lou became president, the Girl Scouts were embroiled in an ongoing controversy over its name with the Boy Scout organization. The Chief Boy Scout Executive, James E. West, believed that the name "Girl Scouts" watered down the meaning of the word "scout." He thought that the similar names of the two organizations discouraged boys from joining the Boy Scouts and reduced monies that were available to the boys' organization.

West argued that the Girl Scouts should be absorbed by the Camp Fire Girls, an organization that had been founded in 1910. Both organizations were dedicated to teaching girls self-sufficiency and outdoor skills together with promoting homemaking. The Camp Fire Girls had been founded by a married couple, and men served on its executive board. The Girl Scouts of America was a wholly woman-operated organization. In West's mind, the Girl Scouts taught girls to "ape men" and "trivialized and sissified" the use of the word "scout." In a move that gave West additional ammunition for his argument, Baden-Powell wrote an article in a 1921 issue of the international Scouting magazine *Jamboree* stating that the use of the word "scouts" suggested that women were entering a man's domain. "Guide," the word used by the girls' group in Great Britain founded by Baden-Powell's sister, better described the ideals to be taught young women.[24]

Lou sought Edgar Rickard's help in resolving the dispute. West's rhetoric generated ill-will between the Girl Scouts and the Boy Scouts, and it created tensions between the Girl Scouts and the Camp Fire Girls. Lou believed that the Camp Fire Girls were antagonistic toward the Girl Scouts, a result of West's insistence that the Scouts disband and become absorbed into the other girls' organization.

Edgar sought out John H. Finley, a former editor of *Harper's Weekly* and a member of the Princeton University faculty, who had joined the board of the Camp Fire Girls in 1921. Finley had close ties with West's personal assistant. Edgar arranged for Finley and Lou to meet in an attempt to bring a resolution between the two scout organizations. "I saw John H. Finley this morning. He knows nothing whatever of the efforts of West to discredit the Girl Scout movement. . . . He cannot understand nor endorse any scheme for attempting to alienate the Girl Scouts from the Camp Fire Girls as he looks upon their functions as distinctive," Edgar wrote Lou.[25]

West was adamant that the organization at least change its name if it were not going to become a part of the Camp Fire Girls. In 1924, he had attorneys prepare a lawsuit charging the Girl Scouts with patent infringement for using the word "scouts." The suit was never filed, but West never abandoned his efforts against the Girl Scouts. The attacks ceased only upon his death in 1941.

Lou's public comments about the purpose of the Girl Scouts demonstrated how sensitive she was to public perception of the organization and the transition occurring in women's roles. A growing number of women now graduated from college, and many were delaying marriage in exchange for a few years of independence. For women of means, the shape of independence was to be active in organizations such as the Girl Scouts that offered leadership opportunities. Women who entered the workforce still encountered restrictions in many professions, but others were incrementally opening their doors to college-educated females. Lou sought to portray Girl Scouts as valuable to a young woman's development, without generating angry reactions from the organization's detractors: "If you should ask me about the Girl Scout movement . . . I would tell you there are three fundamental goods in it. It teaches play, individual helpfulness, and citizenship."[26]

The Girl Scouts' dependence on private philanthropy was another motivator in using cautious language to describe the organization's goals. With annual dues a mere twenty-five cents per year per girl, the Scouts' ongoing success relied on private largesse.

Two months after becoming president of the Girl Scouts, personal tragedy struck. Lou and Bert had been on a trip to Colorado in mid-March, and they traveled from there to their home in Palo Alto. Jean, her daughter Janet, and her youngest son Walter, together with Charles Henry, joined Bert and Lou on San Juan Hill for a family reunion. Walter, aged five, wandered away unnoticed from the family group and was discovered unconscious in the pool by a servant. No one knew how long he had been there. Ray Wilbur Lyman was immediately summoned, but his efforts to resuscitate the boy failed. It was a bitter blow to the entire family, but especially to Jean. In addition to a failed marriage, she had lost her youngest child.

Following Walter's funeral, Lou was left alone in the Palo Alto house. Bert returned east while Herbert, Jean, Janet, and Charles Henry returned to Monterey. Writing to Allan, who had not come west for the funeral, Lou expressed her sadness. She could still see Walter "playing all around the house now, with his adorable smile . . . [His] little sun-tanned sweater [still hung] over the foot of my bed, as though he were going to run in to get it soon."[27]

Lou returned to Washington in early April. She took on a schedule that was hyperactive even by her standards. While most of her activities involved the Girl Scouts, Lou was part of a committee that had organized a musicale as a fund-raiser in support of Wellesley College. She served as a patroness of the tea held for the Florence Crittenton Sunshine Society, an organization that provided a home and care for unwed mothers. She plunged into her duties as president of the scouts, and she had a new organization of which she was equally passionate.

In the prior year, Lou had been instrumental in the creation of the National Amateur Athletic Federation—an organization dedicated to promoting physical activity across the entire spectrum of age, gender, and ability. Now, in addition to advocating for Scouting, Lou was dedicated to changing the face of school-based athletics.

1. Lou Henry, age 9, and her sister, Jean/Courtesy of the Herbert Presidential Library

2. Charles Henry in 1886, in Waterloo, Iowa/Courtesy of the Herbert Presidential Library

3. Lou Henry, age 15, with a group summering on Mt. Wilson, CA. Lou is standing on the right, holding a rifle and looking down/Courtesy of the Herbert Presidential Library

4. Lou Henry, age 21, second left, between her father and an unidentified friend. Jean Henry is on the right/Courtesy of the Herbert Hoover Presidential Library

5. The Henry home in Monterey, CA, where Herbert Hoover and Lou Henry were married on February 10, 1899. Florence Henry sits on the steps/Courtesy of the Herbert Hoover Presidential Library

6. Lou inspects a cannon set up to defend the British concession in Tientsin during the Boxer Rebellion, 1900/Courtesy of the Herbert Hoover Presidential Library

7. Lou Henry Hoover during her stay in Japan for surgery for a back injury in 1901/ Courtesy of the Herbert Hoover Presidential Library

8. Jean Henry, who traveled to Japan and China with the Hoovers during 1901/ Courtesy of the Herbert Hoover Presidential Library

9. Lou Henry in Britain behind the wheel of a horseless carriage, 1903/
Courtesy of the Herbert Hoover Presidential Library

10. Lou and Bert, together with Abbie and Edgar Rickard, in Venice, 1912. The couples pooled their extra money and took off on trips across Europe/ Courtesy of the Herbert Hoover Presidential Library

11. Lou and Bert and their sons, Herbert Junior (far right) and Allan, returning from Great Britain to the United States, 1917/Courtesy of the Herbert Hoover Presidential Library

12. Herbert Hoover, in a rare show of public affection, kisses Lou at a stop during a presidential tour, 1930/Courtesy of the Herbert Hoover Presidential Library

13. Lou visits the Central Union Mission in Washington, DC, where she coordinated the donation of Christmas baskets for the needy, 1932/Courtesy of the Herbert Hoover Presidential Library

14. The Hoover family at Christmas, 1938. Lou holds Allan Henry Hoover Junior, born in 1937. Allan sits across from Lou. Herbert Junior is seated next to his father/ Courtesy of the Herbert Hoover Presidential Library

15. Lou was still actively camping in her early sixties, as shown by her Christmas card for 1939. She is on the left, with friends Augusta B. Hartt and Helen Means/ Courtesy of the Herbert Hoover Presidential Library

16. Lou was an avid photographer. This undated photograph of native Hawaiians was taken during a stop on a voyage to Asia or Australia/Courtesy of the Herbert Hoover Presidential Library

17. Lou and Bert circumnavigated the world at least once a year in the early part of their marriage. Bert managed mines throughout southeast Asia, including India/ Courtesy of the Herbert Hoover Presidential Library

18. The Hoovers traveled to China immediately following their marriage, where Bert managed a mine on behalf of a British firm contracted with the Chinese government/Courtesy of the Herbert Hoover Presidential Library

19. Egypt in the first decade of the twentieth century/Courtesy of the Herbert Hoover Presidential Library

20. Bert and Lou traveled to Australia in 1903 following the birth of their first child, Herbert Junior. In some portions of the outback, Lou was the first woman miners had seen in nearly four years/Courtesy of the Herbert Hoover Presidential Library

21. Lou Henry Hoover bathing her firstborn, Herbert Clark Hoover Junior, born August 4, 1903, in London/Courtesy of the Herbert Hoover Presidential Library

CHAPTER 10

An Organizational Powerhouse

On any given night, one could find a business associate of Bert's, a staffer from Commerce, an engineering colleague, a visiting Girl Scout associate of Lou's, another cabinet secretary, and a friendly journalist dining together at 2300 S Street. Invitations were often issued last minute, and the guests represented eclectic interests. It was from such a diverse gathering that the National Amateur Athletic Federation got its start in late 1921.

It was on one of these evenings that Harding's secretary of war, John W. Weeks, and secretary of the navy, Edwin Denby mentioned that an unusually high number of young men who had been drafted into the Army when the United States entered World War I proved to be malnourished and in poor physical condition. Weeks and Denby remarked on the need to improve the overall health of America's young men in the event the nation needed to fight another war. They talked about forming an organization that promoted physical activity. As a champion of physical fitness for young women, Lou encouraged the two men to include women in their discussions.

Physical fitness was a common topic at 2300 throughout the winter as plans were made to encourage physical activity and wellness. On May 8 and 9, 1922, the Boy Scouts, the Girl Scouts, the YMCA, YWCA, YWHA, United States Golf Association, National Rifle Association, Playground and Recreation Association of America, Knights of Columbus, Lawn Tennis Association, state departments of physical education, as well as representatives from the departments of the army and navy, met at a conference in Washington. The National Amateur Athletic Federation (NAAF) was created as a result of the gathering.

The NAAF officially came into being in December 1922. Henry Breckenridge, a former assistant Secretary of War in the Wilson Administration, was elected president. Elwood Brown, an executive with the YMCA, was chosen executive secretary. Lou, who had hosted some of the organizational meetings in her home, was elected vice president—the only woman to serve on the executive committee.

The NAAF appeared on the scene at a pivotal time in the history of college athletics and physical education programs in the United States. Two organizations had ascended in the world of American amateur sports. The National Collegiate Athletic Association (NCAA) was initially formed in 1905 as the Intercollegiate Athletic Association and changed its name to NCAA in 1910. Its founding was the result of multiple concerns across the academic community. Cheating had become commonplace among teams, and there was no regulatory body to enforce rules. Some colleges hired non-students to play on their teams to boost their chances of winning. When it came to sports safety, injuries in the relatively new game of football had become so severe that President Theodore Roosevelt convened a conference to address the safety and academic needs of college students. The NCAA was formed out of that conference. Its aim was to standardize playing rules and assure that the members of a college's teams were eligible students enrolled in that school. That effort did little to alter the spectator's mindset: By 1922, collegiate sports were a highly popular spectator sport, and a strong source of revenue for colleges and universities.

The other organization that regulated young athletes was the Amateur Athletic Union (AAU). Founded in 1888, the AAU's mission was to set standards for amateur sports. It assumed responsibility for vetting eligible athletes to represent the United States in the Olympic Games when the modern games began in 1896. The AAU considered the formation of the NAAF a direct challenge to its authority.

The NAAF's organizers contended that its goal was to be wholly inclusive and to encourage everyone to be engaged in physical activity. The creation of a Women's Division, dedicated to physical education among women, proved its point. Most colleges and universities had made women's physical education compulsory, and women's teams were formed in several sports that were considered appropriate for women's competitive play. These included swimming, track and field, and basketball (the latter of which was dominated by women in the early years of the sport).

Lou chaired the all-female executive committee of the Women's Division. Its members, representing a cross-section of professionals dedicated to girls' health and fitness, included the physical education director at the University of Wisconsin, the assistant state supervisor of physical education in Massachusetts, the director for physical education and hygiene at the New York City YWCA, and the associate director of the American Child Health Association (ACHA). Bert founded this last association at about the same time as the NAAF got its start. The ACHA's focus was on improving overall child health and nutrition, reducing infant mortality, and eliminating child labor.

Lou privately funded, at an estimated cost of one thousand dollars, an organizational conference to set the goals of the Women's Division in early April 1923. The ideal of the delicate woman who should not exert herself physically continued to hold favor in some influential circles, and newspapers reported that it was Lou's goal to make physically fit goddesses out of women. Detractors claimed the Women's Division planned to adapt military training to make young women physically fit. Pacifists feared that a spirit of militarism would be instilled in women.

None of this was true. The overarching message of the Women's Division was basic:

The purpose of physical activity was to engage in play. Winning in a competitive match was secondary. "A team for everyone and every one for a team!" Lou wrote in the opening line of her foreword to the book, *Play Day—The Spirit of Sport*. Written by two members of the executive committee, the ACHA published the book in 1929 in conjunction with the NAAF's Women's Division.

Play Days encouraged all youth to participate in a sport, regardless of athletic prowess, and to have fun while doing it. "This name focuses on the purpose of all athletics," Lou observed, "—a purpose which many wise people have feared we were in danger of forgetting—which should be relaxation and fun for all, instead of over-exertion for a few, bleacher seats for the many, and too strained intentness for all."[1]

From the start, the NAAF faced financial challenges. Executive Secretary Elwood Brown had masterfully organized funding sources, but these dried up when he died suddenly in 1924 from blood clots that formed as the result of a tooth extraction. By 1925, the Men's Division, facing challenges to its legitimacy by the AAU, struggled to remain effective in amateur men's sports. The Women's Division, however, continued to thrive, in large measure thanks to Lou's expertise as a fund-raiser and her network of donors. It outlasted the Men's, and was folded into the American Association of Health, Physical Education, and Recreation (AAHPER) in the early 1940s. The Women's Division's original goal of promoting physical activity among all women remains the AAHPER's official position.

The view that women should not participate in varsity sports at the same competitive level as men impacted women's athletic programs throughout the twentieth century. Title IX legislation, signed into law in 1972, prohibited gender discrimination in any program that received federal aid. But it was not until 1992 that a lawsuit was successfully argued to address women's sports and establish equality in varsity programming. Of the many organizations that bore the stamp of Lou's leadership, next to the Girl Scouts, her work in the Women's Division held the greatest impact for the longest period of time. In the minds of some today, Lou's stance against women's competitive play at the varsity level held women back from achieving their full potential. While there is merit to the argument, it does overlook how high the barriers to women's physical fitness were as late as the 1920s. The Women's Division, under Lou's leadership, was groundbreaking in identifying the importance of setting appropriate performance benchmarks for women, in addressing concerns about activity during a girl's menstrual period, and even in designing a gym uniform that would be considered modest while simultaneously allowing for full freedom of movement.

Lou took over as captain of Washington-based Girl Scout Troop 8 on March 22, 1923, a position she retained even after she moved to the White House. The troop had been formed two years earlier with fourteen girls and had grown to forty-two by the time Lou took charge. Due to her frequent travel schedule, Lou relied heavily on the young women who served as her assistants and aides. Nevertheless, she got to know each of the girls individually, and she was careful to track the milestones in their lives.

Lou remembered birthdays and graduations, often with flowers. She occasionally arranged to cover girls' college tuition, either through a direct payment or through arranging for employment. Lou stayed in touch with many of the girls after they had gone off to college or married and left the Washington area. Girls from her troop continued to correspond with her well into their adulthood, many sending Lou articles they had published once they were established in their professional lives. Lou's correspondence with the girls in her troop was motherly. She supported and encouraged the girls as they completed college educations and embarked on careers. For Lou, the girls of Troop 8 were the daughters she never had.

In June 1923, President Harding embarked on "The Voyage of Understanding," a 15,000-mile trip to and through the Alaska interior. Its purpose was to escape the pressure in Washington and to shore up the president's reputation with the American people.

History has generally been unkind to the Harding administration, and with good reason. Harding dismissed Charles Forbes, the head of the newly created Veterans Bureau, after it was discovered that he was selling medical supplies intended for veterans to private entities. Yet Harding allowed Forbes to flee the country to escape prosecution. Albert Fall, the secretary of interior, arranged for the transfer of the Elk Hills and Teapot Dome federal oil reserves from the Navy's jurisdiction to his department. Then Fall leased the reserves to private oil companies for a kickback. He was convicted of bribery and was sentenced to nine months' imprisonment. Harry Dougherty, Harding's close friend and engineer of his Republican presidential nomination, served as attorney general. When the oil leases came to light, Dougherty fought to withhold the incriminating documents from congressional investigators. Dougherty was finally forced from office after Calvin Coolidge became president.

The scandals beleaguered Harding. "I have no trouble with my enemies," he said, as each new injurious revelation came across his desk. "I can take care of my enemies in a fight. But my friends, my goddamned friends, they're the ones who keep me walking the floor at nights!"

Bert and Lou accompanied the president and Mrs. Harding to Alaska, along with Fall's replacement, Hubert Work; Secretary of Agriculture Henry Wallace; Alaska's territorial governor Scott C. Bone; and eighty other presidential staff and spouses, and journalists.[2]

The group sailed along the Alaska coast on the USS *Henderson*, stopping at over a half dozen communities, including Juneau, Valdez, and Seward. The party then toured the territory's interior by specially designed car. "The coast of that part of the country is beautiful, and makes one want to go back again sometime, and explore it with much leisure," Lou wrote her friend, Ethel Bagg Bullard, in the breezy tone reminiscent of Lou's early marriage.

"The weather was very pleasant, and we really had great fun. And, of course, there were all sorts of new and interesting things to see."[3]

By the end of the tour, Harding was noticeably weakened. His itinerary along the mainland's Pacific coast was canceled, and the president was rushed down the coastline by rail. He arrived in San Francisco on July 29, where he took rooms at the Palace Hotel. Harding's press secretary reported that he had eaten tainted fish. The president walked up the hotel steps to his room; it was the last time he was seen alive in public.

Bert sensed that something more serious than food poisoning was afoot. He contacted Ray Lyman Wilbur and asked him to come to San Francisco and bring along a heart specialist. By the time the physicians arrived, on August 2, it was too late. Harding succumbed to what was believed to be a stroke. The death certificate cited apoplexy (the then-current term for a cerebral hemorrhage or stroke) as the cause of death.

"It was all very terrible—out there in San Francisco," Lou wrote Bullard. "President Harding had been pronounced well on the road to recovery, and we were all thinking it would mean just many days of complete rest for him. And, then, so suddenly, his heart just gave way, and he was gone."[4]

Lou encouraged Florence Harding with a note and the gift of a jade pendant: "Here is a bit of green for you! Green is the color of hope, you know, and courage—so it is particularly yours. The hope and the trust of the many things very worthwhile that are coming this way in your years to be done,—and the courage which is yours, with which you will meet and do them."[5]

Edgar Rickard, sensing that Lou needed a bit of rest herself, implored her to visit him and Abbie at their Connecticut home. "Abbie and I have had you constantly in mind during this trial of heart and nervous energy," he wrote Lou. "We know how you have given everything in you to help soften the burden of Mrs. Harding. Can't you come to us in Darien and rest and do just as you please all day long? ... [Y]ou know how simple and restful our cottage can be. Please come and stay just as long as you possibly can."[6]

Lou turned down Edgar's offer. She made the unusual decision to skip the annual Girl Scout summer convention, and instead returned to Palo Alto, which had become her personal refuge, to spend time with her sons. Herbert was to return to Stanford in September, and Allan would remain in California for his senior year of high school. She took the boys camping, puttered around her Palo Alto home, and arranged for Allan's enrollment in Palo Alto High School.

The decision for Allan to remain in California for his last year of high school was in reaction to the deplorable conditions of the District of Columbia's public school system. With no autonomy over its own budget, the District depended upon Congress to appropriate operating funds and set the District's budget priorities. The influx of workers during World War I had swelled Washington's population, and the numbers had not abated following the end of the war. Congress, however, had failed to recognize the problem and had allocated no funds for new school construction. Western High School, which Allan had attended in the 1921–22 school year, was so overcrowded that administrators operated the school in two shifts.

Lou was a strong proponent of public education, and she had complained to Senator Frank B. Kellogg, chair of the oversight committee for the District of Columbia, about the poor quality of the city's school system. She acknowledged that she could easily afford to send Allan to one of the District's private schools, but she chose not to do that. When it came to education, she was a small "d" democrat. Lou's astute—and prescient—analysis is still leveled today at American public education.

"Supposed that the conditions became such that I felt forced to send my boy to a private school . . . [to] make room for the children of people who could not possibly send theirs away.," Lou wrote to Kellogg.

> The democracy of our school system will be destroyed, the public high schools . . . will come to be considered for the education only of the children of those who cannot afford anything better. And we will be striking the cleavage of a money aristocracy straight down through our nation to the foundations of our educational system.[7]

Allan's enrollment in Palo Alto High meant that Lou once again depended on others to provide the day-to-day parenting of her child. She hired a Stanford graduate student to live in the house on the hill with Allan. (The young man shared some of Allan's passions, including helping Allan build a car in a room on the lower level of the Hoover's San Juan Hill home.) Charles Henry; Jean; and Jean's children, Janet and Del; moved in for the winter.

With Allan settled, Lou returned to Washington in the early fall and picked up her social duties as a political wife. She hosted a tea for the wife of a new assistant secretary of Commerce. On Columbus Day, Lou presented a talk called "In the Home," part of a one-day conference organized by the United States section of the Pan-American International Women's Committee, an organization of women in the Western Hemisphere that promoted cooperation in scientific endeavors. She continued her work with the NAAF, and she pledged the Girl Scouts' support in raising funds for a memorial to the late President Harding. She also began what became a lifetime friendship with the nation's new first lady, Grace Goodhue Coolidge.

In personality and style, Lou Henry Hoover and Grace Coolidge were opposites: Lou, the take-charge extrovert; Grace, the take-directions introvert. Yet, both women were warm, open, and friendly, considered style-makers during the 1920s, and viewed as supportive wives of their politically ambitious husbands. Their relationship was unaffected by the antipathy that existed between those husbands. Coolidge was a tight-fisted and taciturn Puritan. Bert was likewise taciturn and still governed, to some extent, by his strict Quaker upbringing. Both men had their insecurities, and both could be small minded and petty. Privately, Coolidge derogatorily referred to Bert as "Wonder Boy." Bert was politically savvy enough to know the president held his political future in his hands and showed Coolidge appropriate deference.

Grace Coolidge had earned a Bachelor of Arts degree from the University of Vermont. Upon graduation, she found employment as a teacher of the deaf, a job she retained until her marriage to Calvin Coolidge in 1905. Like the Hoovers, the Coolidges had two sons, although the Coolidges lost their younger son, Calvin, Junior, to sepsis from blood poisoning caused by a blister acquired while playing tennis in the summer of 1924. With their children close in age, Grace and Lou experienced milestones such as college graduations, marriages, and the birth of grandchildren at the same time. The two women had the ability to separate themselves from the limelight, to laugh at their own foibles, and, unlike their respective spouses, not to take themselves too seriously. Their relationship became so close that they wrote poetry to each other and gave each other nicknames connected to flowers each preferred. Lou called Grace 'Lily'; Grace called Lou 'Bleeding Heart.'[8]

Grace jumped into her duties as honorary president of the Girl Scouts, a move that strengthened the bond between her and Lou. Grace was photographed enjoying cookies during Girl Scout Service Week, held in late

October, and she was generous with her time when it came to the scouts. Grace and the president dined at the Little House—the name that had been given to a model home donated to the Girl Scouts by the General Federation of Women's Clubs—where they were served by scouts practicing their hostessing skills.

At the prompting of Helen Ferris at National Girl Scout Headquarters, Lou agreed to write a story about Grace's girlhood for *American Girl* magazine, the in-house publication that was sent to scout membership. The idea for the story emerged following an evening when Grace, Lou, and a friend of Grace's from Vermont, Mrs. John Sargent, lightheartedly reminisced about their girlhoods. Upon hearing about the evening, Ferris remarked to Lou: "You know, we have been publishing a series of true stories about girls who became Presidents' wives. And we have been having another series about the girlhood days of our Girl Scout leaders. And Mrs. Coolidge's story would fit in with both! Won't you ask her to write us the story of her girlhood days?"

Lou replied that Grace was "pretty busy," but agreed to ask.

As Lou had expected, Grace said she did not have the time to write the story. Lou teasingly suggested that she could write the story from her memories of the evening. Grace dared Lou to write the piece. Lou, not one to turn down a challenge, did just that, with help from recollections of Grace's family and Vermont friends.

Lou's story is interesting in the detail it provides about Grace Coolidge's childhood and in what Lou neglects to mention. Lou emphasized Grace's learning to be a homemaker. "Like all the rest of you, even when still very tiny, she was busily doing whatever mother was doing, and early learned to sew, to knit, to dust, to sweep, to set the table, to stand on a little box and help with the dishes at the sink and to dry them shinily [sic] and put them away on the cupboard shelves."[9] Lou went on to describe Grace's love of outdoor activities, her experiences sugaring maple, her faith, and her kindness to others.

The heartwarming story reveals the messages that Lou wanted Scouting to communicate to the public at large. Its omissions of Grace's college education and her years of teaching prior to her marriage are a glimpse into Lou's handling of the criticisms that were being leveled against the Girl Scouts by its detractors. She focused on the way family relationships enriched one's life. Play was an important part of one's day. Community involvement strengthened character. Lou, who privately resented the burdens of homemaking, stressed its value: "And so in her [Mrs. Coolidge's] own little house with her own little babies in Northampton, and later as the wife of the Governor of Massachusetts, and then in the beautiful White House down in Washington, she has always found abiding interest and a chance of beautiful accomplishment in planning and doing the things necessary for the happy running of a household."[10]

Unless a scout was personally acquainted with Lou Hoover, she would never know that the story's author had been taught "masculine" skills as a child, trained as a scientist, was an active member of the Mining and Metallurgical Society of America, regularly attended meetings of the American Association of University Women, and had personally raised millions of dollars in relief efforts. Lou crafted an image of a traditional wife and mother, even though she was anything but. To maintain her image, she avoided profile pieces that delved too closely into her many affiliations and turned the reporter's attention toward the merits of a "cause"—a maneuver she pulled off when she appeared on the cover of *Time* magazine.

On April 24, 1924, Lou Henry Hoover became the second woman to appear on the cover of *Time*, a weekly newsmagazine launched the previous year by Henry Luce. (On July 30, 1923, actress Eleanor Duse became the first woman to appear on the magazine's cover.) The occasion was another of Lou's "causes"—a conference of the Women's National Committee for Law Enforcement that Lou chaired.

The Eighteenth Amendment to the Constitution, otherwise known as the National Prohibition, or Volstead, Act, was the result of years of work by anti-alcohol forces. Congress passed the act on December 18, 1917, and it was ratified by the states on January 16, 1919.

Women had been involved in efforts to forbid the sale of alcohol as early as the 1820s. By the 1870s, they were the face of the movement. Leading the charge was the Women's Christian Temperance Union. The WCTU and other anti-alcohol groups identified liquor as the single leading cause of crime, domestic violence, and spousal abandonment. Alcohol became a scapegoat for social ills brought on by the rapid industrialization of the United States following the end of the Civil War.

By 1924, the promised lawfulness had not materialized. The "noble social and economic experiment," as Bert referred to Prohibition in a letter to Senator William S. Borah, led to the growth of organized crime and its accompanying violence. The decision of many to ignore the Volstead Act generated an anarchic attitude across the nation regarding all statutes.

More than one thousand women from across the nation, most of them members of organizations affiliated with the General Federation of Women's Clubs, women's missionary societies, and temperance organizations, met in Washington on April 10 and 11, 1924, to discuss the problems of general lawlessness. Among the attendees were wives of current and former cabinet members: Mrs. John D. Rockefeller Jr., first lady Grace Coolidge, and former first ladies Florence Harding and Frances Folsom Cleveland Preston (the widow of President Grover Cleveland). Speakers included Attorney General Harlan Fiske Stone, Secretary of the Navy Curtis Dwight Wilbur, and Assistant Attorney General Mabel Walker Willebrandt, who was charged with enforcing Prohibition.

The main message of the conference was a call to action. *Time* referred to the conference attendees as "[t]he avengers of the slandered Prohibition laws." Mabel Willebrandt told the assembly: "[W]omen play bridge at their clubs instead of studying the qualifications of candidates for public office.... Corruption in high places is revolting, but the condition that will prove fatal to this country is lethargy in local government; deterioration and graft in the police force in your city; leniency and pull in state and county courts, and indifference and lack of personal possessory pride on the part of each citizen in the affairs of his local government."[11]

Lou's name as chair lent legitimacy to the nascent Women's National Committee for Law Enforcement, which remained active until the repeal of the Volstead Act by ratification of the Twenty-First Amendment in 1933. The Committee would eventually claim over twelve million members. Lou remained a steadfast proponent of Prohibition, but she never became as active and vocal as her successor, Mrs. Henry W. Peabody, wife of a prominent Boston businessman, who would eventually testify before a Senate committee against repeal of Prohibition.

Lou's decision to assume the chairmanship of the committee on law enforcement was a deft political move. During the same time that she was the face of law and order, Bert's conduct as commerce secretary was coming under the microscope as the Senate investigated the scandals of Harding's appointees.

Bert was not a favorite of traditional Republicans, and his party affiliation did not provide him cover from the senatorial investigations. His administrative fingers were in a lot of pies. While the oil leases were nominally a purview of the interior department, both the Democrats and unfriendly Republicans found it hard to believe that Bert was unaware of their transfer from navy to interior. Furthermore, Bert had been a Harding intimate who often cruised along the Potomac River with the president on the presidential yacht *Mayflower.* Surely, the senators reasoned, Bert and the late president had discussed the actions of other cabinet members in those encounters.

The potential for an investigation into the Hoovers' finances raised alarm bells for Lou. Serving as trustee for the Henry family assets, Lou had housed them within West Branch Corporation, the Hoover family trust. Without Bert's knowledge, Lou engaged the services of William C. Mullendore, an attorney who had once worked for Bert in the American Relief Administration. She asked him to arrange the removal of Henry family monies from West Branch Corporation and transfer them to her sister Jean in a way that avoided a tax burden. Lou and Mullendore corresponded using an agreed upon set of code words in order to conceal Lou's intentions from Bert.[12]

In the meantime, Bert decided it might be advisable to restructure West Branch Corporation so that it would not be perceived that he was trying to evade income or death taxes. His idea was to make Lou sole trustee while retaining "uncontrolled discretion" over the fund's management. She received a telegram on June 20 from Edgar asking her to sign proxy statements representing her shares, and those of Allan and Herbert as their trustee, to be voted at a special meeting called of the shareholders of West Branch Corporation for June 30.[13]

Lou had recently signed the deed for 2300 S Street over to the Corporation so that she would not be listed as the owner, a move intended to protect the property in the event of legal action resulting from the senate investigations. With that move, she did not want to give Bert "uncontrolled discretion," and she did not want responsibility for Bert's financial decisions. Lou may have been willing to drop everything and travel halfway across the country or the world to spend time with her husband, but when it came to money matters, she drew a line. Bert had a reputation for playing fast and loose with his own, and other people's, money. Together, she and Mullendore came up with a plan that allowed her to escape liability.[14]

Fortunately, nothing ever came of the senate hearings. Public attention to the potential for more Harding scandals gave way to interest in the 1924 presidential election. Calvin Coolidge planned to run for a presidential term of his own. The Democratic nomination was contested by Al Smith, the Catholic governor of New York, and William Gibbs McAdoo, a son-in-law of Woodrow Wilson. Neither man won the nomination, but the theater generated by the convention was enough to turn the public's attention away from scandals within what was now Coolidge's cabinet.

On February 1, 1925, Edith Carpenter Macy, the chair of the Girl Scouts' Executive Board, died suddenly from a heart attack while vacationing in Florida. She had served as chair of the Girl Scouts' Executive Board since 1919, and the combination of her financial commitment to the Scouts and her leadership skills meant her death left a void in the organization. Juliette Gordon Low once described Macy as "the pivot that kept our whole organization in harmony."[15] Lou decided that she could better serve the Girl Scouts by stepping into the slot vacated by Macy's death and resigned as Girl Scout president to become the chair of the executive board.

Macy's sudden death left such a hole in the Girl Scout organization that Lou considered its immediate needs to be more important than attending Allan's graduation from Palo Alto High School. She once again asked Allan to forgive her for missing a key milestone in his life. Allan, who idolized his mother, accepted her apologies.

However, she and Bert were both on hand for Herbert's graduation from Stanford on June 22, 1925, and his marriage, three days later, to Margaret "Peggy" Watson, a fellow Stanford student, on June 25. Herbert had announced his engagement the previous year. "We are all extremely pleased over Herbert and Peggy," Lou had written Ethel Bullard when the couple's intentions were announced. To another correspondent, Lou shared that Herbert had been interested in his future bride since their freshman year together in Stanford. Following his graduation and wedding, Herbert and Peggy traveled across the country to Cambridge, where Herbert was enrolled in Harvard Business School. Although his parents and Uncle Tad had done their best to steer Herbert toward the "family business" of mining engineering, the younger Hoover had become fascinated with aviation. He intended to build a career in the fledgling industry.

Lou jumped into her new role in Scouting with the energy and attention to detail of a highly paid CEO. Now thirteen years old, the Girl Scout organization was in its adolescence: Membership was growing at nearly an exponential rate; finances continued to be shaky; and leadership voids threatened the ability to manage such rapid expansion. One of her first efforts was to find a way to supplement the personal income of Sarah Louise Arnold, who would replace Lou as president of the Girl Scouts.

Arnold, dean of Simmons College, had worked with Bert in the Food Administration in 1917. She supplemented her educator's modest income with writing. Lou anticipated that Arnold would not have time to continue writing and to serve in the unpaid position of Girl Scout president. Harry Chandler, publisher of the Los Angeles *Times*, promised $2,500, but Lou did not want Arnold to sacrifice financially in service to the Scouts. Lou wrote Edgar: "Do you happen to know whether any of the old Food Administration crowd,—or anyone else—, is interested enough in Dean Arnold to want to contribute largely (anything from $100.00 up!) to a fund for presentation [as a gift] because she is going to be the next year's President of the Girl Scouts. . . ."[16]

Lou's profound belief in the value of Scouting and the seriousness with which she took her responsibilities is reflected in her first welcoming address to the board:

> Perhaps it is well, as we start out on this our first session after the Convention which elected the first Board of Directors, to consider for a moment what we really are,—for ours is a position of tremendous responsibility. Most of us are in Girl Scouting so completely, I think, because we believe it is the movement of the present fraught with the greatest possibilities for good of any movement in our country,—and the responsibility of endeavoring to guide that movement aright is tremendous beyond conception.
>
> It is within our power to make this a great, living thing, giving and extending in beneficent influence beyond our widest conception now,—or else we let it fossilize into a more or less pleasant, sterile, little organization of no more usefulness or inspiration than a dozen others already in the field. This power is ours,—limitless,—the responsibility for accomplishing, or letting die, this vigorous young thing is ours.
>
> And at the same time, we must not forget that we have lesser responsibilities. We have, for example, the responsibility of managing a public trust.

> Each one of us has her due personal responsibility under law for the administration of a corporation, and for the administration of a corporation backed by contributory funds. This means we must look straight-eyed at the legal necessities here, and be sure that in developing the soul of our movement, we do so only by methods countenanced by the laws of our existence. This means only that we proceed always with due care, and sometimes a little more slowly than our impulses desire.[17]

When the Girl Scouts celebrated its centennial in 2012, it owed a good portion of its longevity to the work Lou accomplished as chair of the Executive Committee from 1925 until her resignation when Bert won the presidency in 1928. She pushed the Scouts to begin to think strategically, and the executive board eventually agreed to develop a five-year budget and strategic plan to secure the Scouts' financial situation. She continued the work started under Macy by promoting professionalized leadership development, including overseeing the construction of Camp Edith Macy, in Westchester, New York, built specifically to train scout leaders. (Lou worked with James Yardley Rippin, the architect husband of the Scout's executive director Jane Deeter Rippin, to design the camp's main hall.)

Under Lou's leadership, sections of the Girl Scout's constitution and bylaws were revised to improve the troop chartering process and to assure legitimacy in earned badges. Jane Deeter Rippin was tasked with overseeing the Scouts' day-to-day operational concerns, but Rippin deemed it wise to keep Lou apprised of even the smallest details, regardless of how petty. When questions about the chartering of Los Angeles' troops arose, Rippin forwarded Lou the contents of the telegram:

> Before issuing new charter you had better investigate Los Angeles Council. Notice fact that names of Scout representatives do not appear on application. We leaders are not satisfied. We are most enthusiastic about our local director and do not want to lose her. So sorry she was not allowed to go to National Convention. We have an actress for a commissioner and would like a Scout.[18]

Lou's business acumen enabled her to pinpoint accounting problems that contributed to the Scouts' annual deficits. In a confidential letter to Abbie Rickard, the organization's treasurer, Lou revealed her dismay at how Rippin accounted for the cost of the Scout publications, such as the Scout handbooks and materials for the leaders. "You may imagine my dismay when I discovered that she [Rippin] has not written into the cost of any of these books the proportion of the salaries of the members of the staff engaged in compiling them!" Lou acknowledged that, as board chair, she should have reviewed the financial statements more closely. Also absent from the calculations were allocations for office space and general office expenditures. "Amongst other things, I was astonished at the cost of handling. In the five main books, the handling percentages run 11 7/8%, 12 2/3%, 23%, 24 2/3% and 31 1/3%. This, it seems to me, is stupendous." Lou suggested that Abbie check with Edgar to find out what constituted reasonable handling charges. The upshot of Rippin's accounting method was that she was showing a tiny loss on the sale of each book on paper, when, in fact, the loss on each sale was significant.[19]

National headquarters also absorbed inventory costs for local Scout stores. Stores returned unsold uniforms to National, and National wrote off the expense. In 1928, for example, the return of equipment amounted to $40,000. That same year, the Finance Committee voted to borrow $20,000 toward balancing its budget, but the National organization needed $120,077 to avoid a deficit. "Would it be possible for you to ask at least twenty-five friends to become contributing members of the Girl Scout organization?" Abbie wrote Lou, after outlining the Scouts' financial woes. "We are anxious to extend the interest in Girl Scouting among a greater number of people, and the Finance Committee would appreciate it if you would ask various friends who have not been contributing to the work."[20] While there is no record of Lou's response in the file, it is quite likely that Lou tapped into resources to help the organization.

Lou turned fifty-three on March 29, 1927. Her hair had begun to turn prematurely grey in the early 1920s, and by 1927, it was white. The lighter color emphasized her blue eyes, but it did not age her appearance. She was frequently photographed in her Girl Scout uniform, which was tailored for the flapper style of the era with a pleated, loose-fitting jacket, drop-waist belt, and pleated skirt. She sported the wide-brimmed hat that Juliette Gordon Low favored, which gave Lou a stern appearance that belied her warmth and vitality. When not in her uniform, Lou dressed modestly, but fashionably. Her clothing reflected the style of the times, including colorful, flowing dresses and gowns, some of which were shot through with genuine gold or silver metallic thread—a popular embellishment in women's clothing of the period.

Since her work with the CRB, Lou had begun a practice of private philanthropy. Through her extensive network of friends and acquaintances in both the United States and Europe, she would be made aware of young people, (usually women), who showed promise, but who lacked the resources to complete their college education. Without revealing her identity, Lou would arrange to have college tuition and/or living expenses paid for these selected individuals. Lou's network of contacts sent her regular reports on the progress of recipients along with an assessment as to whether or not Lou should continue to fund the person's education. In some cases, individuals were made aware of their benefactress, and they would attempt to repay her once they were earning an income. In nearly every instance, Lou returned the check.

Her generosity extended to her family. Lou's niece, Hulda Hoover, decided to marry before she completed her degree at Stanford. Hulda's sister, Louise, had likewise married before finishing at Stanford, where their father, Theodore, was dean of the School of Engineering. Louise had dropped out of college following her wedding, a situation that Lou was hoping to stave off with her younger niece. When Hulda's new husband, Charles McLean, flunked out of Stanford, a family friend arranged for the couple to be accepted at McGill University, in Montreal, Quebec, Canada. Lou helped cover their expenses.

She wrote to Theodore: "I think our children's experiment has been singularly successful. I was sure it would be from their attitude last summer,—but even I confess to being most pleasurably surprised by the way they have met all their new conditions and managed to pull out such good records at the same time. It shows that Charles has the ability as well as the disposition and character. They don't always necessarily go together!"

Lou detailed the monthly stipend she paid the couple, and assured Theodore that she was committed to helping her niece and her husband get a start in their lives together. "I shall continue to send them what they need for the coming year [when they return to] Stanford," Lou assured Theodore, "and afterward to get them whatever destination they choose for beginning their life work."[21]

Lou paid the tuition for private schools for Janet and Del Large. Jean and

Lou had concerns about Janet attending Palo Alto High School because of the large number of Stanford men who sought to date the younger girls. Lou suggested that Jean send her children east. Janet lived at 2300 S Street for a year to attend Holton Arms School, but she faced social pressures from her teachers and classmates that Lou could not have anticipated. Lou thought it would help if Jean came east, but her sister was now a full-time caregiver for their father. Charles Henry had developed dementia. He was prone to violent outbursts which were triggered when someone he did not like cared for him.

"It really would be good if Auntie Jean could be here for a few days.," Lou wrote Allan, asking him if the newly hired caregiver was competent to care for Charles in Jean's absence.

> [T]here are factors in Janet's situation at school that would make it very advisable that her mother could be known before the year is out. So many people are sent to school to be got away from undesirable or undesiring parents, that I think it would be useful for her teachers and our friends to realize what a delightful, modest, unassuming, worthwhile person her mother is.[22]

The following year, Lou enrolled Janet in an arts academy in Vermont run by Lou's friend Katherine Everts. (Lou had provided financial assistance to Everts to get the academy up and running several years earlier.) Del attended Mercersburg Academy, in Pennsylvania, an academy run on the model of the highly respected college preparatory school, Exeter Academy, in New England.

Lou's largesse had its limits. "I am tired of helping educate that great husband of Ethel's [Ethel Minthorn was a first cousin to Bert and Tad]," Lou wrote her brother-in-law. "Don't you think he is educated enough to teach now?" She asked Tad if he thought a conversation with the couple would bring results. "I talked with Ethel one day on the subject,—and she looks as though she had worked herself to a mere thread, and he is too fat and lazy-looking for anything. When I asked when he was going to work, she talked some drivel about the fact that now he had his Master's degree, of course it wouldn't be difficult to get his Doctor's. I told her that I didn't approve of that at all."[23]

Lou's immediate family had also expanded: She was now a grandmother.

Herbert and Peggy's first child, Margaret Ann (known as Peggy Ann), was born two months' premature on March 17, 1926. On November 11, 1927, Peggy Hoover gave birth to her second child—a son named Herbert C. Hoover III, called Pete, to distinguish him from his father and grandfather. "I went to see the baby while Daddy went to St. Louis," Lou wrote Allan on November 21. "He is a nice big seven-and-a-half-pound baby that you can hold—not a frail little one like Peggy Ann. He is very cunning, but doesn't look like anyone in our family. . . . His features are quite definite—and he has a good-sized nose for a baby. In that respect only he resembles you," she teased her son. "But it isn't the same shape as yours. He isn't in any respect like the Hoovers, or Henrys, or Watsons."[24]

By 1928, Lou had settled into a rhythm that suited her. The work with the Girl Scouts, which used her organizational and business skills, provided her with enormous satisfaction. She was a recognized social leader in Washington and had developed a network of like-minded women friends who had the money and the education to move beyond the restrictions placed on affluent women in the previous generations. Lou also reveled in her new role as a grandmother, and her correspondence with friends suggests she wanted to be more hands-on with her grandchildren than she had been with her own children.

Whatever her private thoughts, Lou had accepted the on-again, off-again intimacy in her marriage. She and Bert enjoyed traveling and camping together, but otherwise, she accepted that they lived separate lives. Unless marked "private and confidential," she opened and responded to his mail. Except for his personal investments with Edgar and other associates, she managed Bert's money. She ran his household, and she bought his clothes. She performed these tasks with her usual efficiency and competence, and she added these responsibilities to the many others she handled without evident resentment. Other than desiring to live full time in Palo Alto rather than divide her year between California and Washington, Lou was reasonably content.

The weather and Bert's presidential ambitions were about to upend her contentment.

CHAPTER 11

The Trail to the White House

In late 1926 and into the first three to four months of 1927, the states along the Mississippi River experienced relentless rainfall, brought on by what we today call the El Niño effect. By Good Friday, April 15, 1927, the Mississippi River had flooded several hundred thousand square miles. The water extended as far west as Texas, as far north as Illinois, and devastated the southern states of Mississippi, Louisiana, and Arkansas. In the Commonwealth of Kentucky alone, the Red Cross established twenty-two tent cities on dry ground. New Orleans faced a devastation not seen again until Hurricane Katrina hit the city in 2005.

President Coolidge, following a long tradition of federal non-response to natural disasters, watched as the waters rose. He initially resisted requests for governmental assistance, but when it became obvious that the states could not handle the magnitude of damage caused by the flooding, Coolidge responded. He put Bert in charge of the disaster.

The newspapers announced Bert's appointment with great fanfare: "With Secretary Hoover, wartime relief expert, as active field marshal, the Nation's authorized agencies of mercy mobilized here today to combat the increasing horror of America's greatest Mississippi flood catastrophe."[1]

Bert went to work with the same organizational intensity that he had used to provide relief to Belgium. He formed a committee consisting of elected officials; heads of relief agencies, including the Red Cross; and friends from his network of businessmen. He toured the flooded areas, arranged for the delivery of needed supplies, and inspected the levees around New Orleans. By the end of September, Bert reported to Coolidge the results of the recovery efforts. Over ninety per cent of the communities that had been destroyed by the flood were rebuilding. The remaining eight to ten percent were African American communities that had been ignored by relief teams and short-changed in receiving supplies. Bert omitted these details from his formal report.

Flood relief activities placed Bert in the glare of the national spotlight throughout the summer of 1927. The attention focused on him raised questions regarding Coolidge's plans to run for another term in 1928. Speculation had been rife regarding the president's intentions since the 1926 midterm elections. Some observers noted how deeply the loss of his son had impacted Coolidge, and many doubted that he had the drive to serve for another four years. In the meantime, Bert had been testing the waters for another presidential run. He formed an exploratory committee while doing his best to keep his inquiries as unobtrusive as possible. His relationship with the president was prickly at best. Were the touchy Coolidge to get a whiff of his commerce secretary's ambitions, Coolidge could use his office to quash those ambitions by dismissing Bert from his cabinet, thus robbing him of a ready-made stage.

On August 2, 1927, Coolidge announced from his summer office in the Black Hills of South Dakota that he did not "choose to run for president in 1928." With Coolidge out of the race, the scramble among likely candidates began. The Washington *Evening Star* published a gallery of photographs of the most likely candidates. Bert headed the list, which also included former Illinois Governor Frank O. Lowden; Vice President Charles G. Dawes; Speaker of the House Nicholas Longworth; and Senator William E. Borah, known as the "Lion of Idaho."[2]

Lou remained on the periphery as Bert laid his campaign groundwork. Edgar observed that his friend would only discuss his political plans when Lou was not in the room. She wrote her sons: "[A]ffairs are going with uncanny rapidity towards making your Daddy President. Even he is perfectly amazed at it, and sometimes says it just does not seem possible that it can all be happening on its own impetus, and practically without any effort on his part."[3] Either Lou intentionally ignored the reality in front of her, or Bert purposely mislead his wife. She hoped to finally put Washington behind her and return full-time to California.

The truth was that Bert was as much the master of his campaign effort as he had been the "master of the emergencies," as his biographer Will Irwin dubbed him for a 1928 campaign film. Bert had learned from his mistakes in 1920. This time, he resolved to win.

By the end of January, nearly every state had a Hoover for President Engineers Committee. Men who had met Bert at professional society meetings and remained connected over the years headed the committees. Lou had been active in the various societies' women's auxiliaries, and the women members wanted to form their own committees in support of Bert's candidacy. Thinking it would be a well-received gesture, they asked Lou to serve as an honorary vice president. She was having none of it.

"My dear Mrs. Gilbreth," Lou instructed her secretary to write to Lillian Moller Gilbreth, a fellow engineer and close friend of both Hoovers:

> Replying to your letter of February 17 to Mrs. Hoover, there has apparently been [an] unfortunate impression gotten abroad that she is in some way connected with the Hoover-for-President Engineering Committee,—probably due to the confusion caused by the similarity in names between this committee and the Women's Auxiliary of the American Institute of Mining and Metallurgical Engineers which has just elected her president.
>
> I think you undoubtedly appreciate her position in refusing absolutely to take part in any organization furthering the candidacy of her husband for the Presidency.
>
> Thanking you, for her, for your friendly offer of cooperation.[4]

Nat Carle, another colleague and former Stanford classmate of Lou's, tried to cajole her into accepting the title:

> Someone raised the point that there were many representative engineers among the women of the United States and suggested that they be asked to accept honorary appointments. Among the women mentioned were you, Mrs. Gilbreth, and Miss Kate Gleason. To my surprise, several of the engineers did not know of your technical training in college, and I made a brief statement in regard to same.[5]

"My dear Nat Carle," Lou replied, "I think it was very nice of you to remember enough of our engineering experiences together to suggest that I be an honorary member of any engineering body,—but please don't let it be the Hoover-for-President Engineering Committee!

Yours sincerely, and alarmedly,"[6]

Undeterred, Carle tried once more, eliciting an uncharacteristically sharp-toned note from a perturbed Lou:

> My dear Nat Carle,
>
> I wonder where is your sense of humor,—or my ability to put things over in comprehensible, understandable English? We both had 'em thirty years ago.

She then softened her language, assuring Carle that she did not want the committee to feel obligated to name her as an honorary vice president, ending her letter on a friendly note by encouraging Carle and his wife stop by to visit the next time they were in Washington.[7]

Privately, Lou paid close attention to Bert's campaign progress. She kept a delegate count in anticipation of the Republican convention scheduled for June 12 through 15. She sent regular updates to Allan, who was keenly interested in his father's political future. While attending a Scouting event in Scranton, Pennsylvania in April, Lou reported:

> [Today is Thursday, and] I have not seen Daddy since Saturday night, really. I left Sunday night,—but he was busy with men all day Sunday, so I did not even see him at meals. . . .Nothing has happened against our hero,—but a number of unexpected advantageous things have happened for the opposition. While it is fine for the country to have the rotten condition of Illinois get a jolt, it means that there are probably that many votes for Lowden or Dawes [both from Illinois] direct, instead of being in the hands of the recent robbers, and being given later to L or D for a price.. . . . Some well-balanced people like Mr. Sullivan say this is their last gasp, and that Daddy's innings begin now.[8]

Bert had solid support in cities and heavily urbanized states, such as Massachusetts, but his support in rural areas was tepid. Farmers had not forgotten the economic pain he had caused them during World War I. In his negotiations with brokers during his time with the CRB, Bert pushed to get the lowest possible price for wheat. As Food Administrator, he created the United States Sugar Equalization Board, Inc. and the Food Administration Grain Corporation to control prices. When contracts that had been signed prior to the Armistice for wheat deliveries were dishonored once Europe restarted its own agricultural production in 1919, American farmers suffered a significant loss of income. By 1928, they still had not recovered.

Lou, however, insisted to Allan that Bert had always supported farmers. In explaining the rural-urban divide among Ohio's delegates, she told her son:

> It is funny the way the real farmers let the farm agitators put over all this stuff about Daddy being against the farmer, when he never has been. Even in the war, when his one thought and aim was to get food for the armies and the starving, he always protected the farmers from possible loss. But instead of remembering that, they make up all this absolute falsehood about his missing the farmer then![9]

Even if facts indicated the contrary, Lou always expressed strong support for Bert and his integrity in letters to her sons. As a trained scientist and a competent businesswoman, she was experienced in drawing logical conclusions from observations and analysis. But when it came to protecting Bert's reputation and encouraging her sons to love and support their father, she often ignored the facts.

As Bert oversaw his campaign, Lou kept track of Allan's activities in Palo Alto through a combination of letters and telegrams. She paid Allan, now a student at Stanford, a salary to serve as a host for guests and maintenance superintendent. Vaal Stark, older sister of Lou's assistant Dare Stark, managed daily affairs, which included keeping track of the revolving door of students and visitors who were offered lodging on the Hill. Lou directed visiting Girl Scout colleagues to San Juan Hill and wrote Vaal to arrange a lunch or a party in their honor. In the case of one pair of scout leaders, Lou told Allan: "I also said [to Vaal] that if the house were not full, you might invite them up to sleep there and have breakfast with you,—or alone, if you have to dash off to an eight o'clock."[10]

Envisioning the house as the Hoovers' western headquarters, Lou instructed Allan to inventory furniture and identify pieces to be replaced. She outlined plans for the renovation of some rooms, and entrusted Allan to work with Birge Clark on the remodeling. Concerned about the external appearance of the property, Lou instructed Allan:

> Tell Clarence [the Hoover's handyman], he must get out of sight always, any rubbish. But especially now, to take away all the bricks and mortar and

> stuff the workmen threw from our roof down on [the next door neighbor's] lot. And any time you see any kind of rubbish lying around on any of our property in sight from the roads, or any one's house, for more than a day or two, tell him I told you to have him keep all our land tidy from the roads and paths and houses. Big dead weeds (and living ones!) I also consider rubbish.[11]

She supported Allan's newfound passion of aviation and his efforts to receive his pilot's license, as long as he was pursuing his interest because he was "overwhelmingly thrilled," and not because he needed something to do. Aviation had captured the imaginations of both Hoover young men to the point where Herbert was engaged in it professionally. In 1928, the Guggenheim Fund for the Development of Aeronautics had employed Herbert to survey West Coast air routes. Even Lou expressed an interest in this new form of travel, admitting to Allan that she had "always intended to take it [flying] up sometime, so will join you."[12] But she drew the line at his flying across the country to visit his parents. She and Bert preferred that Allan choose transportation that kept him on the ground.

Like his mother, Allan explored a range of interests, including the start of a rose-growing business. He and Lou exchanged letters about color selection and production costs. She encouraged her son's entrepreneurial endeavors, stressing the value of good time and financial management: "Now that you have gone into the rose growing business, don't let it monopolize too much of your time," she cautioned Allan. (In the same letter she warned him not to sell anything that belonged to her to support his interests in flying.) "You did so remarkably well without roses last year, that now if you have a few, don't spend your entire time wearing them and sharing them with your friends—ladies and gentlemen! Some roses, some golf. Marks always up to date." She outlined what she saw as Allan's priorities: "[M]arks first, golf next, roses and their accompaniments next, before anything else [such as flying] is contemplated."[13]

From the public's vantage point, Lou saw [herself as] a woman who continued to be engaged in her own activities while Bert directed his campaign operation from his office at the commerce department. In the custom of the time, neither of them traveled to Kansas City, Missouri, to attend the Republican National Convention. Allan, however, wanted to attend, and

Lou, with the help of Bert's campaign organization, provided her son with a ticket to the convention and arranged for him to room with the son of New Jersey Congressman Franklin Fort, an active organizer on behalf of Bert's candidacy.

Bert held a majority of delegate support from the start. Former Illinois governor Frank O. Lowden and Kansas senator Charles Curtis were distant seconds. However, Bert's people had concerns that Caucasian delegates from the more heavily rural southern states might not stay loyal to him if there were multiple ballots. A common practice to secure delegate loyalty was for candidate organizations to give payments to defray delegates' travel expenses. Bert directed that only white Southern delegates receive money and that none go to African American delegates.

Lou refused to acknowledge the discrimination when she reported the decision to Allan. "Daddy has given absolutely mandatory orders that there wasn't a dollar to be spent on colored delegates, if he lost them all," she wrote. In spite of that, two or three of his supporters did send money to African American delegates from the South without letting Bert know, which "made him extremely angry, as you can imagine," Lou added. "Then in Florida, where so many Northern whites are settling, there is growing a large Republican population. There were enough of them down there to join the Republican organization and put out the old time colored bosses. Everybody should be extremely pleased over this."[14]

Lou shared the prejudices that were common to white Americans of the era. She had written to one friend that a prospective businessperson born in Portugal had not lived up to his full potential because he was typical of his people. She retained the anti-Oriental prejudices she had acquired during her years of living in the Far East. She showed concern for the welfare of her Hispanic and African American employees, but she drew a line at becoming too familiar and believed they were better off living in their own communities. Her letter to Allan indicates a tacit approval of Bert's decision to marginalize the Republican African American delegates. If she thought there would be long-term political repercussions, she did not discuss them in her correspondence. What neither she nor Bert could foresee was that this seemingly small decision during the 1928 convention would initiate a shift among African American voters away from the party of Lincoln to the Democratic party and remake the electoral map.

Bert won the Republican presidential nomination on the first ballot. Charles Curtis, who had won sixty-four ballots to Bert's 837, was chosen as his vice-presidential running mate. The Democratic National Convention, held at the end of June, nominated New York governor Alfred E. Smith, the first Catholic presidential nominee. Senate Minority Leader Joseph T. Robinson of Arkansas was the vice-presidential nominee. Smith's religion, together with his support for the repeal of the Volstead Act, would be major factors in the campaign. Bert had a strong reason to put to rest any rumors about his and Lou's alleged Catholicism.

Anti-Catholic sentiment was strong during the 1920s, fed, in large measure, by a resurgent Ku Klux Klan. The original Klan had been founded after the Civil War. Initially a social club, it gradually became an underground organization dedicated to terrorizing free African Americans and fighting racial equality in the United States. The Klan faded into the background following the end of Reconstruction and the passage of Jim Crow laws, upheld by the Supreme Court's decision in *Plessy v. Ferguson*, in 1896. In 1915, William Joseph Simmons, an Alabama native and graduate of Johns Hopkins University in Baltimore, held a meeting at Stone Mountain, Georgia, to reorganize the Klan. The group's message was strongly nativistic, anti-Catholic, and anti-Semitic.

The United States' entry into World War I diminished support for the Klan, but the economic downturn following the Armistice and the influx of immigrants from Eastern Europe created a new opportunity for the Klan to gain members and influence. Simmons hired two marketing professionals to promote the organization. They were successful enough to generate electoral majorities that affected the gubernatorial elections in Oklahoma, Texas, Oregon, Indiana, Maine, and New Jersey. In 1924, the Democratic Party had officially denounced the Klan at its convention. Coolidge, however, refused to condemn the organization, and communicated his displeasure when his running mate, Charles Gates Dawes, criticized the organization at a rally in Maine.

The Klan was still a political force to be reckoned with in 1928. Rumors that had circulated in 1920 that Lou was a Catholic because a priest had performed her wedding ceremony resurfaced. Some rumors asserted that both Lou and Bert were secretly Catholic. Others claimed that Bert was an atheist and Lou was a Catholic, influencing her husband's decisions based on her presumed religious beliefs. Lou received letters from around the country asking her to confirm (or deny) the couple's Catholicism, questioning whether Herbert and Allan had attended (or were attending) Catholic schools, and if the Hoovers attended church regularly.

Lou did her best to correct people's impressions: "All of the nice little details were made up of absolutely whole cloth or their imaginations.," she wrote to one woman.

> They made an ardent Episcopalian out of me without much foundation. One half of my family were Episcopalian, the other half Presbyterian—(and I was quartered and eighthed into absolutely every known Protestant religion of the colonies)—but they were so tolerant that I went to church or Sunday School according as the conditions of the town we were in dictated.

Of her wedding ceremony, Lou explained, "My father simply asked him [Father Mestres] if he would come and do it [the wedding ceremony], and he said that he would be delighted."[15]

Lou's private denials were insufficient to end the rumors entirely. They persisted through the entire presidential campaign, and Lou wrote to Father Ramon Mestres after the November election:

> Now that the smoke of battle has cleared away and one is living in a normal world again I want to assure you,—what I believe you must always have known,—that neither my husband nor I ever gave any single statement about our wedding to the press; that all the weird accounts were either circulated as trouble makers by the "opposition" or by overly enthusiastic supporters of my husband who were using their imaginations as a basis instead of ascertaining facts.
>
> Sometime the simple facts will be recognized. In the meantime, little effect is made one way or the other upon the general mind. But I hate to have the faintest suspicion myself that you might have any question as to our attitude upon the subject. I was even worried by the absurd tale that my husband had not remembered your name and had to telephone me for it,—lest you might think that was true! Of course, it was pure fiction,—he never was interviewed by anyone on the matter.[16]

Lou's letter is reminiscent of her correspondence with Alice Dickson during the year that Alice packed up Red House and implored Lou to respond to her letters. Just as her hastily written notes to Dickson, Lou's letter to Father Mestres assumes that he understands how busy she has been and overlooks his feelings. She did not apologize for the press hounding him; neither did she ask forgiveness for the anti-Catholic tone that permeated the last months of the campaign. It was an insensitivity that surfaced when Lou was in a situation requiring that she express approval for Bert's actions—whether overtly or tacitly. There is no record of a reply from Father Mestres.

As Bert met with his advisors to develop a campaign strategy, Lou handled the challenges to the family's privacy. She instructed Allan to order and install gates at San Juan Hill for additional security. "Tell Roth Dad asks for appropriate not ugly not too expensive gates or barriers on our road," Lou instructed Allan in a telegram.[17]

Bert and Tad's elderly aunt, Ann Minthorn Heald, was besieged by as many as five reporters daily after Bert became the nominee. Her children, Ethel and Bertha, were at work during the day, and "Aunt Ann of course has not the courage to or force to stand these people off," Tad wrote Lou. He hired a companion, and he told Lou, "the cost thereof which will not be large, should, I think, be charged to the Honorable Herbert Hoover's campaign expenses."[18]

Lou concurred. "I think you were quite right about the Presidential Nominee being responsible for paying Aunt Ann's protection from newspapermen and photographers."[19]

On July 5, Charles Henry took ill while camping with Jean and her family in the California mountains. She took her father to a sanitarium in Placerville. Doctors expected him to make a slow recovery, assuming he did not develop pneumonia. On July 9, based on an optimistic update, Lou joined Bert for a victory train ride to Palo Alto with various stops along the way.

On July 18, Allan cabled Lou from Placerville: "Grandfather passed away this morning." Charles Henry was eighty-four. Lou, who was in Grand Island, Nebraska, wired Allan with detailed instructions regarding her father's funeral arrangements, adding: "We are sorry you have all these sad duties the first day of your twenty-second year, but know these things will be well attended in your hands."[20] Bert continued to greet crowds at each of the train's stops, but Lou retired privately to grieve. Their train arrived in Palo Alto the morning of Friday, July 20, and Charles's funeral was held at the chapel at Stanford that afternoon.

Lou disappeared from public view following her father's death. Charles Henry's health had been declining in the years since his wife's passing, and Lou had monitored his condition through regular communications with Jean and Allan. However, one is never fully prepared for the death of a parent, and Lou was no exception. Her natural ebullience deserted her, and she spent hours alone. Duty helped her cope. As trustee for the Henry Family, she oversaw matters concerning her father's estate and took steps to ensure financial security for her sister. Over the years, the two sisters had jointly purchased residential properties and rented the homes, providing a source of needed income for Jean and supplemental income for Lou.

Political life pulled Lou back into action. Bert was officially notified of his nomination and delivered his acceptance speech on August 11 to a packed Stanford University stadium. His message was carried over radio. Behind the scenes, Lou took on the familiar role of managing the logistics of her husband's life.

"Why wouldn't it be a good idea (for me!)," Lou wrote to her long-time friend, Sue Dyer, "for you to take on the job of rather official hostess on the hill for the next month? A few people will be staying with us,—and by that I have no idea whether it will be two or three,—or sixteen with a cot in every hall! Bert does in such matters what appeals to him at the moment."[21]

In accepting a friend's offer to use her home as headquarters for Bert's campaign operation, Lou wrote:

> [Bert] dislikes the idea of having any kind of headquarters or offices in downtown office buildings,—while the possibility of using a few rooms in a house such as yours in the immediate neighborhood would be perfectly miraculous, so that the visiting delegations of Serbs, Croats, and Slovenes or of the Republicans from Massachusetts will be received with distinction in your house without meeting in the front hall my departing tea party, or the Congressman from Massachusetts, or the Secretary of State, or Dr. Work [chairman of the Republican National Committee] dropping in for a friendly conference.[22]

Minor differences existed between the major parties' platforms. The Republican Party called for lower taxes, maintaining the protective tariff, the "observance and vigorous enforcement" of Prohibition, the creation of a Federal Farm Board, and disclosure of campaign finances.[23] The Democrats sought the establishment of a Federal Farm Board to oversee loans to farmers and proposed the establishment of major public works programs to help resolve the unemployment problem, including flood control projects—a response to the 1927 disaster that had propelled Bert to frontrunner status for the Republican nomination.[24]

Ignoring the similarities between the platforms, Bert couched the Democrats' and Smith's vision for America as one of "state socialism," a loaded phrase that belied the numerous federal regulatory programs Bert had enacted as US Secretary of Commerce. Prohibition was a hotly debated topic. As governor of New York, Smith signed the Culliver Law, which reduced New York State's participation in the enforcement of Prohibition restrictions. Bert, who enjoyed a private drink on occasion at the Belgian Embassy in Washington, publicly supported the full enforcement of Prohibition. The underlying subtext to the Hoover-Smith campaign was Al Smith's Catholicism.

In his formal acceptance speech at Stanford, Bert committed to a stand for religious tolerance, but privately, he did little to stop the rapidly growing anti-Catholic campaign gaining ground nationwide. Catholics were not well-known outside of the heavily industrialized northeast and Midwest, and the southwestern states, which had originally been settled by Catholic Spaniards. (Some Spanish missions dated to the 1600s.) Anti-Catholic publications and lecturers warned that Smith's election would mean the country would be forced to pledge allegiance to the Pope. Handbills promoted lecturers who claimed that the purpose of Catholics was to murder Protestants and destroy the American government. A handbill entitled, "10 Reasons Why Al Smith Should Not Be Elected," listed alleged statements by Catholic clergy claiming that Catholics had taken an oath to unite church and state.[25]

Smith courageously denounced the bigotry and hatred as un-American in a speech on September 20 in Oklahoma City, the heart of Klan country. Bert not only chose to ignore the issue but proceeded to give a blow-by-blow account of the many slurs that had been uttered about him, with the implication that Bert had been as much a victim of bigotry as his opponent.

Rather than play an advisory role where she called her husband to account for his slanted view, Lou turned a blind eye to the bigotry that influenced the campaign and echoed Bert's rhetoric and viewpoint. "Religion is not a matter for a political issue, pro or con," she wrote Edgar.

> I myself am in a position to know with what very great regret very many leaders on the Republican side in the campaign saw that this religious issue might become involved, as they realized what it might mean in creating inflammatory groups in certain sections of our country. . . . I myself have heard and seen the orders going out that no matter what individuals or certain ardent groups in certain sections of the country might feel on this subject, that it was not ever to be utilized directly or indirectly by the Republican leaders.[26]

Lou insisted that the Republicans were not behind the whispering campaign against Smith, and that it was Smith and the Democrats who had launched whispering campaigns about Bert. These included lies about his racial prejudices: "[H]e carries on his practice of discrimination against [the Negroes] in favor of the whites in his Department." She cited charges that Bert had profited from his deals to purchase sugar, wheat, and corn for Belgian relief, and reminded Edgar (who needed no reminders) of the financial sacrifices Bert had made as head of the CRB.

Lou repeated Bert's assertion that the Democrats had a responsibility to speak against the lies leveled at him, even as Bert remained silent regarding the blatant falsehoods circulating about Smith: "[I]nstead of attempting to see justice done [for] an opponent and a fight carried on, on honorable lines,— while they would not stab him or another enemy in the back themselves,— they stand quietly by and watching it done by those of their colleagues without an audible protest."[27]

Lou's letter to Edgar was her way of venting her frustration over campaign rhetoric. She had become as thin-skinned as Bert and could not turn a deaf ear to attacks on his character or actions. However, there were kernels of truth to the charges. Bert's behavior during his management of the 1927 flood, and his actions during the convention, convey a pattern of racism. While he did not officially draw a salary as head of the CRB, he continued to earn income from his worldwide mining interests. Edgar, who managed the Hoovers' finances, knew Bert's finances as well, or perhaps better than, Lou.

Lou campaigned with Bert throughout September and October. She appeared on the back platform of the train at each of its many whistle stops, and she joined Bert to watch a baseball game between the Washington Senators and New York Yankees at Washington's Griffith Stadium. Newspapers captured her smiling at a 20,000-strong rally in New York's Madison Square Garden in late October. She declined a large number of invitations to speak on her own publicly, and she carefully kept her Girl Scout responsibilities separate from her campaign activities.

The prospective first lady enjoyed favorable press. The journalist Adela Rogers St. John wrote a flattering portrait of Lou for the weekly general interest magazine, *Liberty*. "[Y]ou probably would imagine her as the president of some big woman's college, such as Wellesley or Vassar or Bryn Mawr. She has that air of understanding, coupled with authority and adequacy and infallibility, which I have found only in women used to deciding and commanding in some intellectual sphere." The article included a photo of Lou receiving her second honorary Doctor of Letters from Whittier College, (her first had been awarded by Mills College in 1923).[28]

The National Republican Committee used a flattering article published in the *Buffalo Evening News* to introduce Lou to the nation: "[S]he is not 'just Mrs. Herbert Hoover,' but definitely herself, a woman finely reared and educated, a woman who could walk impressively on her own two feet had she not Secretary Hoover's two successful feet to keep in step with."[29]

Lou and Bert returned to Palo Alto on Election Day to cast their ballots. Bert won in a landslide, carrying forty of the forty-eight states, including the southern states of Florida, Kentucky, North Carolina, Tennessee, and Virginia. Smith did not even carry his home state of New York. Congratulatory telegrams poured in from friends, family, and the Coolidges. David Starr Jordan wrote to Lou: "We have watched you and Herbert as closely as though you were runaway students; and I congratulate you on all the splendid things you have said and heard. . . . . A happy year is assured with Saint Herbert's Day on March 4th."[30]

Lou enjoyed a brief respite on the Hill. "The days have been joyous ones," Lou wrote Grace Coolidge, "delightfully broken up by playing with the babies."[31]

The rest in Palo Alto was short-lived. Inauguration day was not until March 4, 1929, and Bert was too restless to knock around San Juan Hill for four months. He and Lou, together with a group of friends, boarded the USS *Maryland* on November 19 and sailed from Los Angeles harbor to Amapala,

Honduras. It was the first port of call for a ten-week, ten-country tour of Central and South America. The ship proceeded along the Pacific coast of Central America, with stops at El Salvador, Nicaragua, and Costa Rica. Bert met with the presidents of each of these countries on the respective stops.

In Ecuador, the Hoovers transferred to the USS *Cleveland*. "Affectionate greetings from the other side of the equator," Lou telegraphed Grace Coolidge, whose son, John had recently married. "[A]nd may you and the President be as happy in your new daughter as we are in ours."

The trip continued its sojourn along the Pacific coastline of South America with stops at each country along the way. They rounded Argentina at Tierra del Fuego and proceeded up the Atlantic coastline on the USS *Utah*. "You would be amused if you could see me propped up in my bunk (which is really a very nice bed)," Lou wrote to Ethel Bagg Bullard. It was clear that Lou had not lost her sense of adventure or her joy in travel. "We are having a glorious voyage,—most interesting visits ashore with every minute filled, and day by day I find myself with more Spanish words added to my vocabulary!"[32]

The Hoovers arrived in Florida at the beginning of January and rented a home on Belle Isle, in Miami. "My dear," Lou wrote to Allan, "we have been running true to form. So busy you couldn't shake a stick at us and find us not twice in the same place."[33]

Bert went out daily for deep sea fishing, sometimes joined by Lou, and other times accompanied by the men in his traveling party. Lou enjoyed the scenery, which she described to Allan as "really prettier than I thought it would be,—mostly flat and palmy and piney, with pretty good Hollywood kind of California houses." The canals reminded her of Venice, "only it is very new and not all huddled up together like Venice."

Despite her enjoyment, Lou wanted to go back to California. She told Allan that the real purpose of her lengthy, descriptive letter was "all of which is more or less to show that I have not yet been able to catch Daddy alone long enough to talk California to him."[34]

In the meantime, Lou worked on the inauguration guest list and ordered furniture and selected paint and wallpaper for the Oval Office. She arranged housing for the large number of friends and colleagues who planned to come to Washington to help the Hoovers celebrate. Abbie Rickard and Alida Henriques met to discuss Lou's staffing needs. She planned to retain as her social secretary Mary Randolph, whom Grace Coolidge had brought to the White House. Randolph would be joined by Lou's long-time secretaries, Mildred Hall and Ruth Fesler, whose salaries Lou paid from personal funds.

Expectations of Lou as first lady were as high as those of Bert as the incoming Chief Executive. During the campaign, Colorado attorney L. Ward Bannister delivered a speech in support of Bert's candidacy that had been broadcast over Radio KOA, Denver. Bannister told his audience of Bert's other achievement: "He married Lou Henry—intelligent, sympathetic, capable, charming, fully qualified in her own right, and as a woman among women, to sit as the nation's hostess in the dining room of state."

The Washington *Evening Star* lauded her qualifications: "From an educational standpoint no former mistress of the White House has surpassed her, while in travel and worldly knowledge her experiences even exceed those of Mrs. Taft."[35]

There had been no previous first lady who was as familiar with the inner workings of the White House as Lou. Grace Coolidge generously helped Lou understand the variety of duties that she would oversee—housekeeping, menu planning, and East Wing staffing. The one thing that Lou would have to learn on her own was how to navigate the public's expectation of her role as first lady. She had managed her public persona as the wife of a cabinet secretary, often using her Girl Scout responsibilities and her retreats home to Palo Alto to be with her sons as acceptable means of avoiding the glare of the public. The White House afforded no such shelter. Events would conspire to make it all the more difficult for Lou to avoid the spotlight.

CHAPTER 12

An Independent-Minded First Lady

Bert took the oath of office on a cold, blustery, rainy March 4, 1929, while Lou looked on from the first row, dressed in a plum-colored velvet coat and matching cloche hat. Water dripped from the new president's face and soaked his suit as he delivered his speech from the unsheltered inaugural stand erected on the East Portico of the Capitol. It was the first presidential inauguration to be recorded on newsreel.

The dismal weather did little to dampen the ambitious schedule for the afternoon. The Hoovers returned to the White House following the ceremonies to host a buffet luncheon in the State Dining Room for three hundred family members, friends, Cabinet officers and their families, members of the military, and others in official Washington. At the conclusion of the meal, the presidential couple braved the weather again to watch the inaugural parade from a protected reviewing stand. They returned to the White House and hosted a tea for state governors and their respective staffs. Lou and Bert did not attend the charity inaugural ball held at the Mayflower Hotel that evening. Vice President Curtis and his half-sister, Dolly Gann, who served as his hostess, represented the new administration at the event.

Lou is not remembered as a fashion icon, but she maintained the standard set by Grace Coolidge for sartorial elegance. Washington society writers had praised Lou as one of the more fashionably attired of the cabinet wives. When her outfits came under closer scrutiny after she moved into the White House, Lou was admired for her excellent taste.

Lou was the first president's wife to be photographed for *Vogue* magazine, a tradition that would be maintained for each successive first lady until 2017. Renowned photographer Edward Steichen took the pictures, which *Vogue* published in its May 11, 1929, issue. Lou wore a light-colored dropped waist dress with a pleated bodice and a straight skirt. A thin, waist-length gold necklace with a circular pendant was her only jewelry. Her white hair was parted in the middle, with no hint of the length that was wound in a coil and secured at the nape of her neck. At age 55, she still looked youthful, but Steichen captured a hint of sadness in her eyes in this portrait as Lou looked straight into the camera.

A different Steichen portrait of Lou graced the cover of the May 13, 1929, issue of *Time*. In that photo, Lou wore a simple black velvet dress and a lengthy strand of pearls. The photographer masterfully captured her understated elegance and warmth. Once again, Lou gazed straight-on at the camera, but this time, there is the hint of a smile and the glint of mischief in her eyes.

At the turn of the century, Edith Roosevelt determined to establish the nation's first lady as the pre-eminent social leader in Washington. She was the first presidential wife to hire a non-family member or close friend to serve as her social secretary. Isabella "Belle" Hagner, who was listed as a clerk on the White House employee rolls, became Edith's social secretary. Hagner had served in that same capacity for wealthy Washingtonians and had worked for the *Social Register*, a listing of socially prominent families. Hagner helped the first lady navigate the ins and outs of Washington society, briefed society reporters, and organized the teas, musicales, and receptions that were expected in social Washington. With the employment of Hagner, Edith set a new standard for her successors: The first lady was considered a social doyenne, and the press expected the same type of access to the first lady that it had to the president.

By the time Grace Coolidge took office, the job of managing the first lady's image with the press had become an art form. Like Hagner, Mary Randolph had deep connections with social Washington and Grace benefitted from Randolph's insider savvy. The first lady relied on her social secretary to create the guest lists, menus, table settings, and details of the many events hosted at the White House. Randolph also briefed society writers who covered the first lady.

Randolph believed that the social demands of a first lady differed from those of a Cabinet wife. She began her employment with Lou expecting the new first lady to understand the distinction and to be as teachable and compliant as Grace Coolidge. Inauguration Day disabused Randolph of that perception. Lou had hosted dignitaries around the world for nearly thirty years.

She had firm ideas about guest seating, place settings, table decorations, and menus. Furthermore, Lou despised publicity. Bert's team had managed Lou's press coverage over the years, mainly by restricting access to her. She had no desire to make herself available to journalists. Lou believed it was Randolph's job to take direction from the first lady, not the other way around.

Randolph lasted a little over one year as Lou's social secretary. Observers at the time suggested that Randolph resigned after a disagreement with Lou over proper place settings for a White House dinner—the culmination of tensions that had been building between the two. According to Sue Dyer, Randolph could not control Ruth Fesler and Mildred Hall, who understood how Lou wanted things done and did them without question.

Lou's papers indicate that Randolph had health issues in late fall 1929. When Randolph resigned on May 27, 1930, Lou sent her a short, friendly note: "This is just a line to say goodbye, and to express my earnest hope that you may soon be entirely restored to health."[1]

Randolph's replacement, Helen Greene, lasted less than four months and was gone by the end of September. After Greene's departure, Lou never installed anyone else in the official role of social secretary, a decision that raised eyebrows in social Washington. Lou's personal secretary, Ruth Fesler, served in that capacity. Fesler followed Lou's guidance in dealing with the Washington cliff-dwellers—a term that referred to the arbiters of the archaic rules that governed social Washington. Lou also continued the practice she had started years ago of hiring newly graduated, single young women from other parts of the country to work for her. None of these women had the experience or the social savvy to know how to navigate the vipers' nest that characterizes the Washington political and social scene. Author Frances Parkinson Keyes, the wife of a US senator, wrote of Lou's secretaries: "The girls from the great open spaces had been catapulted into positions for which they were handicapped by their inexperience."[2]

One of Lou's first disagreements with Randolph was Lou's decision to invite Jessie De Priest to tea at the White House. Jessie's husband, Oscar De Priest, was the first African American elected to Congress since the end of Reconstruction. He represented the South Side of Chicago and had been chosen by the Cook County Republican Party to replace Martin B. Madden, a Caucasian who had served as the chair of the powerful House Ways and Means Committee and had died in office the previous year. In the 1920s, the Republican Party dominated Chicago politics, and a nomination by the party's central committee guaranteed election.

Tensions were already high among southerners at the prospect of accepting De Priest on equal terms. De Priest had been charged with sponsoring and protecting vice and gambling in his district, but he was cleared of any involvement. Nevertheless, the accusations provided a handy excuse for southern members of Congress to attempt to prevent De Priest from being sworn in and taking his seat. Lou's friend, Ruth Bryan Owen, who had been elected to the House from Florida, suggested to House Speaker Nicholas Longworth that he replace the traditional ceremony of swearing in members by state delegation with a corporate swearing-in of all members simultaneously. Longworth circumvented the southern challenge by doing just that. Undaunted, southern representatives refused to sit on committees to which De Priest had been assigned, and they refused to accept office assignments near the Chicago congressman. De Priest's ostracism in Congress extended to his wife, who was excluded from social events for congressional spouses.

One of those events was the customary reception held by the first lady for all the wives of senators and representatives to coincide with the convening of Congress. Unlike other social events swirling around the nation's capital that had excluded Jessie De Priest, the new first lady's reception would be different.

A few weeks after Congress convened on April 15, Lou instructed Mary Randolph to write to Bert's aide Walter H. Newton:

> In connection with the projected congressional teas, the question arises as to what can be done about the family of our new colored representative. Mrs. Hoover wishes me to ask for your suggestion, and to remind you that we must think not only of this occasion, but of what is to be done during the entire term of the representative.[3]
>
> Will you please let me have an immediate reply.[sic]

Newton's answer is not included in Lou's papers, but a notation at the top of the invitation list for the first gathering indicates, per Newton's recommendation, that the congressional wives were to be invited to a series of teas in groups arranged in alphabetical order.[4]

An average of 150 women was invited to teas hosted between May 27 and

June 4. Social Washington would have quickly scanned the lists and noticed that Jessie De Priest had been excluded when others with last names starting with "D" had been invited. Unbeknownst to them, a small tea, with fifteen invitees, was scheduled for June 12. Jessie De Priest received a hand delivered invitation to the event on June 4th. The messenger was sworn to secrecy.

The women who gathered for tea that Tuesday afternoon included three wives of members of Congress from New York, Pennsylvania, and California. Lou's sister Jean was present. Gertrude Mitchell, wife of the Attorney General, changed her travel plans to attend. Lorna D. Sharpe Metcalf, wife of the Rhode Island senator, replied in her RSVP: "My dear Miss Polly [Mary Randolph's nickname], Will be delighted to go to the White House tomorrow. I regret that I may be a few minutes late as I have asked some women to lunch and a sail which was to have terminated at 4, but I will try to cut it short and get there as early as possible."[5]

Lou's invitation—a White House invitation—gave Jessie De Priest the social legitimacy that Washington had denied her.

Initial reaction to De Priest's presence at the White House was incredulity. A Virginia Republican committee member wired Lou: "Please wire me if Southern papers are correct in their morning statement that you entertained a Negro woman at tea yesterday. I have been a lifelong Democrat, but stumped the entire state of Virginia for Mr. Hoover last fall. We are to hold a semi-[R]epublic[an] convention in Roanoke, Va., June eighteenth. Very important I have your reply to read to this convention."[6]

Lou forwarded the telegram to her husband's staff. Referring to herself in the third person, she wrote:

> Will you take this up with the President at the first opportunity? And report back to us as soon as possible. We realize that Mrs. Hoover is perhaps not the one to make the statements in the questioned paragraphs. But perhaps it would be wise if those facts should get across by somebody else?[7]

Bert's press machine sought to limit the political damage. To fend off the charges that Mrs. De Priest had been granted social equality (which, of course, she had), the White House insisted that the teas were simply official events, and not social ones. "It has been the custom for years for the White House to entertain at official receptions the wives and members of the Senate and House of Representatives in accordance with official lists furnished by the printing clerk of the Senate and the clerk of the House. No names have been omitted from the official list."[8]

On June 16, Walter Newton released another statement: "The incident was official, not social," and to have snubbed Mrs. De Priest would have been an act of "official discrimination" by the White House. Newton then provided a list of all the other times African Americans had been entertained socially at the White House. The list included President and Mrs. Cleveland hosting Frederick Douglass and his Caucasian wife to dinner; Theodore Roosevelt inviting Booker T. Washington to dine with Roosevelt's family; and the Wilsons hosting the Haitian minister, Solon Menos, and his wife, at five different diplomatic functions between 1914 and 1917. What was carefully omitted from this recounting was that Douglass's visit had been loudly criticized by Southerners, and the rancor and racial hatred generated by Booker T. Washington's dining with the Roosevelt family reverberated for years following the event.

State legislatures jumped into the fray to express their outrage. The Texas legislature formally censured Lou on June 24. Three days later the Georgia state legislature, in 179–5 vote, declared "its regret over recent occurrences in the official and social life of the national capital, which have a tendency to revive and intensify racial discord." The Mississippi state senate and the Florida state legislature condemned Lou for hosting an African American woman at the White House.[9]

Support for Lou's actions came from the International Club of Detroit and the Women's International League for Peace and Freedom. William Lloyd Garrison, editor of the liberal publication *The Nation*, praised Lou for her courage. Northern and Midwestern newspapers wondered what the uproar was all about. "The entertainment of the wife of the one Negro member of Congress at the White House caused a lot of needless excitement," wrote a columnist for the Philadelphia *Ledger* on July 4. "There is nothing unusual about a member of the colored race being a guest at the President's mansion."

A writer for the Des Moines *Register* drew a distinction between Roosevelt's choice to invite Booker T. Washington to the White House and Lou's social obligation to extend an invitation to Jessie De Priest. "The present White House host had to include the wife of the Negro congressman in some one of the series of teas—or else be guilty of a discrimination so wanton that it would be construed an injustice."[10] The Chicago City Council passed a resolution calling Lou Hoover's act 'courageous,' and the national African American press spoke in glowing terms of Mrs. Hoover's decision.

The controversy continued to drag through the newspapers throughout the summer months. Some of the flames were fanned by the national speaking tour that Oscar De Priest embarked upon. He ignored death threats and traveled through the South, charging the segregationists with cowardice and working to raise money for the NAACP.

The De Priest incident took place two months after Lou's first confrontation with Washington's cliff-dwellers. Tradition held that the wife of the vice president, who served as the president of the Senate, ranked second behind the first lady. Since Dolly Gann was the half-sister of Vice President Curtis, Alice Roosevelt Longworth, wife of the Speaker of the House, believed that she had pre-eminence at social and diplomatic events. Following the election, but before the inauguration, the Senate Ladies Luncheon Club decided that an official hostess could only be the wife of an official. Outgoing Secretary of State Frank B. Kellogg endorsed the Club's decision and stated that it would apply to diplomatic ranking at official dinners. Incoming Secretary of State Henry Stimson refused to comment on Kellogg's ruling.

Lou considered the controversy needlessly time-consuming and senseless. Rather than acquiesce to Mrs. Longworth's demands, Lou did not invite the two women to the same receptions. That allowed Mrs. Longworth to be second to Lou in the absence of Dolly Gann, and Gann was second-ranked at any event where she was present. Longworth, seeing that she had been bested, announced that she had never considered the ranking to be a serious issue.

Mary Randolph wrote in her memoir that Lou did herself, and ultimately the president, a disservice by refusing to acknowledge Washington's way of doing things. Randolph had encouraged Lou to take things slowly, but Lou was determined to make her own decisions. Indeed, some of Bert's struggles to work with a recalcitrant Congress, especially its Southern members, to pass legislation to provide aid to financially strapped Americans, may be traced to a simple invitation to a White House tea. One afternoon at the White House upended the Southern strategy Bert had employed to gain the Republican nomination and, ultimately, the presidency.

Lou arranged and furnished the rooms in the family quarters and Oval Office with an eye to Bert's comfort. She asked a handful of New York-based furniture companies to send sample desk chairs for Bert to try out. Fabric swatches and paint samples were delivered to the White House at her request. White House carpenters were instructed to build bookcases to accommodate Bert's numerous books. Bert rearranged the furniture multiple times, tried out different rooms for his private study and his bedroom, and finally settled on a corner study at the opposite end of the hallway from the room he claimed as a bedroom. His study is today known as the Lincoln Bedroom. In late May, Lou wrote her sons: "We are beginning to feel perfectly at home."

Lou respected the historicity of the White House and its furnishings. She worked throughout her four years as first lady to preserve the character of the presidential mansion and to educate people on its rich heritage. A new interest in the historic nature of the White House and a move to have the public rooms reflect a nineteenth century appearance took hold during the Coolidge years. Grace Coolidge had requested Congress to authorize the White House to accept gifts to induce donations from people with period-appropriate artifacts. She worked with an advisory committee of experts led by Harriet Barnes Pratt to refurbish the Green Room. Its refurbishment was still under way when the Hoovers moved into the White House. Lou continued to meet with the Pratt Committee, directed it to follow through on work it had discussed with Mrs. Coolidge, and kept Grace apprised of the progress.

In keeping with the renewed interest in period-appropriate furnishings, Lou researched the furniture from the Monroe presidency. James and Elizabeth Monroe were the first presidential couple to occupy the White House after the British burned it in 1814. When the Monroes moved to Washington in the fall of 1817, they brought their own furniture with them. Several of the pieces had been made in France and acquired by the couple when James Monroe served as the American ambassador to that country.

In January 1930, Lou undertook the selection of fabrics to recover a Monroe sofa that was in the East Room. She sampled three or four different chairs to be used for White House musicales to ensure they were appropriate to the time period, ultimately selecting fifty gilded chairs in the Louis XV style, which she had upholstered in blue damask.

A year later, Lou contacted the Monroes' descendants, who were living in Fredericksburg, Virginia. Laurence Gouvernour Hoes and his mother,

Rose Gouvernour Hoes, still owned a number of the Monroes' furnishings. Lou sought their permission to copy the desk on which Monroe had signed the Monroe Doctrine and its companion chair, Elizabeth Monroe's bureau, a marble-topped tea table, a Hepplewhite card table, and a dainty three-legged table. The marble top for the tea table had been made in Vermont and shipped to France to complete the furnishing. The fall-front Monroe desk was made of mahogany and brass, with an inlaid fluted brass strip at each corner. The desk contained a secret compartment that required a complex combination of key turns to unlock, along with a series of interconnecting drawers that added to the complexity of the desk's construction. Lou hired Morris Walter Dove, a Russian immigrant living in Washington who had trained in European cabinetry, to create the copies. Laurence Hoes praised Dove for "so faithfully reproduc[ing] this exquisite workmanship."[11]

Since it was uncertain whether Congress would appropriate funding for the reproductions, Lou requested the Hoeses' permission to have the selected pieces copied with the understanding that it was likely that she would pay for them herself. In that event, they would not remain in the White House, but would become part of the Hoovers' possessions. The Hoeses agreed. Lou paid for the furniture and the insurance on the original pieces to cover possible damage while it was made available for the reproductions. Dove's final invoice was $1,480. There is no confirmed evidence that Congress passed an appropriation to reimburse the Hoovers for the Monroe reproductions, and a letter from Hoes to Lou implies that she took the pieces home to San Juan Hill when she left the White House. (They are now in the White House.)

Lou also commissioned a copy of Elizabeth Monroe's portrait. The original had been painted by Benjamin West, a noted portrait artist of the first quarter of the nineteenth century. The copy was made by a Washington artist, Eben F. Comins, who had recently completed a portrait of Bert's Secretary of Labor William N. Doak. Comins' copy was donated to the United States. Today, it hangs in the Blue Room of the White House.

Lou wanted to share her passion for the White House furnishings with the general public. Dare Stark McMullin had joined Lou's staff in 1930. Dare researched the provenance and cataloging of each item of furniture, including urns, candelabra, statues, and mirrors, in the President's House. Records associated with many of the pieces were archived in federal records, but the

National Archives and Records Administration had yet to be formed, and the information was not publicly available. McMullin had access to the records as an employee of the first lady; she also interviewed contributors and others knowledgeable about the furnishings.

Lou paid for photography of the private family quarters from her own funds. These were the first photographs ever taken of that section of the White House. McMullin's manuscript was completed at the end of 1932. Lou's goal was to fulfill her long-time dream of publishing a book for general readership, but political events made it impossible to find a firm willing to take a risk on a book with a Hoover author. Two copies of the manuscript were produced of the detailed and historically important document. One languished in Lou's private papers for seventy-five years, and the other existed in the White House archives. The manuscript was finally published as an insert in an issue of *White House History Quarterly* in 2017.

Lou sent sections of the manuscript to Edith Wilson and Grace Coolidge and asked if they would review the material for accuracy. "I want to know if you will be good enough to read the chapter dealing with what Mrs. McMullin has found regarding 'Wilson' acquisitions," Lou wrote former first lady Edith Galt Wilson, "and correct any misstatements in it, and add any details our ignorance has omitted? It would be most kind if you would do this, not only kind to Mrs. McMullin and me, but to all in the future who may have any kind of interest in the furnishings of the White House."[12]

Grace Coolidge was delighted by Dare's work and wanted to know more about individual pieces she recalled from her White House tenure. "I was so delighted to have your letter on the furniture chapter and to find that you were interested and so very helpful!" Lou wrote Grace. In answer to some of Grace's questions, Lou responded with details about the disposition of a variety of small items that decorated the public rooms. It was clear that Lou had become intimately familiar with the many and varied furnishings inside the mansion. "Someone in the house told Mrs. McMullin the story of the little marble urns going upstairs, and my later taking them to the Red Room. . . . The small table in the Green Room,—the one with the sliding screen,—went away when the Pratt committee put the finishing touches on that room."[13]

Unfortunately, Lou received few accolades for her efforts to preserve the Executive Mansion's furnishings. Her dedication and hard work were casualties of her aversion to publicity. It would remain for historians to praise her for what Laurence Hoes described as "a rarely cultured and farseeing First Lady [who] found time to give an unselfish thought to history and posterity."[14]

Presidential retreats had become routine as far back as the Grant administration, when Ulysses S. Grant bought a beach cottage known as Long Branch, in Elberon, New Jersey. The Clevelands had a home on the Tenallytown Road, in what is now known as the Cleveland Park section of Washington. Theodore Roosevelt and his family returned to Sagamore Hill, on Oyster Bay, New York.

Lou looked for property in Chevy Chase, Maryland, a bucolic community within easy reach of the White House, but she decided that not even a tree-shaded, suburban home would offer relief from Washington's heat and humidity. After studying the elevations of the region within a reasonable drive from Washington, Lou climbed into her Cadillac and toured the Virginia countryside. Virginia's Shenandoah Valley, 2,500 feet above sea level, offered proximity to Washington and escape from the swampy conditions of the nation's capital.

On Lou's recommendation, Bert dispatched his aide, Lawrence Richey, to identify properties that would meet the first couple's needs. Richey contacted postmasters within a 100-mile radius of Washington and investigated the acreages they recommended. Word of Richey's mission reached the ears of Virginia members of Congress, and a campaign was launched by various representatives and area chambers of commerce to lure the Hoovers to their specific communities. A bill was introduced in Congress to fund the construction costs of a retreat. The Hoovers, anxious to move forward quickly and without the restrictions imposed by federal funding, committed to purchasing the land with their own funds.

Six weeks before Bert took the oath of office, Lou traveled to Virginia to check out the sites identified by Richey. A ranger in the Shenandoah Park directed Lou to a 146-acre parcel that was ideal. The higher elevation promised cooler summers. The Rapidan River ran through the property, and locals vowed it teemed with trout. What would become Camp Rapidan could be reached from the White House in less than a half day.

Lou once again chose architect James Yardley Rippin to design the buildings on the site. Tents would be erected the first year, but Lou envisioned a "rather biggish establishment. . . .We look over some miles of a fair fishing stream with picturesque wooded foregrounds, and not bad high hills,—or very low mountainous,—background," Lou wrote to James and Jane Rippin. "A goodly number of campsites presented themselves, all of value chiefly because they are such a short distance from Washington,—not quite two and a half hours on a good motor trip."[15]

Lou detailed her ideas for structures to James Rippin: "There must be room for 18 or 20 people to eat, with a feeling of spaciousness,—architecturally, not gastronomically! And for the same number or more to sit in another portion of the same structure,—probably the two to open into each other, or to be a part of the same 'room,' to help with this feeling of spaciousness. And naturally it must have a field stone fireplace!"[16]

The Hoovers' cabin was to include a study for Bert and a workroom for Lou, in addition to the necessary bedrooms, bathrooms, and dressing rooms. Separate guest cabins, offices for people to work, and accommodations for the servant staff were to be erected. At its completion, Camp Rapidan comprised thirteen cabins and a separate camp for the marines assigned to accompany the president when he traveled. Lou contracted with local carpenters and furniture makers for the interior furnishings for each of the cabins. Partial invoices for bed frames, mattresses, and pillows alone, purchased from J. N. Clore in Madison, totaled over eight hundred dollars.

The camp was located near Dark Hollow, a community near Criglersville. Virginia, in Madison County. Criglersville was little more than a wide spot in the road with a population numbering one hundred and a general store that served as the grocery, post office, and gathering spot. Dark Hollow was even more isolated, marked by a small cluster of cabins and out of touch with the outside world. Madison, the namesake county seat, boasted a population of five hundred. The town paved the portion of the state highway within its boundaries after the Hoovers announced plans to create a private retreat nearby.

Tent camping did not deter either the Hoovers or their guests, and the neighboring community became accustomed to the presidential traffic winding its way through the area each Friday afternoon during the Hoovers' first summer there. Commander Joel Boone, the naval physician assigned to the White House, joined the Hoovers on most weekends. During one visit, Boone met an eleven-year-old boy by the name of Ray Buraker, who lived nearby with his parents and eight brothers and sisters. Boone shared his encounter with Bert, who asked the physician to encourage Ray to pay the president a visit. As an incentive, Bert offered to pay the youngster five dollars if he would bring a live possum. On Bert's birthday, August 10, Ray arrived at Camp Rapidan with a gift for the president.

Charles Lindbergh was visiting at the time, and Bert introduced Ray to the aviator, who had gained fame in 1927with his solo flight across the Atlantic Ocean. Much to the surprise of Bert and his guests, Ray had never heard of the flier. The boy had never been to school; there was none close enough for the children of Dark Hollow to attend.

Lou and Bert undertook discussions with local and state officials about establishing a school near Camp Rapidan. Together with the authorities, it was agreed that a building would be constructed to serve as a combination school, community center, and accommodation for a teacher. The plans included two additional bedrooms for guests or for children unable to return home because of bad weather. An experienced contractor oversaw the work of local residents who comprised the labor force. The idea was to teach skills that the adults could use to repair and improve their own homesteads.

Lou took the lead in hiring a teacher. She contacted Berea College, located in Berea, Kentucky. The school offered a tuition-free college education to young people from the impoverished Appalachian region in exchange for working on the college farm or on campus. Berea imbued its graduates with an ethos of giving back to the community. Lou chose Christine Vest, a practical, no-nonsense teacher who had experience in communities similar to Dark Hollow.

When word got out about the school, donations of books and supplies came in from around the country. The Hoovers supplied most of the financial support for the building's construction and operation. Lou paid Vest's salary, set at $1,500 annually, nearly three times the average wage for a teacher in a rural, one-room school.

Lou took a special interest in Vest's success. She arranged to have a horse delivered so that Vest could visit families in the community and go to the store. Lou made inquiries regarding a suitable bank and recommended one where Vest could deposit her money (an important decision in an era before depositors' insurance). Lou routinely stopped by the school to join the children for a picnic lunch on her way to Camp Rapidan, and Vest sent regular reports about the students' progress. She found her students eager to learn and a community highly supportive of education. The Hoovers treated the students to a day at the Madison County Fair in fall 1930 as a reward for their diligence.

The President's Mountain School, or as some called it, the Hoover School, generated national attention. Lou received letters from all over the country, praising her decision to erect a school in the mountains. Educators clamored to have an opportunity to visit. An English teacher in Delaware wrote to Lou: "May I congratulate you upon the dynamic and concrete way in which your program contributes to the growth of [better citizenship]. . . . I am teaching English and Music in the Delaware Schools, and when my vacation begins in June, I have a sincere desire to visit your mountain school en route to my home in Virginia."[17]

Lou's response, written by her secretary Ruth Fesler, reflects Lou's trademark impatience with people's ignorance. "I am wondering if you know how difficult it is to get to the President's Mountain School? There are no transportation facilities provided from Criglersville to the school which is a nine or ten mile trip, and only a Ford can get over the last mile of the road. In rainy weather it is difficult going in one sense even over the newly constructed, wide, well-graded mountain road."[18] Fesler urged Miss Rollings to contact Christine Vest several days before the proposed visit.

The rural superintendent for the Orange County (Virginia) Public Schools wrote Lou shortly after the school opened: "I am writing to ask that several of us who are supervising rural education in the neighboring counties be granted permission to visit and observe the work of Miss Vest the rural specialist who is teaching in the Hoover School which is being conducted in Madison County. . . .We feel that by this observation of the methods used by Miss Vest we may gather much that will be of benefit in our work in similar sections of our counties."[19]

"In another term or another year it would be a matter for Miss Vest to decide," Lou tactfully responded. "But now when everything is new to her in one sense, and her whole time and attention are needed for getting the work organized, her plans made and developed, except for her own county and the State education people, we do feel that she should have the opportunity to meet her problems without possible handicaps by visits and other things."[20]

The President's Mountain School operated for five years. The building and the homes of the families in Dark Hollow sat on land that became incorporated in the Shenandoah National Park. (The Hoovers had donated Camp Rapidan to the National Park Service upon leaving office after the Roosevelts expressed no interest in using the facility as a retreat.) In preparation for the official opening of the park in 1935, the park officials relocated the families of Dark Hollow and closed the school.

Christine Vest left Dark Hollow, married one of the marines who had been assigned to Camp Rapidan, and lived all over the world. In an interview in 1961, she observed:

> When [my students] moved from the mountain because of the park, the older ones went to work, and the younger ones found their place in the regular schools where they moved. I often wonder what their lot would have been if they had not had all this preparation before leaving their mountain. Because of the school, they were able to take their place in a normal way and many have done very well and have nice homes and fine families of their own today.[21]

Lou's interest in education extended to the emerging field of Adult Education. In late April, she had met with Bill and Lucy Adams, a young couple living in California. Bill Adams was the son of a Stanford professor, and he wrote material for some of the Girl Scout publications. The couple met with Lou to explain and secure her support for the California Association for Adult Education. The association encouraged civic education and discourse and had developed programs to encourage adults to discuss many of the issues of the day—ranging from the growth of socialism and communism in Europe to labor unions and the economy. The Carnegie Foundation funded the work, and Lucy Adams served as program administrator. The goal "is . . . trying to get adults to keep on thinking,—[rather] than educating them in the largely accepted way," Lou explained to her son Allan in a letter.

Lou thought it would be worth Allan's time to contact the Adamses and to introduce Bill to some of his connections in Palo Alto. She preferred that the program educate people on "the Republicanism that Daddy stands for," but the concept of adult education fascinated her. "If I were not married to Daddy or connected with him in any other way, I could think of so many exciting things to do—like the area that this opens up."[22]

Lou's correspondence with Allan is a mix of motherly love and advice, political reporting, and emotional honesty. The two had a special bond. They could go months at a time without writing, then easily pick up the thread of their discourse as if they had been in touch daily. Allan's easy-going and cheerful nature resonated with his mother's warmth and tenderheartedness. His personality elicited Lou's fun-loving spontaneity, and his sunny disposition re-centered his mother. "My dear old boy, I've been wandering around in a pleasant, absorbed, teary trance all day—partly due to my sadness at your going away, and partly to my great joy at your being in existence,—at the fact that I can always have your memory with me, always be thinking what you would do or say that moment if you were here. . . . For you may know hereby that you always cheer up the occasion when you are present, either in memory or imagination."[23]

The bond required a high level of understanding on Allan's part. Lou missed her son's graduation from Stanford on June 17, 1929. Allan anticipated that his mother would not make the trip across the country and had written her in April that she need not feel obligated to attend. In acknowledgment of his accomplishment, Lou cabled her son on the seventeenth: "I am distressed beyond words that I have demanding duties here which prevent my actually seeing you walk the plank but you know I will be right there anyway."[24] She teased Allan about his decision to follow his brother's footsteps and enroll in Harvard Business School: "I hope you are going to like Harvard, although to me it is quite a comedown from Stanford!"[25]

With his intentions to go to graduate school in the East, Lou planned to rent San Juan Hill to a suitable tenant. She did not want anyone prying into personal family possessions and assigned Allan the massive task of going through all of his family's personal effects in the fifty-seven room house. Lou wrote a lengthy nine-page letter instructing her son on how to deal with papers, collectibles, financial records, jewelry, and other assorted memorabilia in each room of the spacious home. As reinforcement to her instructions, Lou followed up with a telegram:

> If feeling well enough, please go thoroughly over house so every foot is in order to leave indefinitely. News clippings, old check books, and accounts should be well-packed as usual in strong, cheap new trunks and checked with your baggage. Bring those small things of Grandma's and Aunt Jen's which you mixed in upstairs drawers. Also, bring old photos. Is there time for letters before leaving?[26]

Although Lou was now officially the honorary president of the Girl Scouts, she maintained an active role in its operations, especially in keeping the organization true to its mission and financially healthy. In late fall 1929 Lou expressed her concerns regarding the content of the *American Girl* magazine to Jane Deeter Rippin. The magazine had started as a publication targeted to member scouts. Over the years, in efforts to make the publication self-supporting, Rippin and her team accepted outside advertising. The impact of the business decision was seen in the changed content. Rippin acknowledged Lou's concerns: "Your letter regarding the *American Girl* comes at a most opportune moment. Only the other day, at staff meeting, I brought up the point which you mention—only two pages of Girl Scouting. And there have been several criticisms on the way in which this material is presented." Rippin hired a business manager for the magazine who was committed to devoting "more space to Girl Scouting and present it so that the girls will look forward to receiving the magazine for their Girl Scout pages rather than for the stories."[27]

Lou raised the issue of sufficient funding for *American Girl* with Edgar Rickard. She was, she wrote Edgar in December 1929, pleased to see the board move toward a five-year budget, which she saw as an improvement over the year-to-year operational budgeting under which they had been functioning. She also acknowledged the board's plans to launch a fund drive in spring 1930. However, Lou had concerns about the money allocated to both the magazine and to camping activities. "It can scarcely be hoped that the whole of the desired amount [from the proposed fund drive] will be obtained before next spring, and it seems to me most vital that at least two of these projects should be well underway with assured funds for their completed program before that time."

The American Relief Administration was still operational, and it had provided funding for the launch of *American Girl*, which helped to keep the magazine afloat. Reminding Edgar of the ARA's previous assistance, Lou requested him "to propose to the ARA to allot to the Girl Scouts a sum sufficient at least to meet the demands of these two departments [the magazine and camping] for an adequate development for the next five years." Lou requested a total of $500,000. "I know of no cause at present more worthwhile in the guidance of our youth than that of the Girl Scouts, and it seems to me these two projects are of the most importance at present in the program."[28] The ARA's board approved the request.

Aside from the De Priest incident, the Hoovers basked in the warmth of widespread public approval for the first eight months of their White House tenure. Bert got off to a good start. The automotive, machinery, iron, and lumber industries were producing at record highs, and the stock market had steadily increased in value since 1921. The non-farm sector of the United States economy enjoyed seemingly unstoppable prosperity. High short-term gains on stocks lured individuals into speculative investing. Normally conservative banks had succumbed to the attractiveness of rapid returns on their money and loaned large sums to these speculators without requesting collateral. Privately, Bert was one of those who believed that the current rate of economic growth could not continue indefinitely. In a time when business was booming, it was difficult for his voice to be heard.

He was not alone in believing the economic expansion would reverse course. Former vice president Charles Dawes, who headed his family's multiple businesses, had instructed his brothers to begin liquidating their stock holdings as early as 1927. Dawes's concern was that credit had become too easy to obtain, and he expected a contraction of credit to correct the market at some point in the next few years. Even Dawes, who had been a banker before entering public life, could not convince others outside his intimate circle of friends that a market correction was on the way.

Correction did come. In early August 1929, the Federal Reserve Bank responded to the large portfolio of speculative lending by raising the interest rate to its member banks from five percent to six percent. The increase set the law of unintended consequences into motion. The discount rate hike did little to deter speculative lending, but it slowed industry expansion and small business growth because the cost of capital increased by twenty percent. The European central banks, never having completely recovered from the economic effects of World War I, raised their interest rates as well.

The stock market did not initially respond to the credit tightening. However, by mid-October, there were signs that the days of wild speculation might be closing. On Wednesday, October 23, the Dow Jones Industrial Average lost 6.33 percent. The following day, October 24, known as Black Thursday, losses totaled $4 billion on trading of six million shares. In the following week, panic selling dominated market trading. In the final week of October, the stock market losses totaled $30 billion.[29]

Bert responded to the market crash with his customary energy. In the first two weeks of November, he met with industry leaders, financiers, cabinet members, and other officials to outline a plan to restore confidence to the nation's stock market. He assured the public that the fundamentals of the nation's economy were sound, which, at that point, they were. He gained commitments from the CEOs of DuPont, Ford, General Motors, Sears Roebuck, Standard Oil, and General Electric that they would not lay off workers or cut wages. Labor leaders committed to cooperating with management. Congress agreed to cut corporate and personal income tax rates. Bert announced federal investment in shipbuilding. The Fed lowered its discount rate to spur borrowing, and Bert encouraged businesses to take advantage of the rate decrease.

The initial response to Bert's leadership was largely positive and encouraging. Previous downturns had been painful, but short. The Federal Reserve had been created in 1913 in response to the Panic of 1907, and here was its first chance to prove that it could reduce the impact of a downturn on the overall economy. Bert was the first president to implement interventions rather than let a slowing economy run its course. There was no hint of what was on the horizon.

The Hoovers' first Christmas in the White House in December 1929 could be considered an omen of things to come. The couple was hosting a party in the State Dining Room, located in the East Wing, for their family and the children of aides and friends, when White House usher Ike Hoover whispered in Bert's ear that the White House was on fire. Either a blocked chimney vent or defective electrical wiring had sparked a blaze in the West Wing executive offices. The blaze was fueled by over 200,000 pamphlets that had been stored in the attic since the days of Theodore Roosevelt. Fire tore through the Oval Office and the White House press office, destroying the reporters' files and notes.

Allan Hoover, Lawrence Richey, and George Akerson rescued the contents of Bert's desk in the Oval Office, along with his flag and chair. Ike Hoover covered the desk with a tarpaulin to protect it from damage. The four-alarm blaze brought a total of 130 firefighters to the White House—nineteen engine companies and four truck companies. Pumpers used waters from hydrants up to five blocks away to fight the blaze. The freezing temperatures caused sheets of ice to form, hindering the firefighters' efforts. Two firefighters collapsed and were taken to the hospital; both recovered.[30]

In the meantime, Lou calmly continued the party in the State Dining Room, where the Marine Band was playing. She dispensed gifts (the Hoovers would give toy fire engines to attendees at the following year's party), and continued to host the children's activities without giving a hint as to the frantic efforts taking place on the other side of the mansion. After the party ended at ten p.m., Lou and her sister Jean joined Bert, who was standing on the West Terrace smoking a cigar and watching the firefighting efforts.

The firefighters extinguished the blaze by ten thirty. The West Wing's floors, attic, and roof were damaged. The smoke-smudged walls were in good shape. The White House was not insured, and Congress was asked for a special appropriation to repair the damage. Work began on January 4. Bert moved back into the West Wing on April 14. The White House had been restored. The economy still needed work.

Volunteerism and Private Philanthropy

January 1930 marked the Hoovers' first New Year's Day in the White House and the start of Washington's traditionally busy January social calendar. "President and Mrs. Hoover Caught in the Social Whirl of the Nation's Capital," read the society page headline of the Washington *Evening Star*.

The year began with the traditional New Year's Day diplomatic reception. Begun in 1801 by President Thomas Jefferson, the event was greeted with anticipation by diplomats, members of Congress, non-elected government officials, and the public. Undaunted by the damage caused by the Christmas Eve fire, Lou rose to the occasion. The press praised the presidential couple for their willingness to stand indefinitely to greet everyone who stood in line. Society writers wrote approvingly of Lou's blue, heavy silk crepe gown with an uneven hemline and a round neck with a lace collar, adorned with a brooch.

Social events filled the first weeks in January. The Hoovers attended the German Grand Opera's performance of Wagner's *Die Walküre* on Monday, January 6. On Tuesday, they dined with Vice President Curtis and Dolly Gann at the Mayflower Hotel and then adjourned to a reception held in the Hoovers' honor at the Congressional Club. Lou hosted the annual reception in honor of the Judiciary on Thursday, and plans were on the calendar to attend events hosted by each member of the cabinet throughout the social season. Accompanied by her sister Jean, niece Janet, and friend Sue Dyer, Lou attended a performance of William Gillette in his signature role as Sherlock Holmes. Lou and Bert had hosted Gillette, a noted playwright, actor, and stage manager, at a White House luncheon earlier that day.

The event that won the most accolades was a reception held for the members of the Senate on January 30. "The President and Mrs. Hoover paid the

Senate the highest possible compliment in holding in its honor last night the first reception ever given in the White House exclusively in honor of that body," reported the Washington *Evening Star*.[1] Lou wore a gown constructed of soft silver metal fabric, with a long train that flared in the back. The skirt had an over panel which fell from the bodice, and the cape-like collar was made of silver lace. The reception scheduled for the House of Representatives at the end of February, which had the potential to resurrect the De Priest incident, was cancelled upon the news that former president and chief justice William Howard Taft was dying.

By early February 1930, the stock market crash had been forgotten by the press. Congress returned to debating the two prevailing issues of the day—the repeal of the Volstead Act and disarmament. Legislators appeared to pay scant attention to the economy. With the temporary close of the social season, the Hoovers departed Washington for a week's vacation in Long Key, Florida. "Six days of doing nothing but sitting on the deck of a boat, or fishing," Lou reported to Allan as the respite ended. She enclosed a political cartoon showing Bert heading to Florida with fishing rods under his arm and fishing lines hooked to his suit jacket. Men representing the special interests of the day held the rods: Drys; Wets; Office Seekers; Congress; A Friend of Senator So-and-So; Delegations from Far and Near. No one represented the failed stock market.

Most economists believed that the October stock market crash was an overdue market correction. Although the Dow Jones Industrial Average was lower at the start of 1930 than it had been six months earlier, the value of the market steadily trickled upward during the first half of the year. Likewise, gross domestic product was lower than it had been a year earlier, but it, too, showed improvement by the second quarter. The real story of what was happening in the economy lay in the unemployment rate. The captains of industry, having given Bert assurances that they would not lay off workers, could not deny the numbers on their income statements.

Unemployment inched up through the year. In January 1930, the unemployment rate was 2.2 percent (it had been statistically at zero in August 1929). In July, unemployment was five percent. By the end of 1930, the rate was 11.89 percent.[2] Depending on the estimate, somewhere between 4.3 and 6.9 million people were out of work.[3] While Bert was not a true free marketer, his inclination in the early months of 1930 was to give the economy time to correct itself, an approach Lou supported in her letters to Allan.

In early April, Lou attended the annual meeting of the Society of Friends, held in Philadelphia, accompanied by Mary Vaux Walcott, a fellow geologist and the widow of the former director of the Smithsonian Institution. In the face of the charges leveled against them during the 1928 campaign that they were secretly Catholics, the Hoovers decided it was important to solidify their affiliation with a non-Catholic church. Likewise, the Hoovers' donation of the seed money to build a new Society of Friends' meeting house in Washington, which was dedicated in January 1931, was a combination of their generosity and statement of their faith to the public.

Shortly after her return from Philadelphia, Lou slipped on a freshly waxed floor in the White House and hurt her back, aggravating her old bicycle injury and requiring the use of a wheelchair for six weeks. "I wrote Dr. Boone that I believed I knew the exact spot where you slipped," Grace wrote in a sympathetic note. "Wilkins keeps those floors so slick that there are a few well-known treacherous ones. I used to go skating around the edge of some of those corners on the outer edge of one of my heels."[4]

The wheelchair restricted Lou's mobility, and she spent most of her time in the family's quarters on the second floor, where she continued to receive guests, manage the White House, and handle Girl Scout matters. Jane Deeter Rippin had resigned her position as the organization's executive director in late March, a move anticipated by Lou. "While I think the situation very unfortunate, I really cannot blame her at all and would certainly pursue the same course myself if I were in her place," Lou wrote Abbie Rickard after receiving a copy of Rippin's resignation. "I don't think she could stay unless three [members of the board] who are there left,—and of course that is not a demand that one can make, as I said to you once in the winter."[5]

Rippin had dedicated eleven years of her life to building the Girl Scout organization. She was the day-to-day guide who managed the Scouts' rapid growth and contributed to the development of a dependable donor network. She and Lou shared a common view that leadership should be professionalized through training and national standards. At the time of Rippin's resignation, Scout membership stood at two hundred thousand. There were chapters and leadership teams in all forty-eight states, the territories of

Alaska and Hawaii, and Puerto Rico. Girl Scout camps had been constructed throughout the country.

Lou expressed her support and admiration for Rippin's service in a letter to Mrs. William H. Hoffman, president of the Girl Scouts. "I am completely at a loss for words adequately to express my feelings about what Mrs. Rippin has meant to this organization and what she has accomplished for the Girl Scouts of our country. Her ability, resourcefulness, untiring energy, devotion, forbearance, tolerance, and intense loyalty, are qualities that rise tumultuously one upon another in my mind."[6]

Lou suggested to Abbie that the board consider offering the Executive Director's position to Lillian Gilbreth: "I can think of no one half so good." Lou recommended that Gilbreth be offered the same salary that had been paid to Rippin, although Lou suggested "one might offer a couple of thousand less for the first year with the understanding that it might be increased either gradually or at the end of the first year if the experiment proved a success. . . . I think she would be immeasurably better than any of the old welfare workers about New York or than the people of our staff, old or new."[7]

Psychologist and engineer Lillian Moller Gilbreth was a friend and professional colleague of Bert's and Lou's. Gilbreth pioneered the field of time-and-motion studies to attain organizational efficiency, and she was the first woman to be elected to the National Academy of Engineering. The Society of Women Engineers issued her "Membership #1." The mother of twelve children, a son and daughter immortalized her story in the semi-autobiographical *Cheaper by the Dozen*. When Gilbreth's husband, Frank, died in 1924, she traveled to Europe to deliver a paper to an international engineering body on his behalf. She continued to operate the engineering firm founded by the couple after her husband's death.

Gilbreth had been invited to attend the inauguration, and she was a regular visitor to the White House. She shared Lou's commitment to Scouting and Bert's interests in engineering. In late September 1929, Gilbreth had a half hour appointment with Bert to discuss the upcoming World Engineering Congress, to be held in Tokyo, which Gilbreth was scheduled to attend. He spent the time talking about shared engineering interests and showing her his "Chamber of Horrors," the room where he kept the political cartoons that he collected. Gilbreth stayed for dinner as a last-minute invitee.

The meal was a typical Hoover evening. Twenty guests were seated around a formally set table with china and silver and decorated with flowers and Japanese ivories. Lou had written a card for each guest that identified who was seated on each side and the person's interests. What seemed effortless to Gilbreth was artful on Lou's part.

Lou continued the habit she had begun in the early years of her marriage to assure an interesting group of dinner guests nightly to engage Bert and help him relax. She once apologized to Jean for not having her to dinner at the White House one evening when she had come to visit. "It seems that all the women we know have lately been flocking down on us, and men have been scarce; with the result that I realize that Bert goes into himself at the table and keeps on thinking about the problems he has been dealing with during the day instead of being lured out of the thoughts of the daily grind into other fields."[8]

The last-minute dinner invitations were part of the unflattering gossip about the Hoovers' insensitivity to the impact of their lifestyle on the staff that filtered out of the White House. Lou received the brunt of the criticism, even though most of the invitations were issued by Bert, frequently without Lou's knowledge. She complained in letters to Jean and Allan about Bert's habit of inviting people to dinner on the spur of the moment, but she also had trouble understanding why the White House staff could not adjust to the couple's lifestyle. "It is a funny house downstairs here, not like 2300, where old Butler or Lucille or almost anyone could stay on and concoct small meals for us in the kitchen," she wrote Jean shortly before her sister was due to arrive for a White House visit. "It seems to necessitate three or four cooks here if they [guests] get some soup and a steak and dessert."[9]

Lou viewed journalism as an unworthy and unwholesome activity. Her antipathy toward the press allowed gossip, rumor, and innuendo about her management of the White House to go unchallenged. She had no champions among the women journalists, who covered only society news. To be able to have a scoop about the first lady, a special sit-down interview, or be invited on a trip would have boosted the journalists' morale and provided material for stories about Lou's graciousness and personal kindnesses—similar to the flattering press coverage she had received as a cabinet wife. However, Lou chose not to follow the practice of either Grace Coolidge or Florence Harding of inviting members of the Washington Women's Press Club to tea or on an annual trip on the presidential yacht *Mayflower*.

Lou did not connect the need to befriend women journalists in the same way she would warmly welcome women in science, Scouting, or the arts. "I think it is difficult to exaggerate the resentment toward the White House felt by the women who do newspaper work in Washington. I think it isn't so much personal as professional," one reporter wrote in a letter to fellow woman journalist, "Missy" Meloney, editor of *Sunday* magazine.

> Frankly I am very much surprised that Mrs. Hoover has not done as her two predecessors did about us working members of the Press in Washington. Knowing her as I do, and loving her and admiring her most devotedly, I expected that she would realize how much these things mean to these women whose lives are really for the most part very fine and yet have so little of the charm and pleasure that are common to you and me.[10]

Meloney sent the letter to Bert's press secretary, Lawrence Richey, who shared the correspondence with Lou and her secretaries (likely Mildred Hall and Ruth Fesler). They defended Lou. In an unsigned response, the secretaries explained they had used guidance provided by Mary Randolph during the year she was employed. Randolph had (supposedly) explained that neither Grace Coolidge nor Florence Harding had invited the women journalists on a *Mayflower* excursion until the second year in office. "As far as any one of us knows, it has never been suggested to us that anything be done for this organization." The secretaries added, in what is an interesting twist for the rationale given for having Jessie De Priest to the White House, to have invited the women journalists to a social event at the White House would have been considered political, not social.[11] Given Lou's years of experience in Washington, and her efforts to craft Bert's image during his presidential campaigns, her reluctance to court the press was amazingly short-sighted.

Unfortunately for Lou and Bert, their reputation regarding the unkind and inconsiderate treatment of the White House staff has persisted into the twenty-first century. Recent transcriptions of oral histories from employees who were backstairs at the White House reveal actions more in keeping with Lou's compassion. One of those histories is from Alonzo Fields, whose story was depicted in the film *The Butler*: "You never had to go to Hoover and say, 'Fields is sick, and his wife is in poor condition, and they're in need.' Somehow or other, they would always seem to know it. And you would receive benefits without anyone pleading to them."[12]

Fields shared the story of how Lou ordered cream to be delivered to the home of another White House employee, Wilkinson, who had been diagnosed with ulcers. The common treatment of the day was to encourage drinking milk and cream. "[Wilkinson] was a houseman, and I bet a dime on it that he only got about forty-three dollars every two weeks, about eighty some odd dollars a month. And he had five in the family. This going on a cream diet for him was completely out." When the milkman delivered cream to Wilkinson's door, Wilkinson said he had not ordered any cream. "Well, I'm sorry, cream has been ordered for this residence. . . .[T]his has been taken care of."[13]

The President's Cookbook, published in 1968, confirms Lou's generosity with the staff.

> The best of everything was served. . . . And this policy extended to the servants, who were apt to be cheered, when home ill, by a basket of food and flowers sent with Mrs. Hoover's card. Mrs. Hoover never questioned the amount of food consumed or its cost. Her only requirement was that it be of the best quality, well cooked, and well served.[14]

Lou's empathy extended to those with family members who contracted tuberculosis. The disease was one of the six leading causes of death in the United States in the 1920s and 1930s. In the days before the discovery of antibiotics, little could be done for a tubercular patient than to order rest and a retreat to a drier climate.

Herbert was diagnosed with the disease in mid-1930. "Daddy and I very well," Lou cabled Allan in early September. "Illness here [Herbert's diagnosis of tuberculosis] definite and demanding immediate treatment but not critically dangerous."[15]

It was an unfortunate time for the Hoovers' elder son to be sidelined. He had earned his own *Time* cover on July 14, 1930, with his election as the first president of Aeronautical Radio, Incorporated, a non-profit corporation created by Western Air Express (Herbert's employer), Boeing, and American Airways, to serve as the industry's sole licensee and coordinator of radio communication outside of the federal government.

Herbert had combined his fascination with radio and electronics and an interest in the infant aviation industry to develop systems that improved aviation's safety and enabled it to expand into passenger transportation. He had set up stations across the country on behalf of Western Air Express to allow communication between radio-equipped aircraft and ground crews. Herbert had gained well-deserved recognition in the industry for his expertise, efforts begun during his year as a Guggenheim fellow.

With the confirmation of his tuberculosis, Herbert initially took up residence at Camp Rapidan, in the care of one of Joel Boone's assistants. Herbert's wife Peggy was with him. The group stayed until late October, when "[i]t has gotten so cold up at camp that everybody has been ordered down except Herbert and Fox [Boone's assistant]," Lou wrote Allan from the White House. "The water pipes have frozen and they are living on buckets of water carried to them and heated over something. They are expecting to bring Herbert here on Wednesday for a couple of days, and he and Dr. Boone will take the Friday night train to Asheville [North Carolina] where they arrive early Saturday morning."[16]

Under the assumption that Herbert would convalesce somewhere in the desert southwest, Jean had offered to help Peggy manage her household in California. However, the family decided that Herbert would go to Asheville, where Lou rented the eight-room, two-bath Blue Briar Cottage atop Sunset Mountain once owned by William Jennings Bryan.

> Jean, most privately. . . . [The doctors] said that for the present, until Herbert was able to get about, it was just as good for him in the places that have proven salubrious in the East as places in the West. . . . But while he has to be lazy, he can just as well be on this side of the Rockies. . . . We have discovered that Bert is going to be so restless if Herbert is west that as much for his father as for him, we want them to be together. Asheville has very large sanitariums,—one of the largest of the national ones is there, and a number of private ones.[17]

During his time in Asheville, Herbert became active in the local amateur radio club. Peggy and her three children (the youngest, Joan Ledlie, had been born on April 12, 1930), divided their time between Asheville and the White House.

When White House butler Phillips Brooks developed tuberculosis, Lou hired his wife, Katurah, as her personal maid so that the family would continue to have an income. Lou encouraged Katurah to visit her husband in the Maryland sanitarium where he was convalescing. After one visit, Lou perceived that Katurah was upset.

Keturah acknowledged that she was. "I went out to see Phil this afternoon and when I got to where he was, the bottom of his bed was full of snow," she told Lou.

Lou "jumped up and . . . went to the telephone and called this hospital and said she wanted him to have special service and to be put in a place where there would be no draft or anything," Katurah Brooks recounted in an oral history. "[B]ecause she wanted him to get thoroughly well, and if they couldn't do that she would see that someone was placed at the head of the hospital who would. I never will forget that. She was so interested in his welfare."[18]

The position of first lady has no job description, but there are common threads that unite the presidential spouses and hostesses who have filled the position. A hidden aspect of the role is the perception among some Americans that the first lady has the influence (and power) to secure a local federal job, such as postmaster (in the days before Civil Service), or that she has a pot of government funds from which she can disperse aid. Correspondence to the nation's first ladies includes many such requests for help.

As the economy worsened, the number of letters asking for Lou's assistance increased. Philippi Harding Butler screened the letters and passed along those whose needs seemed legitimate and verifiable. Lou then contacted her nationwide network to learn more about each situation and to get recommendations on where her help could make a difference. When Lou provided money, she did so anonymously. Through Bert's associate George Barr Baker, Lou provided initial aid of twenty-five dollars to two elderly sisters, and she committed to sending them ten dollars monthly. Florence Henry's former housekeeper wrote Lou that she was about to have her property in Whittier, California, foreclosed. Lou asked Allan to look into the matter. When Allan determined that the bank was too far into the foreclosure process to reverse it, Lou instructed him to see that the former housekeeper received a small bequest from an "unknown person" interested in the woman's welfare. An untold number of people benefitted from Lou's private philanthropy, including members of her and Bert's extended families. In the deteriorating economic conditions, even a small, one-time monetary gift was a lifeline.

Conflicting economic signals made it difficult for Bert and his advisors to determine how to manage the nation's economy. Although the unemployment rate had tripled in the six months between June and December, the nation's gross domestic product had improved slightly. The decline in GDP at the beginning of 1930 was minus 8.5 percent; at year's end the GDP was minus 6.4 percent.[19]

What economists could not account for was the beginning of a severe weather event taking place in the Midwestern and southwestern states that would tip the scales toward a deeper depression. The two heavily agrarian regions suffered economically. Bank failures, triggered by multiple mortgage foreclosures, were common occurrences. One North Dakota newspaper described agriculture as groaning under a seven-year depression. "[F]armers have been crying for help so long that their voices are all husky."[20]

America's corn and wheat belt experienced a drought unlike anything that had been recorded since the founding of the nation. "The summer of 1930 will long be remembered as a 'humdinger,'" began an article in the Washington *Evening Star* titled, "Enigma of the Great Drought," "when heat over half the United States was violent and continuous, when our fields and lawns lay parched, when crops were burned up, when forest fires raged and cattle thirsted for water."[21]

The 1930 drought was the first in a series of drought events that would be remembered as the Dust Bowl. Agricultural historians have since confirmed that the drought was exacerbated by farming practices implemented during the 1920s. Soil conservation was in its infancy, and only a tiny handful of people saw a connection between the drought and plowed acres.

A decade of depressed commodity prices, combined with a move toward mechanized agriculture which increased operating expenses, had forced farmers to clear marginal land and put more acres under cultivation. Growers hoped to offset the low prices they received for their crops with higher yields. The additional acres of exposed soil upset the normal evapotranspiration cycle—the means by which water evaporates from plants into the atmosphere and is returned as rain.

One-fourth of the United States labor force was engaged in agricultural production in 1930.[22] As farm incomes decreased, mortgages went unpaid, limiting the available liquidity so crucial for banks to continue operating. Demand for manufactured goods—the goods that would keep people employed in factories in the cities—declined. The traditional cyclical downturn in the economy combined with the drop in demand from one-fourth of the nation's labor force and its families, the instability of the stock market, and a weakening international economy converged to send the United States' economy into a tailspin.

Bert was a numbers man who valued objective data. By the end of 1930, however, objective data sent conflicting signals. Bert refused to buy into the pessimistic voices around him, reiterating his belief that the economy was fundamentally sound and merely experiencing a normal correction. He did not support calls for relief bills and bond sales to fund unemployment benefits, believing it would wreak long-term harm on the nation's economy. As the clamor for federal aid grew, Lou observed to Allan: "No country yet has been able to take the weight of paid unemployment from Roman times, fore and aft."[23]

Neither Lou nor Bert grasped the connection between the farmers' struggles and the nation's economic depression. Lou placed blame on the banking industry. "He [Bert] saw this depression coming," she wrote Allan a year to the day of the market crash,

> and its world causes, and tried in vain to get the leaders to act who might have averted it. He also saw the stock market collapse coming and months before begged the leaders of the NY Stock Exchange and the NY Bankers [sic] to take steps to avert it. They only scorned him and proceeded to augment it.

Bert's detractors, Lou observed, forget "that he has little power to act,—beyond what the law provides and what the group leaders will help put over voluntarily."[24]

Bert fell back on the approach that had worked so well for him as Food Administrator: He called for a national commitment to volunteerism. As part of that call, Bert formed the President's Emergency Committee on Employment (PECE) in late 1930. The advisory board consisted of dollar-a-year-men-and-women—recognized business leaders who gave their talents to the government for the salary of a dollar a year. Lillian Gilbreth headed up the Women's Division of PECE. In the early months after its creation, the Women's Division promoted a "spruce-up-your-home" campaign, an updated approach to the Better Homes movement Bert had championed as commerce secretary. Women were encouraged to find small, odd jobs that local men could complete and thereby earn a little money. The concept promoted volunteerism and community support.

By early 1931, PECE was falling apart. The *Nation* magazine referred to its work as "Relief by Publicity." Gilbreth had initially supported the concept behind PECE—to provide national, moral leadership in encouraging local efforts. However, it was clear by the spring that much more was needed to address the depression. Gilbreth's and Lou's mutual friend, Alice Dickson, wrote Lou that she and Gilbreth were returning home to their regular paying jobs.[25]

In the face of PECE's disintegration, Lou addressed the nation by radio on March 23, 1931. Flanked by two local girl scouts, Lois Kuhn, of Bethesda, Maryland, and Peggy Starr, of Hyattsville, Maryland, Lou praised the work of the Girl Scouts and the many women's organizations that were engaged in assisting those hard hit by the drought and unemployment. Lois Kuhn opened the program by delivering a report on scouts' work in canvassing needy cases in the girls' communities and helping to provide aid.

Lou began her address by thanking the scouts for their report. Then, she proceeded to speak to the challenges faced by so many: "Because of a devastating drought that has fallen upon the just and the industrious almost as hardly as upon the unjust and the lazy, there is a great want of these necessities over larger areas of our country." There was hardly any place in the United States, Lou continued, where a Girl Scout did not know someone who was in dire need.

Lou showcased the work of girls and women in her speech, mentioning the efforts of groups as diverse as 4-H, Campfire Girls, YWCA, Young Women's Hebrew Association (YWHA), Catholic Welfare Clubs, the Women's Clubs of the General Federation of Clubs, PTAs, and the Business and Professional Women's Association.

> You who are listening in at the other end of this wonderful newly discovered thing called radio, each and every one of you has been doing what you could to help your own neighborhood; you have given additional work where you could; you have postponed the burdens of full payment of debts, of rents, of loans, of mortgages of those of whom fate and not their own shortcomings have handicapped. . . .
>
> The President, I know, is most appreciative of the achievement of the

> organization with which you are all cooperating, the women's division of the President's Emergency Committee on Employment. He said, as the coming clouds of depression threatened, that a very large proportion of the work and the spirit that would make the storm pass without consummate destruction would be due to the way in which women met it.[26]

Lou championed the Girl Scouts' volunteer role in helping communities face the impact of the Depression. In mid-September, she invited the Executive Council of the Girl Scouts to Camp Rapidan. At that meeting, a decision was made to revise the scope of Girl Scout assistance from canvassing community needs to providing help with gardening, canning, and other homemaking skills that would help families save money. Some historians credit Lillian Gilbreth as the author of the new approach, dubbed the "Rapidan Plan." The Plan mirrored the efforts of the Women's Division of POUR, The President's Organization for Unemployment Relief, which was the successor to PECE. Others credit Lou. Regardless of the idea's originator, the Girl Scout leadership departed the Shenandoah Mountains with a unified commitment to encourage scouts to offer direct assistance to the needy in their communities.

Lou was sensitive to public perception of family members working for pay in private industry or working in unpaid government positions. She had a more comprehensive understanding of the economic pain inflicted by the Depression than she has been credited. As with so many of Lou's achievements, her reluctance to turn the spotlight on herself and her achievements concealed from the public the depth of her compassion.

She encouraged her nephew Del to agree to work without a salary. Allan had graduated from Harvard Business School in June 1931. When Bert considered appointing him to an unpaid position in the Department of Commerce, Lou knew the move would be fraught with political peril. She disabused Bert of the idea, basing her argument on what we would today call the optics. "Even though in this season of depression you should work for practically no salary at all, and thus not be taking a paying job away from someone in need of that, few people would realise [sic] that, and most who are out of work, or working with the unemployed of hearing about them, would think that here was Daddy getting well paid Government jobs for his own son."

Lou encouraged Allan to avoid going into government service until he had a chance to understand how businesses were built and sustained. She was also skeptical of businesses that had achieved success by creating what, in her mind, was an artificial demand for products.

> At the same time, I think you need to study a little about what is so-called success today. People have been thinking too much in terms of quantity and not enough in terms of quality. And men of the Ford, Rockefeller, Wooley type have been making great "successes" because they have been producing so very much of something,—and not content with filling the demand for their respective articles, they have specialized men going around making a fictitious demand for it. . . .To fill a need until it is filled is a legitimate ambition. To create an artificial demand for a thing, I think is of more doubtful benefit to all concerned. Times are going to be very "hard" for most of the world.[27]

Heeding his mother's advice, Allan took a job in banking in California, launching him in what would become a successful career in finance.

Bert presented his legislative plan to Congress when it convened in December 1931. Acknowledging a $2.1 billion projected budget shortfall for the coming year, Bert intended to slash the federal budget by $4 million and called for a tax increase to balance future budgets. He called for action to stabilize the nation's banking system, including insurance programs that would protect depositors, a home-loan discount bank system, and the ability of the Federal Reserve Bank to be able to liquidate the holdings of failed banks. Bert also sought a national finance corporation that would help industries get needed funding to retool.

"Your Daddy . . . is working as hard as ever," Lou wrote Allan. "And it is mostly with the country's woes, thus far." She was optimistic that the country was about to turn the corner, a sentiment that Bert had expressed in his message to Congress. "But there are many rifts of brightness shining thro' now, and I think he can spend more time in the future in truly constructive things rather than in the prevention of threatening disasters. It is a pity that there is so much of the latter necessary, as they do not show their accomplishment at all." Echoing her thoughts from previous letters, she added, "[S]ome of the worst [disasters] that have hit us, he saw coming, and tried to prevent, but could get no cooperation from the people who might have accomplished it."[28]

Bert's desired banking reforms required the cooperation of Senator Carter Glass, a Virginia Democrat. Glass repeatedly blocked Bert's proposals from reaching the Senate floor for a vote. Lou fumed that Glass's resistance had everything to do with politics and reflected a pronounced lack of concern for the problems facing the country. She predicted that if Bert lost the election in 1932, the next president would gain approval in Congress for Bert's proposals and be given all the credit. Her observation proved prophetic. A caption in a political cartoon by Jay "Ding" Darling, the Pulitzer Prize winning editorial cartoonist of the Des Moines *Register*, read: "We pick out an engineer for his ability to run the train and then elect men to the United States Senate who do nothing but tear up the track."[29]

Lou remained averse to large-scale federal funding to address the nation's unemployment problem. She believed that such funding would be fiscally unsustainable over the long term and politically slide the nation toward socialism. For Lou, socialism gave the state too much power over its citizens and robbed them of initiative. Her answer was to promote private philanthropy and individual assistance between neighbors within their communities. An avid knitter, she donated hand-knit sweaters to Washington's Red Cross chapter as part of an effort organized by Dolly Gann to gather clothing for needy families. At the end of January 1932, Lou organized a series of five benefit concerts featuring the renowned pianist Ignaz Jan Paderewski. Paderewski had become a friend of the Hoovers, and he stayed at the White House during his time in Washington. The pianist agreed to donate the proceeds from ticket sales to the unemployed. Lou headlined a committee that included Vice President Curtis, Chief Justice and Mrs. Charles Hughes, Secretary of State and Mrs. Henry Stimson, Helen Taft, and Edith Wilson, among others.

In a nod to the struggling cotton farmers in the South and to encourage women to buy cotton fabric for clothing, Lou wore a white dimity gown woven with blue threads in a cornflower pattern at the reception she hosted in honor of six cabinet departments, including agriculture, interior, and commerce. The gown copied a dress worn by Lou's mother dating to the 1870s and featured a tiered, floor-length skirt with a scalloped train, ruffled sleeves that reached to her elbows, and a close-fitting bodice with a scooped neck. Lou accented the look with a black velvet ribbon choker. One of the elderly guests at the event recalled that the last time a cotton gown had been worn at the White House was during the Civil War, when the guest attended a reception hosted by President and Mrs. Lincoln. Lou furnished a portrait of her in the gown to the Congressional Club, who used it as the frontispiece of the program for the Annual Breakfast held in her honor.

In one of the only formal interviews that she granted as first lady, given at the start of what would be her last year in the White House, Lou echoed the messages promoted by Lillian Gilbreth's Women's Division of POUR. Lou reminded women to look for the odd home repair or home renovation project that could employ a local man. She stressed the value of maintaining a positive attitude and reminded people that an optimistic outlook was contagious and would benefit all at home and in their community. It was a case of mind over matter, and Lou believed that changes in attitudes about the economy would bring about changes in people's financial circumstances. The inveterate optimism was vintage Lou Henry Hoover.

While Lou maintained an upbeat attitude in public, she privately prepared her sons to expect the worst. She wrote a letter to Herbert and Allan advising them that their annual incomes from their trusts would be less than what they had received in the past. She encouraged both of her sons to find ways to economize and cautioned them not to expect to see an improvement in financial position in the near term. In rare candidness, she admitted that it was possible that Bert might have difficulty paying for a private assistant if things did not improve.

Bert and Lou privately questioned the stability of the nation's political and economic structure. Bert had expressed his concerns to Lou regarding the government's capacity to respond in a timely manner to the stresses placed upon it by the Depression. The government, Lou observed to Allan, could "fail in people's imaginations, if not in fact. . . . Have you had the time yet," she asked him, "to question to yourself as to what you thought was right and what needed change in our accepted system? And if you had decided ideas as to needed changes, if you had any thought as to how they could be accomplished, and where individuals without making a 'cause' or 'reform,' could be helping in starting desirable improvements?" She continued:

> Daddy is extremely fearful of the conditions of things in the last few days. This is May 29th. He thinks things in the nation are hanging on the ragged edge of financial collapse, due to the long inaction, and sometimes

> crazy action, of Congress. He thinks it very largely due to the fact that most of the members just have not the understanding of what it is about, and with what disastrous conditions they are playing. And that many, although knowing that the condition of the country is very bad, but not realizing quite how bad,—are still playing politics for their own next election,—while they are really pushing the election to a place where an election won't matter.[30]

In the twenty-first century, when Americans have become accustomed to the nation's first ladies sometimes taking the bully pulpit on behalf of their husbands, it is natural to question why Lou did not make more of an effort to put forth Bert's thinking to the public. She was a gifted public speaker (more so than Bert), and effectively communicated her warmth and friendliness in her radio addresses. But both Hoovers were reticent about sharing their innermost feelings publicly. That reluctance, combined with their inbred distaste for dealing with the press, played a large factor not only in Bert's defeat in 1932, but in the subsequent legacy of both Hoovers.

The Republican National Convention was held in June, and Bert was renominated as the party's presidential candidate. The absence of jubilation at the convention prompted Lou to discuss Bert's plans after leaving the White House, hinting that she expected her husband to be a one-term president. "As far as I am concerned, or even Daddy, I don't think the election will make much difference in our life. He will be just as busy at something and everything will go along in exactly the same old way as it has for the last thirty years whether it's in the White House or somewhere else."

Lou already understood that Bert had no plans to return to California and occupy the house on San Juan Hill. He would remain in the east, where "the kind of people he deals with happily in all his various enterprises grow so much thicker in the square mile on this side of the Mississippi that I fancy he will be in California only for short periods, or when he has some definite piece of work to do there."[31]

For her part, Lou was ready to leave Washington and undertake a life where she had more control.

> Your Daddy is taking this election just as he takes everything, which means in his own particular engineering way. Which means that at first he looked the whole proposition over, and said there is nothing else to be

> done but go for it. Whether I think I have done enough of my duty by my country now, or not, whether I think it is an entertaining job or not, can have no bearing on the case, as very much more important things are at stake than any wishes of mine.[32]

Mary Austin published her biography, *Earth Horizon*, shortly after the Republican convention, where she again took aim at the Hoovers. She revisited her anger at Bert for refusing to give her employment with the Food Administration by criticizing his management style. Bert, wrote Austin, "had the conception of great ideas, but could never bring them to birth. . . . He had devoted followers about him who made an impregnable wall between him and the sort of people I had in mind [who could help him promote his ideas]."[33]

Austin took a shot at Lou as well. In a reversal of her fond remembrances of the Hoovers' Red House, Austin described the gatherings there as "thoroughly American talk, and a great deal also that was boring. Mrs. Hoover's kindness was such that she was always remembering in the midst of her entertaining some poor soul who would have 'so enjoyed' meeting interesting people that the interesting ones were usually sandwiched in between social dubs to the loss of the general character of her entertainment."[34]

Rather than ignore the pettiness, Lou bristled at Austin's portrayal. The book's publication, combined with the ongoing political attacks on Bert, propelled Lou to craft her version of his career and motives in a series of letters written throughout 1932 that she sent to Jean and her sons. "I was incensed at much reading one morning of Democratic and 'Progressive' effusions about the President's having no thought for the little man but bending all his energies toward saving the bloated plutocrat. The absolute injustice and downright lying of these statements infuriated me,—and there rushed through my mind a whirlwind mind-movie of how all that he has been doing so endlessly and so courageously has been for the small individual, the millions of them."

In Lou's recounting of his career, Bert was consistently the humanitarian, not a hard-nosed businessman. He did not cut the wages of Australian miners to show more profit to the shareholders; he cut wages so that they could retain employment in a depressed market. He did not line his pockets with funds donated to the CRB; he risked his own fortune.

Bert had not pursued public office—it had pursued him. She omitted any mention of his lobbying to secure a job in the Wilson Administration upon the United States' entry into World War I, and she ignored his efforts, in which she had been a key player, to secure the presidential nomination as early as 1920. "Your father did not want the Presidency himself, or for himself, or the reputation it might bring him," Lou told her sons. "For years he scoffed at the friends, and often strangers—who came to him proposing some step or avenue leading to it.

"The honors, the pomp, the circumstance surrounding it, did not appeal to him. The duties he thought it entailed were very objectionable in his sight—being largely to his vision public-speaking and republic-functioning!"[35]

In the midst of defending her husband, Lou pulls back the curtain of her own disappointment in the way her married life developed and the changes that occurred in Bert that affected their relationship. It is a rare insight into her thoughts about the personal cost of Bert's ambition and his pursuit of public service. "Those years of his life,—and ours,—he gave up to the cause of the little man, millions of him. And not only those years, but most of the kind of happiness of pleasure, that had been his before. A certain definite, original kind of joy of life was stamped out of him by those war years."[36]

She was contemptuous of Franklin Delano Roosevelt, the New York governor who had won the Democratic presidential nomination. "[S]uch a texture of misrepresentation, insinuation, suggesting absolute falsehood, quotation of misleading sentences without amplifying context,—and downright untruthful statements,—one does not remember seeing in a supposedly reputable document," she fumed in a letter to her sons after reading a campaign speech of the Democratic presidential nominee.

Lou saw a parallel between Roosevelt's attacks on Bert and the concealment of the seriousness of Roosevelt's paralysis, resulting from having contracted polio in 1921. In her mind, Roosevelt had a "fake attitude" regarding his illness. "If he accepted frankly that he had a very serious illness, and had providentially recovered in all but the use of his legs, but could not stand alone or walk without support, and so went around in a wheeled chair, I should think it would win him commendation of everyone.

"But this posing before the world as a normal, sturdy man (although compelled to use a mere cane), and going to any amount of trouble and subterfuge to hold the truth of it from the public, shows up painfully a flaw in the man's own truthfulness and forthrightness."[37]

Roosevelt delivered the speech Lou found so offensive two weeks after an incident in Washington that many believed permanently doomed Bert prospects for reelection.

In May 1932, an estimated group of twenty thousand World War I veterans descended on Washington to demand full payment of a bonus promised them by Congress in 1924, but not payable until 1945. Reports conflict as to where the marchers encamped. Some are said to have occupied buildings slated for demolition, other reports indicate that the men erected tent cities along Constitution (then B Street) and Pennsylvania Avenues, and along a thirty-acre site across the Anacostia River on Anacostia Flats.

Initially, the marchers were treated sympathetically. District police superintendent Brigadier General Pelham D. Glassford requested a $75,000 appropriation from Congress to feed the marchers. (The District of Columbia's budget is set by Congress.) Congress turned down the request, but local residents donated funds to feed the men. Lou quietly provided food and blankets. She referred desperate families to local agencies that could provide help, and she assisted some from her private funds. Lou's largesse went unnoticed by the press.

The House of Representatives voted to pay the bonus, but the Senate rejected the measure. Bert had promised to veto the bill if it came to his desk. Some marchers departed after their efforts to get their bonuses failed, but new veterans arrived. Although there are no firm figures, it is estimated that between ten and twenty thousand men and their families occupied tents and empty buildings in the District.

The marchers remained in the District well into July, when efforts were made to evict them from buildings and move them from Washington, beginning on July 21. On July 28, after some marchers rushed Glassford's officers, Bert ordered the secretary of war, Patrick Hurley, to clear the area immediately. General Douglas MacArthur, who would go on to lead the United States' forces in the Pacific during World War II, had the command. His soldiers advanced using tear gas, clubs, and bayonets. The cavalry moved forward with swords drawn. The veterans and their families responded by throwing bricks. Hundreds were injured and an infant died.

Secretary of War Hurley twice sent orders to MacArthur indicating that the President, worried that the government reaction might look overly harsh, did not wish the army to pursue the Bonus Marchers across the bridge into their main encampment on the other side of the Anacostia River. But MacArthur, according to his aide Dwight Eisenhower, "said he was too busy," did not want to be "bothered by people coming down and pretending to bring orders," and sent his men across the bridge anyway, after pausing several hours to allow as many people as possible to evacuate. A fire soon erupted in the camp. While it is not clear which side started the blaze, the sight of the fire became the signature image of the unrest and the treatment of war veterans.[38]

Both the president and General MacArthur asserted that the Bonus Marchers were infiltrated by Communists, a claim Lou repeated in her recounting of the event in a letter to her sons. MacArthur told the press that if Hoover had not ordered their removal, there would have been a revolution: "It is my opinion that had the President permitted this thing to go on twenty-four hours more he would have been faced with a grave situation which would have caused a real battle."[39]

The Scripps-Howard newspapers printed lies about the incident, Lou wrote to Herbert. "Of course, as we said when you were here, investigations showed that a very large number, if not the majority, of the men had never been in the army—or any government service." Many would have taken jobs if they had been available, "[b]ut more had no desire to work, only to agitate." Lou was critical of Glassford's handling of the situation, believing that he encouraged the marchers to remain in Washington instead of departing.

Lou acknowledged that there had been some violence when the army came to evacuate the marchers: "Remember this. The Army never fired a shot or levelled [sic] a gun at anyone. It did not club or threaten to club anyone. It did not use any 'forces' whatever." The Army used 'harmless' teargas. All the stories of shooting and clubbing and fighting by the soldiers are absolutely made up, and all such pictures are fakes." The Anacostia camp caught fire, Lou reported to Herbert. The soldiers denied starting it, claiming that it started as a result of either an accident or confusion. Lou believed that the Communists in the camp started it to promote their own propaganda.

The fire was something "Daddy was particularly sorry for. But you had better have no knowledge of the episode until you hear it from him."[40]

Hoover's handling of the Bonus Marchers—his refusal to sign a bill that would have immediately released their bonuses, the removal of the marchers from Washington's streets, and the horrors of the fire on the Anacostia

Flats—overrode all that Bert had done over his career to provide for the proverbial "little man."

The incident proved to be a public relations disaster, and Bert's and Lou's shared contempt for the press overrode their advisors' pleas for them to show their softer sides. Bert often invited orphaned youths to meet with him at the White House. He became childlike in the youngsters' presence—a brief return to the "fun-making, fun-enjoying" man of Lou's remembrance. Press secretary George Akerson begged Bert to allow reporters to capture those very human moments. Bert, however, insisted on privacy. He refused to use the image of his meeting with orphaned youngsters for political gain.

The campaign likewise encouraged Lou to engage more with the press, but Lou did not cooperate. Reporter Bess Furman was assigned to cover Lou on the campaign trail, and Lou gave Furman one interview as Hoover's campaign train traveled through Ohio. Near Wooster, Lou told Furman that her great-grandfather had founded the town, but she insisted that Furman not cite Lou as the source of the information.

Lou expressed her views about the press to Allan, who was being asked to give an interview about his parents. "Yes, I know just how you feel about interviewing and publicity. Isn't it terrible? But just refuse. I tell myself I am going to keep 'pleasant, affable, and firm,'—but always saying 'no.' " She would make one possible exception to her refusal to talk with the press, and that was when they "come up with some perfectly preposterous story about Daddy's honesty, then I should not say anything about that one—in particular—but might say that I knew him and his ways of life and principles so intimately, that I knew such a tale was perfectly unfounded."[41]

Bert's political advisers remained optimistic and reported that his prospects of winning reelection were still high. Bert disagreed, and he became gloomier as election day approached. The result of Maine's state elections, held in September, set the stage for the expectations for November. The usually Republican state gave a majority to the Democrats in statehouse and congressional elections. A headline in the Washington *Evening Star* read, "All GOP States Seen as Doubtful: Result in Maine Presages Big Swing to Democrats and Wets."[42]

Lou campaigned with Bert through the fall, usually receiving more favorable press than her husband. She often said a few words to the crowds, careful to appear maternal, not political. Even though she saw the crowd sizes and reactions on the campaign trail, Lou had become uncharacteristically suspicious by the time October rolled around. She was scheduled to deliver a radio address to the Girl Scouts from Virginia Beach to be broadcast nationwide. A technical problem that Lou attributed to "Virginia Democratic hooliganism," prevented the broadcast. She delivered it successfully to the country the following week.

Lou cautioned Allan to "[b]e very careful of your engagements the next few weeks. Don't get lured into any kinds of parties where you don't know and trust every member—nor to any [party] held in any place you don't know well."[43]

On October 30, she told her son: "Be ready to meet a surprising defeat."[44]

CHAPTER 14

Out of the Limelight

Bert and Lou took a final campaign swing by train through the midwestern heartland on their way home to Palo Alto. Bert urged loyalty among his supporters at each stop and warned them of the dangers to the country if the Democrats won the election. Privately, the couple was reconciled to a defeat.

Intimate friends were confident of victory. On Election Day, Abbie and Edgar wired:

> We have exercised the high privilege of casting our four votes and my hometown will give you an enormous majority. It has been a distinguishing mark of honor to have been identified as a standard bearer in the army of men and women who are registering their approval of your unsurpassed record and who will, by their vote today, insure your leadership for another four years. And as devoted friends our only concern and our constant hope is that the burden will be lighter for you.[1]

Abbie sent a telegram to Lou following Bert's St. Paul speech, delivered the day before the election. "Know that your audience at St. Paul and the millions listening in must have felt as I did when the President referred to women's service that you stood at the head of the line in unselfish devotion to family, country, and friends and surpassed them all in constructive accomplishment."[2]

Herbert Hoover lost the election in a reverse of the landslide that had carried him to the presidency in 1928. Franklin Roosevelt won 472 electoral votes to Bert's fifty-nine. Roosevelt captured sixty percent of the vote. He was the second Democrat to be elected to the presidency in thirty-six years, and his victory initiated a realignment of American politics. The impact of

Roosevelt's policies, encapsulated in his "New Deal," has governed nearly every sector of the United States economy, even into the twenty-first century.

Since Labor Day, Bert had discounted his advisers' assurances that reelection was certain. "He is getting gloomier by the day," Lou told family and friends in the weeks before the election. The reality of the loss left Bert in shock.

Bert struggled to come to terms with his defeat. He was withdrawn and morose among intimates; too exhausted to participate in the banter and good-natured kidding that was typical of him with close friends. The same friends assured Lou that Bert would return to his usual self in a few weeks. Like their interpretation of the mood of the electorate, the Hoovers' inner circle was overly optimistic.

Lou prevailed on Bert to get away from the White House for a vacation. "You can toss up whether you think he stays or goes," Lou had written Allan while Bert waged an internal battle about taking time away from the White House, "but I am betting on the going." Driven by a sense of duty to the nation, Bert was not comfortable leaving the White House to enjoy himself while the country suffered. Between Lou's persistence and the counsel of friends, he finally decided to depart Washington for the Christmas holidays and to cancel the traditional New Year's Day diplomatic reception, a timetable that met with Lou's approval. "The White House was comfortable if you were just living in it," she confided in Allan, but if you get "enmeshed in Christmas and New Year festivities and occupations, it will be a devil of a bother."[3]

Social Washington treated the cancellation as a serious faux pas: It was one more opportunity to criticize the Hoover White House. "Whenever a change is made in the routine of Washington's official entertainment a long cry goes up that sacred precedent has been ruthlessly violated and just now there is a terrible ruction in the social ranks," the Washington *Evening Star* declared indignantly on page one of its Sunday social section. "No New Year Day reception and no diplomatic breakfast according to the old schedule." Little did the *Evening Star* reporter know that a precedent was truly set: The New Year Day reception hosted by the Hoovers the previous year, 1932, was the last to be held at the White House.[4]

On January 5, former president Calvin Coolidge died suddenly of a heart attack. The Hoovers had just returned to Washington. Bert sent a condolence telegram, and Lou followed up in a more personal tone to Grace. "We are so distressed by this sad, sad word of the loss of your husband. . . . [M]y heart is with you in your great personal sorrow."[5]

Grace denied requests for her husband's body to lie in state in either Boston (he had served as Governor of Massachusetts), or in Washington. She quickly organized a service, held in Northampton, Massachusetts, where the couple resided. Lou and Bert, together with Vice President Curtis, Chief Justice Charles Evans Hughes, several members of Bert's cabinet, and congressional leaders, boarded a train in Washington on the morning of January 7. They arrived in Northampton at ten o'clock as scheduled. The funeral service was held after all of the dignitaries, which included Eleanor Roosevelt as her husband's representative, arrived. The Hoovers made a brief, private condolence call on Grace following the service and then departed with their party for Washington by noon.

In late January, Lou composed a poem and sent it to Grace, along with an offer to come for a visit:

Up and down and around about
The house, you have gone with me.
In years gone by, it has often been,
But in these days, constantly.

The house of beauty, the house of joy,
The house of sadness, of history.
Some ghosts are stately, and some grotesque,
Some tragic, some gay, some humoresque.

Dear,—halls, and stairs and chambers wide
Still treasure the touch of your footstep light
And long for another glimpse of you.

"Do you want to visit the White House once more, to relive an old memory, to see a place one more time?" Lou asked. "We could be very quiet,—and see no one unless you wished. Or perhaps you want memories only, for a time."[6] Grace, lost in her own grief, did not make the journey south.

Other than the cancelled New Year Day reception, Lou hosted the usual Cabinet and diplomatic receptions that were traditionally held in January and February. She asked her sons and long-time colleagues such as the Rickards to suggest the names of their friends who might appreciate an evening in the White House. Many of the attendees mourned the end of the Hoover administration, but Lou, with her traditional joie de vivre, dispelled the gloom with her smiles and warmth.

That warmth did not extend to Eleanor Roosevelt's visit to tour the White House, the first formally scheduled tour between the outgoing and incoming first ladies, set for January 28. Mrs. Roosevelt turned down an offer of a car to pick her up from her hotel and walked to the mansion alone and unaccompanied by Secret Service, arriving shortly before the scheduled time of eleven o'clock. Lou and her secretary, Mildred Hall, showed the future first lady the public rooms and shared with her some of the history of the Monroe furnishings in the Green Room. In the family quarters, Lou explained which of the furnishings belonged to the Hoovers and which belonged to the White House. She pointed out paintings that were on loan from the National Gallery of Art and showed her the sleeping quarters used by Lou's secretaries on the third floor of the residence. Eleanor turned down an offer of refreshments, saying that she "didn't want to take up too much" of Lou's time, and prepared to leave after a brief, forty-five-minute stay. It was as the future first lady prepared to leave that Lou realized they had not visited the kitchen and food preparation area of the White House. Lou excused herself, and Mildred Hall took Eleanor to the kitchens. The visit lasted just one hour.

Lou had enjoyed warm relationships with all of her predecessors. Edith Wilson was a neighbor on S Street. Lou attended social events at the White House and had been with Mrs. Harding at the time of her husband's death. The friendship with Grace Coolidge would extend beyond Lou's White House years. But there would be no closeness between Lou Henry Hoover and Eleanor Roosevelt. When Lou became president of the Girl Scouts in 1935, she instructed scout leadership to show Mrs. Roosevelt honor and respect at Girl Scout functions, and the two women attended some of the same conventions, but they did not appear on stage together. The sisterhood of first ladies that had crossed party lines for nearly half a century came to a temporary halt.

On Saturday, March 4, 1933, the Hoovers departed the White House for the final time. Franklin Roosevelt's inauguration day dawned gray and cold, but without the rain that had dampened Bert's inauguration four years previously. He and Lou spent the morning saying good-bye to each of the White

House staff and finalizing their departure arrangements. Herbert and Allan had arrived from California. Herbert would accompany his father to New York; Allan would return with his mother to Palo Alto. Furniture was placed in storage. The Hoovers' dogs, Weegie and Pat, were taken to Union Station to wait for their owners.

The family traveled to Union Station after Roosevelt had completed his inaugural address. Several thousand well-wishers thronged the train station to say good-bye to the Hoovers. People pushed flowers and candy toward them and clamored to shake their hands. "We'll see you in 1936!" their supporters shouted. Bert did not respond to calls to make a speech, but the tears in his eyes reflected the depth of his appreciation for the show of support. Ray Lyman Wilbur, a long-time friend of Lou's since her first days at Stanford University, took her arm to protect her from the press of the crowd and helped her onto the train. Family and friends rode together to Philadelphia's Broad Street Station.

Bert had always needed approbation, and he took his electoral defeat as a rejection of him as a person, not as a rejection of his actions as president. For fifteen years, prior to the October 27, 1929, stock market crash, he had been the "master of emergencies"—the man who could find a way to make the impossible possible. He fed starving Belgians. He had made sure that the Allies on both sides of the Atlantic had enough food to eat after the United States entered World War I. He had shepherded the United States into a new era of technology with the introduction of radio and the start of television, and he had managed the devastation of the country following the Great Mississippi Flood in 1926. But the Humpty Dumpty of the United States economy had fallen off the wall in 1929, and all of Bert's good ideas, dedicated efforts, and men and women who helped on PECE and POUR could not put Humpty back together again.

Franklin Roosevelt's actions in his first one hundred days of office added to Bert's depressed state of mind. Nearly every piece of legislation that Roosevelt successfully navigated through Congress during that short time, especially the ones related to the banking sector, had its origins in Bert's administration. Rather than credit his predecessor with laying the groundwork for the new initiatives, Roosevelt deftly cast Herbert Hoover as the economic bogeyman responsible for the nation's continuing woes. The name "Hoover" became synonymous with the depression.

Roosevelt reflected public sentiment. Shantytowns that sprung up across the Midwest and west were called Hoovervilles. A Hoovercart was the name given to a contraption invented by farmers: When gasoline became too expensive, they hooked their cars, or parts of their cars, to a team of horses or mules as an alternative means of transportation.

Lou returned alone to Palo Alto, prepared to put the defeat behind her and to begin the life she had envisioned for herself for nearly two decades. She reconnected with activities on the Stanford campus and built friendships with women faculty members. Lou opened her home to Stanford's women students, and she regularly invited small groups to tea. Shortly after her return to Washington, Lou hosted the Whittier College Glee Club at 623 Mirada, the street address assigned to her imposing home on San Juan Hill.

Bert joined Lou in Palo Alto at the end of March, but he was too restless to stay put. He and Allan embarked on an extended road trip, heading east toward Wyoming then circling back through Nevada and Southern California. Lou joined the pair in early April and replaced her son as Bert's travel companion. The trip frustrated her. Bert did not want to see or talk to anyone. He refused to linger for a few days in some of the picturesque communities they encountered along the way; he was ready to move on within five minutes.

While Bert turned his anger inward into depression, Lou turned her anger outward toward the newspapers that she believed misrepresented Bert's efforts and falsely reported the news. She cancelled her subscriptions to the two Hearst newspapers, the San Francisco *Chronicle* and *Examiner,* and subscribed to the San Jose *Mercury*. She appreciated the defense of Bert's administration on its editorial page. Lou was blunt in her assessment of the new president: "The present Administration is stealing [Bert's] ideas and taking the credit for them as original. Every other paper in this part of the world is letting them get by with everything. . . . Communist paper[s] could not do better."[7]

She became uncharacteristically paranoid in the months following her departure from Washington. "You can write me anything, of course, by posting it in some outside letter box, and especially by addressing it to L.H.," Lou wrote Allan. "But I cannot write you anything which we do not want anyone in the hotel [where Allan resided], or elsewhere, to read. Your name would be a temptation for many people to open your letters for what they might get." She went so far as to suggest they adopt pseudonyms for their correspondence: Allan and Lou would be the brothers Alvin Henry and Louis Henry, whose stepfather was Corbert Cooper.[8]

Lou believed her telephone was wiretapped, and she urged Allan to be cautious about what he said on their calls. "I have known for a long time that our line was often listened in on,—but your father did not seem to think so,—and talked anything over it. He has been told definitely of a leak through it however, lately."[9]

Lou's paranoia had some justification. The Internal Revenue Service audited all four Hoovers' tax returns for 1933, and in early 1935 the agency asked for an estimate of Lou's income for the coming year—a request that baffled Edgar Rickard, who served as the family's tax accountant. There was no firm way to know what Lou's earnings would be from her rentals or investments. Edgar expected that the 1934 tax returns would be examined as well. It was difficult to think that the audits were random.

By late spring 1933, Lou had plunged into the operational details of the two women's organizations that meant the most to her—the Girl Scouts and the Women's Division of the National Amateur Athletic Association. Both still struggled financially. The ARA, with Lou's prodding and Edgar's championing, continued to make donations to help the two groups stay afloat. However, by 1936, members of the ARA board were becoming impatient with the Girl Scouts. The organization ran an annual deficit, and it had come to depend on the ARA to make up the shortfall. The Publications Division, which had long been a concern of Lou's, remained a drain on resources. *American Girl* magazine, which Lou had hoped would revise its content to have greater appeal to Girl Scouts, still lacked strong editorial direction.

The executive directors who had succeeded Jane Deeter Rippin lacked her fund-raising skills. By the mid-1930s, many of the original network of donors had aged, died, or lost interest in the Scouts. Lou re-joined the board in 1933, and it elected her national president in 1935. She served in that role until 1937. In those two years, Lou sought to revitalize the Scouts' donor base and encourage the hiring of professionals such as Rippin, who would manage the Girl Scouts' operations effectively. Lou attended the annual conventions and visited camps and gave radio speeches on behalf of the Scouts, including a nationally broadcast address in 1937 to honor the twenty-fifth anniversary of the Scouts' founding.

The Women's Division of the NAAF likewise struggled with the dual challenges of limited funding and limited national support. Rippin had become the executive director of the Women's Division upon her departure from the same position with the Girl Scouts. By 1935, she had resigned her post, although she remained on the board. Lou was impressed with the work of the Women's Division, and she sought ways to reinvigorate national interest in its programs.

There was a distinct contrast between the NAAF's emphasis on inclusion of all people in physical activity, and the AAU's ethos of professionalizing amateur sport. "All of the saner groups in Women's Athletics and Physical Education are in favor of this organization [the NAAF]," Lou told Edgar in a letter asking for his help in finding an acceptable director and funds to continue. "Of course, the women and girls interested in AAU events, Olympics and such spectacles, and the exploitation of girls in public baseball, track meets, and the like, for the benefit usually of their employers in industries, have no use for [the NAAF]."[10]

Recognizing that the Women's Division was unlikely to survive as an independent organization, (it merged into the American Alliance for Health, Physical Education, and Recreation in 1940), Lou turned her attention to promoting physical education on Stanford's campus. "Mrs. Hoover was interested . . . particularly in the physical education program," recalled Helen Pryor, MD, director of Stanford's Women's Health Service. "It was perfectly natural for her to do this because her interest in the whole area was so apparent and so real."

Lou's desire to break down barriers was evident in her encouragement that Pryor oppose a university rule that only men could teach the professional physical education courses. "[W]e opposed it successfully. She encouraged me to plan new curriculum for women in this man's institution."[11] Lou also believed that physical education should be a compulsory part of the college curriculum. Although Pryor did not like the idea of forcing students to take physical education, she respected Lou's viewpoint.

With Lou's support and encouragement, Pryor pursued a curriculum in physical therapy, a then-emerging field of study. "I wanted to put in physical therapy, and she backed me one hundred percent. I am sure that her influence in high places was very instrumental in the success of that endeavor. . . . [S]he thought it was just as important as nursing." Stanford implemented a physical therapy major, which continues to be part of the university's curriculum with specialty residencies in the medical school and hospital.[12]

Two memoirs that contained unflattering portraits of the Hoover White House were published in the three years after Lou and Bert left Washington. The *Saturday Evening Post* serialized *Forty-two Years at the White House* in late 1933, and the book was released the following year. The posthumous memoir was ostensibly written by Chief Usher Irwin "Ike" Hoover (no relation to Bert). The chief usher had died in September 1933.

Ike Hoover had served in the White House since the Benjamin Harrison administration (1889–1893) and had retired shortly after Franklin Roosevelt took office on March 4, 1933. The book was widely accepted by the public as true, but Lou and Grace questioned Hoover's authorship. The chief usher criticized the Hoovers for the remodeling they did to the family quarters. Lou was described as a "fast and consistent talker." One of the staff would announce: "The madam is broadcasting." Ike Hoover acknowledged that Lou may have been a "great talker, but a most interesting and intelligent one."[13]

After reading an advance copy of the *Post*'s article, Lou wrote to Grace Coolidge:

> He was such a dear soul and took his duties and responsibilities so seriously,—and I discussed this whole subject with him so particularly at one time or another,—that I feel very strongly that I have ample justification for thinking that he never wrote that article. When other people's articles on intimate White House affairs appeared, he was very outspoken in his condemnation of their betrayal of confidences.[14]

Grace agreed with Lou. "It does seem a shame that these articles should be printed under Usher Hoover's name for they consist in so large a measure of material which he would have been the last to sanction."[15]

The two women speculated that the chief usher, likely in need of money beyond what he received as his pension, agreed to have the book ghost written with use of his notes. Lou was still expressing unhappiness about Hoover's book a half year following its release and considered writing a rebuttal. Grace suggested that it was time to let it go. "As I expressed myself in our talk in Northampton," Grace graciously observed, "I feel that the 'Ike' Hoover articles are unfair and unjust not only to those about whom they were written but also to [Usher] Hoover himself. In my judgment, it is better not to dignify them by making any reply however indirect. This position has also been taken by some of Mr. Coolidge's most trusted advisors."[16]

Two years later, Mary Randolph published *Presidents and First Ladies.* While the former social secretary complimented Lou on her energy and hospitality, she suggested that the Hoovers could also be unreasonably demanding and insensitive to the White House staff. Randolph described her one year as Lou's social secretary as "'The Big Top,' with plenty of side-shows and lots of ballyhoo."[17]

> The Hoovers turned the White House into a sort of continuous performance of "Alice in Wonderland," and in their day, the Ceremonial Officer reminded me of the "White Rabbit"—always running up and down corridors murmuring: "The Duchess! The Duchess! Won't she be savage if I've kept her waiting!"—while I sometimes felt like "Alice" after she had eaten the cake, and at other times like the "Alice" who had sipped from the black bottle.[18]

Unlike her strong reaction to the Ike Hoover memoir, Lou brushed off Randolph's book. Bert had regained his interest in public life and sought to establish himself as a voice against the Roosevelt administration, and Lou was engaged in her Girl Scout activities and efforts to assist Republicans in the 1936 election.

In 1934, Bert had published *The Challenge to Liberty*. Lou had worked with him on the book and had asked friends for feedback on the tone. "A few weeks ago, we finally succeeded in getting my husband to get to work on his view of the present condition of our country and how it came to get there, and how it could get out,—all of course, in rather general terms," Lou had written her friend Agnes Morley Cleaveland. "I think he may have taken a little too much for granted in the average citizen's knowledge,—rather than in intelligence." She asked Agnes to read the galley proofs and offer her opinion on: "What Mrs. Average Citizen would think of it and get from it?"[19]

The book reignited Bert. He traveled the country to make speeches and took positions against the actions of the New Deal that concerned him. As Lou had anticipated, Bert headquartered in New York, and he lived in the couple's apartment in the Waldorf Astoria Hotel. Edgar resumed the role of keeping Lou abreast Bert's activities. "Your husband continues to do well," he wrote Lou. "He should watch what he eats, although it does not seem to bother him."

In California, Lou kept up with the news and the mood of the nation. Roosevelt's sweeping overhaul of the executive branch had ignited calls for a constitutional convention. She wrote Allan:

> Some one feature is radically wrong, [so] let's scrap the whole thing. It is as though they had an automobile that was not running well, and should say, 'Let's run it into the ditch and leave it, because it is not pulling well,' or steering well, or what not. A sensible owner or a good mechanic would recognize that it was an excellent car, in more than fair condition, but had the steering gear too tight or too loose, or otherwise badly adjusted, or the valves needed to be ground, or the carburetor needed adjustment, or perhaps it only needed a thorough cleaning. Perhaps, even a few indiscreet purchases of bad gasoline had simply corrupted the motive power!
>
> Do we thus want to "scrap" our Constitution? Do we not want to make a careful study of it, see if in any near-vital matters it does need remodeling, and bring it up to date?[20]

Friends' letters reinforced the Hoovers' sentiments about the direction of the country under the Roosevelt administration, and many asked Bert to consider running for the presidency in 1936.

Lou recounted a visit of two Stanford students who were sons of friends of the Hoovers. Lou and Bert talked with the young men about their views on the political condition of the country, and both thought that Roosevelt was doing his best under the circumstances. Bert, who had become increasingly concerned that the nation was moving toward a form of socialism, asked the boys their thoughts on that system of government compared with America's government system. "[T]hey looked very blank and one said, 'Why we haven't got a system, have we?' And the other one rather giggled and said, 'No, haven't we just grown up like Topsy?'

> They knew their ancestors had fought for freedom, but they really didn't have any idea of what that freedom was, or of how said ancestors thought they had anchored it. They frankly had never heard of our old friend, The Bill of Rights. They hadn't the faintest idea of what the first amendments to the Constitution [were] nor how they came to be incorporated, al-

though they did confess to having read the Constitution in high school but not to having really studied it.[21]

These were more than average American boys who were preparing to graduate from Stanford University, Lou commented to Agnes, but they had studied more about communism and socialism than they had about their own system of government. In response, Lou worked with Agnes and other friends, including Sue Dyer and Ruth Hanna McCormick Simms, to promote civics education through Republican organizations. Four years later, she continued to express concerns regarding the direction the nation had taken under Roosevelt: "We are charging so consistently along the path that totalitarian states took more or less twenty years ago in all their development!"[22]

One of those organizations was Pro America, a group in which Cleaveland had initially been active. The founder, Elizabeth Hanley, hoped that Pro America would be recognized as a legitimate affiliate to the Republican Party (what we today would refer to as a Political Action Committee or PAC). Pro America attracted Republican women and Democratic women unhappy with the direction of the country under Roosevelt's New Deal. Hanley had approached Lou about affiliating with Pro America during the 1932 election. However, Lou believed at the time that the strength of the Republican Party lay in its building up its own committees. Now Lou thought the organization might help defeat Roosevelt in 1940. She contacted her first lady predecessors—Mary Harrison, Helen Taft, and Grace Coolidge—to ask them to join her as honorary vice presidents of the organization.[23] Unfortunately for the Republicans, the nomination process at its convention was fraught with internal divisions between isolationists, represented by its eventual nominee Wendell Willkie, and internationalists, represented by Robert Taft, son of the former president. Bert had even made an effort to secure the nomination, but instead threw his support to Willkie. Roosevelt was handily elected to an unprecedented third term.

Lou continued her practice of private philanthropy in her post–White House years. Among those she funded was a young woman of color who was enrolled in the Hampton Institute, in Virginia. Lou covered her tuition, books, and room and board, asking that her name not be revealed to the student. However, Lou was known to a young Hispanic woman who needed money to complete her studies to become a beautician. Upon her graduation, Lou wrote her a letter and enclosed a check with instructions that she use it to buy "some extras" that she had not been able to afford while she had been in school.

Allan married on March 17, 1937. His bride, Margaret Coberly, known as Cobey, was from Los Angeles. The small wedding took place in her parents' home, with Herbert serving as his brother's best man and his daughter, Peggy Ann, as one of the flower girls. The couple flew east for their honeymoon, which included a visit to 2300 S Street (Lou still owned the property), to see if they might like any of the furnishings from Allan's teenage years that were still in the home.

Allan and Cobey's first child, Allan Junior, was born the following year, and a photo taken Christmas 1938 shows a proud Grandma Lou holding her newest grandchild. The couple would have two more children, Andrew, born in 1940, and Lou Henry, born in 1943.

In summer 1937, Lou embarked on an extended camping trip with her eleven-year old granddaughter Peggy Ann, her friend and former secretary Philippi Harding Butler, and Butler's daughter Patsy. They traveled to Yosemite National Park and rented a cabin at Camp Curry. On Thursday, July 22, the party mounted horses and rode through the park. Their trail took them to Illilouette Falls, Vernal Falls, and Nevada Falls, through the Little Yosemite Valley, and to the Merced River. They returned to camp late Friday afternoon and embarked on a second horseback riding expedition Saturday morning that lasted five days, taking them up steep trails to the tree line. The best souvenirs of the trip were considered to be a catalog of the wildflowers that the group saw and their fond memories of the excursion.

At the end of the year, Lou completed her term as president of the Girl Scouts and began to pull back from active engagement in its work. The death of her dear friend Abbie Rickard played a role in Lou's withdrawal from her Scouting activities. Abbie had been one of Lou's first recruits in the service of the scouts and had served as treasurer and overseen the troublesome Publications Committee since the early years of Lou's involvement on the national board. As Lou had added more and more responsibilities to her own plate, she had come to depend on Abbie to play a supporting role in the same way that Edgar supported Bert. During Lou's White House years, Abbie often shopped for gowns and dresses in order to maintain Lou's anonymity. On some of the occasions when Lou had been ill, Abbie had filled in as hostess at White House functions.

Abbie had suffered either a heart attack or a stroke in 1935. Edgar gently suggested that Lou scale back requests to her friend, which could come across as demands. "I am very anxious to see the Girl Scout organization successful," Edgar wrote Lou in September 1935, shortly before Lou assumed the national presidency,

> but I am more interested in keeping Abbie well. She is under quite a strict regime, which includes, among other things, ample time to rest in the middle of the day and before dinner in the evening, and I do hope they won't pile too much on her so that she will feel she cannot take these rest periods, which she very much needs. The consequences will be serious if she gets back to the shape she was in this last spring.

I know that you will help in this respect, and, incidentally, I would have preferred if she had not undertaken this particular trip [likely to the annual Girl Scout convention]. You know that Abbie never complains and is very unlikely to let anyone know when she is completely exhausted.[24]

It was difficult for Abbie to slow down. Her letter to Lou in 1936 that provided the details of the Girl Scout board meeting where member Julian Barnes had accused the staff of mismanagement, especially in the Publications Division, indicated that Abbie was still emotionally and physically engaged in her board responsibilities. By 1937, Edgar had sent Abbie to the home of friends in Nassau, Long Island, in the hope that distancing her from her day-to-day activities would enforce rest. But Abbie's condition continued to deteriorate. She was hospitalized in January 1938. Visits from everyone, including Edgar, were severely restricted. Abbie passed away on February 8, 1938.

Lou wired Edgar: "Our thoughts are with you all every moment. It seems to me that I cannot really stand the loss in my life so I can realize what it is going to mean to you. Our dearest love is with you all." The signature included Lou's, Allan's, and Cobey's names.[25]

With her scout years behind her, Lou turned her organizational skill and energy to the establishment of the Friends of Music on the Stanford University campus. The seed for Friends of Music was planted by the musicales Lou had scheduled during her White House years.

Elizabeth Sprague Coolidge, (no relation to Calvin or Grace Coolidge), was a trained concert pianist and philanthropist who devoted considerable sums of money to promoting music and musicians. Her philanthropic gifts include Sprague Hall—the music building at Yale University—and the establishment of the Elizabeth Sprague Coolidge Foundation, which built an auditorium and an organ for the Library of Congress in Washington in 1925. The Foundation promoted chamber music through commissions, public concerts, and festivals.

At a White House tea, Coolidge asked Lou if there were an opportunity to bring chamber music to California. Lou connected her guest to Sue Dyer. Since Stanford did not have a music department, Sue referred Coolidge to Mills College, located in nearby Oakland. As a result, the college, in collaboration with Coolidge, established a seasonal concert series.

Lou undertook the organization of the Friends of Music in early 1937. She promoted the Friends as a way to address the gap in musical offerings available to the Stanford community since the school lacked a music department. With a light, humorous touch, she wrote individual letters to selected friends and acquaintances to solicit their support:

> This summer during the time of Mrs. Elizabeth Sprague Coolidge's visit here when she gave us these really wonderful concerts,—(were you here to enjoy them?) a number of us in the neighborhood had crystallized a vision which has been vaguely intriguing us a long time.
>
> Since the Trustees haven't the money to give us a real school of music, and the fairy godmother has not yet appeared with her wand, many of us have long felt that we should at least find some method whereby we might give some training in the appreciation of music to our students in other departments.[26]

Stanford University president Dr. Ray Lyman Wilbur supported the idea of a Friends of Music, but he had concerns about how such an organization would be structured and how the funds would be managed. Lou hosted a number of meetings to create bylaws, define how funds would be handled, and secure committed donors. In the meantime, Coolidge funded performances by the Roth Quartet, the Pro Arte String Quartet, and the Kolisch Quartet. Lou hosted a performance of harpist Mildred Dilling in her home.

Lou worked on her donor lists that fall. On December 31, 1937, she triumphantly wired Warren D. Allen, a pianist associated with Coolidge: "You can assure Mrs. Coolidge on the first of the year that we have the $2,000 promised to meet hers and doubtless a few hundred more for secretarial and other expenses."[27]

By 1939, the Friends of Music offered a robust and varied program to the Palo Alto community. The offerings for July and August of that year alone included Bach and Mozart programs, a Coolidge Foundation Concert series performance by the Roth Quartet, a string ensemble serenade, three organ recitals, and a lecture and recital featuring Mussorgsky's "Pictures at an Exhibition."

Through her work with the Friends, Lou became well acquainted with many of the musicians who performed. She developed a friendship with Dilling and helped to promote her career. Lou also followed the career of the pianist and vocalist Nicholas Goldschmidt, the opera director at the San Francisco Conservatory of Music. Goldschmidt directed opera performances at Stanford from 1938 until 1942. In 1940, Stanford University inaugurated a new Music Department. The program was a direct result of Lou's organization of the Friends of Music.

Across the ocean, Europe was at war. As Hitler marched across the continent, Goldschmidt expressed his concerns for his aunt and uncle, who lived in Belgium. Belgian King Leopold III, Rremembering the suffering of his people during World War I under his father's reign, surrendered to Germany in 1940 rather than endure invasion. Lou worked with her contacts in the State Department and European relief agencies and secured a visa and passage for Goldschmidt's uncle and aunt, only to have the offer declined due to the uncle's poor health. In March 1941, Goldschmidt learned of his uncle's death. "Our very great sympathy goes to you on this tragic occasion of your uncle's death," Lou wired Goldschmidt. "You must rejoice that you had many years of his friendship and also that he is spared long future years of serious illness. Please convey our deepest sympathy to your aunt when you write her. Lou Henry Hoover."[28]

Hitler's invasion of Belgium galvanized Americans who had been active in the World War I work of the CRB. Suzanne Silvercruys Stevenson, who led the Women's Division of the ARA, asked Lou to serve on a Women's

Committee. Lou, knowing that Bert would be involved in anything having to do with Belgian relief, sent a copy of Stevenson's request.

On May 31, Bert hosted at his Waldorf Astoria apartment a meeting of representatives from a handful of relief organizations with ties to Belgium. They included the Red Cross, the French and British Relief Fund, the Community Chest Funds, the CRB, the Paderewski Fund, and the Queen Wilhelmina Fund. On June 5, Bert advised Lou: "We have been trying to get up some sort of coordination amongst the various relief bodies. I send you herewith a copy of a memorandum which was the result of a preliminary conference a few days ago. I understand, however, that some of them do not want to go ahead with that agreement–and today it is all off. As a matter of fact, nothing can be done until the present battles are over and we see what Europe looks like. Love, H."[29]

Lou's initial response, after learning that nothing definite had been decided about coordinated Belgian relief, was to send a telegram to Suzanne Stephenson accepting the offer of honorary membership. But a week later, Lou sent a lengthy letter in which she rescinded her commitment. She also turned down offers to serve on honorary committees to help Finland and to assist those living in the occupied Islands of Guernsey. In each case, Lou shared her concerns for the plight of those suffering under Hitler. She then gently explained that she was busy serving as a trustee of several colleges, including Whittier and Mills, active in the Red Cross and Salvation Army, and still doing occasional work with the Girl Scouts.

Lou did take time to write a letter to Madame Chiang Kai-Shek, at the request of Carrie Chapman Catt. The occasion was the fourth anniversary of the Japanese invasion of China on July 7. Catt had written to Lou: "The July 7th anniversary, now a symbol of China's will to resist and of her national unity, will be this year a day of thanksgiving and rejoicing in China because of her successful resistance of four years of aggression.

"The women of China, under Madame Chiang's leadership, now occupy a place in Chinese public life unequaled in any other country and fill scores of positions not usually occupied by women in warring nations. This is all the more remarkable, since women participated little in China's national life before the present war."[30] Lou expressed her admiration to Madame Chiang:

> American women admire the selflessness and courage that Chinese women in all walks of life have shown the past four years of China's magnificent defense against aggression.
>
> Both the enslaved peoples of the world and those still free can take heart in the pattern of courage for all people that has been set by the Chinese people, above all by China's women, who today are playing so vital a part in their country's national life.
>
> Since July 7 is a national holiday in your land, celebrating the same principles for which our democracy stands, we can think of no more fitting day on which to express the friendship of American women for the women of China, and to wish them well in the weeks and months ahead.[31]

Lou's commitment to the Salvation Army replaced her work on behalf of the Girl Scouts and the NAAF. Her interest in the Army began when she sent an anonymous ten-dollar donation in 1922. The absence of bureaucratic inertia in the Salvation Army's organizational structure and its willingness to move quickly impressed Lou. She increased her gifts over the years and eventually made herself known as a donor. Upon her return to Palo Alto in 1933, Lou helped raise funds to support the Army's coeducational orphanage at Lytton, California. She was especially impressed with the physical education facilities at the orphanage's school, which included a gymnasium, swimming pool, playgrounds, and wooded areas and fields which the children were encouraged to explore.

Lou spoke at commissioning ceremonies for new officers and handwrote notes to each one. She could be counted on to assist with fund-raising efforts, including donating items for bazaars, contributing articles to the Army's national and regional newsletters, and speaking at different ceremonies and events.

Lou became a member of the Salvation Army National War Service Advisory Council, and she agreed to chair a committee "of prominent western women" who organized a drive for clothing for women and children on behalf of the Army's London office. The items would be collected by American children and brought to their schools where the Salvation Army would pick up the donations and transport the clothing to its London office. The garments were destined for those living outside of the Nazi-occupied territories.

Lou threw herself into the effort with her trademark energy and cajoling. "I quite understand your wanting to know about the obligations [regarding] joining the Salvation Army Committee," Lou wrote to the wife of Ward Bannister, long-time friends of the Hoovers. "With your conscientious devotion to duty you wouldn't shirk work that you found before,—even though it was much more than you expected!"

She assured her friend that she herself never took on any committee work unless she knew exactly what was involved, and she assured Mrs. Bannister that she would not really need to spend a lot of time handling committee responsibilities. "It strikes me that the work is really the Salvation Army's and the school childrens'! (And their mothers'!)"[32]

It was the classic steel grip in a velvet glove that Lou had honed through years of organizational leadership. She recruited twenty-five women in the targeted eight western states: Arizona, Idaho, Montana, New Mexico, Oregon, Washington, Wyoming, and, of course, California. Her recruitment list included the actress Mary Pickford Rogers. The drive accumulated an estimated four million garments. In a note on the report, Lou wondered if the count included small articles such as children's socks and underclothes. Her efforts were noticed by the founder of the Salvation Army, William Booth. The manager of the Army's London headquarters shared a picture of then-Queen Elizabeth visiting the Army's "Comforts Department," well-stocked, thanks, in part, to Lou's dedicated efforts. (The Army's London headquarters had been bombed a week before the Queen paid her visit.)[33]

On December 7, 1941, war became close and personal. At 7:55 a.m. local time, the Japanese launched a surprise attack on the United States Naval Base at Pearl Harbor, on the Hawaiian island of Oahu. "Joke! We're under attack! And we thought it was a sham battle!" Jean Henry Large wrote to her son Del and his wife, Jean (referred to as "Little Jean" in the family).

Jean had traveled to Hawaii to be with her daughter, Janet, who was living and working at the base. "The first morning Janet had to sleep late in weeks," Jean wrote, in a storybook style reminiscent of Lou's breezy letters. Life near the base had accustomed the residents to planes taking off and landing at all hours, so the first thoughts were that the sounds were a drill. The Commander in Chief of the Pacific dispelled any notion that this was business as usual. He sent out a single line dispatch: "Air Raid on Pearl Harbor x This is not a drill."[34]

Jean had discussed with Lou earlier in the year Lou's plans to visit Janet in Hawaii. Lou had suggested waiting until the summer or early fall and cautioned Jean to wait and see if the United States went to war with Japan. When war did not seem imminent, Jean traveled to the islands.

The attack stranded Jean on Hawaii and affected her communications with her family on the mainland. A brief note describing the attack, dated December 7, 1941, was finally delivered in a censored envelope to Del in California on February 4, 1942: "We are having a very noisy Sabbath right now. Guns are roaring in the offing, clouds of black smoke rising down below, and airplanes sailing round in a 'hit and miss' manner. . . . Just a thought, you don't suppose it is the real thing, do you? I miss you all very much, although enjoying of course the unusual life I am living."[35]

Del's wife was expecting the couple's third child, and Jean was anxious to be back in California where she could help care for his other children and see her new grandchild. Lou used her contacts in the military to see if she could arrange passage for Jean's return to the United States, but the letters that Lou asked Bert to write were not mailed as needed. Janet remained in Hawaii, and an undated letter, thought to have been written in 1943, indicates that Jean and Janet may finally have been able to return to California sometime that year.

As Jean sought a way to return to California, Lou closed up 623 Mirada for the final time. In November 1943, she wrote to her sons:

> "Dear Herbert and Allan: I have a will somewhere. I have not seen it in years, and it probably would be very hard to find if wanted suddenly. So, I will replace it with this,—just a series of friendly requests which I make to you both,—and to your father."

Lou gave Bert all of the community property that the two had accumulated during their lives together and all of her investments. "You have been lucky boys to have had such a father,—and I a lucky woman to have my life's trails alongside the paths of three such men and boys." The boys were to receive the remainder of any funds left in her bank accounts and in small securities after her debts had been paid. They were to "share and share alike," including dividing her personal effects as they saw fit.[36]

The letter was a holographic will.

Lou Henry Hoover walked out of 623 Mirada for the last time in late fall,

1943. She had been a familiar figure on the streets of Palo Alto for the last ten years. Residents encountered her doing her own shopping and carrying her groceries home by herself. Students had been warmly welcomed into her home. She had been an influential force in the growth of Stanford's curriculum programs.

Friends speculated that Lou had a premonition that her time was short. She had become physically weaker, and her doctor advised her to limit her activities. Just a year earlier, she was boasting to Jean that as soon as a muscle strain in her leg healed, she would be back to walking, bicycling, and riding the occasional horse. She had already talked to Peggy Ann's younger sister, Joannie, about going on a camping trip like the one Lou had taken with Peggy Ann through the Yosemite Valley.

It is generally believed that Lou never told Bert that she was unwell. Perhaps the reason could be traced back to her childhood years, when she saw how Florence Henry's illness dominated family life. Or Lou may have wanted to enjoy her remaining days without causing worry or being fussed over by family and friends.

On Thursday, January 7, 1944, Lou spent the afternoon with a friend attending a recital by Lou's friend, harpist Mildred Dilling. Following dinner, Lou and her unnamed companion started to walk back to the Hoovers' apartment. "Let's take a cab," Lou suggested. "I'm not feeling very well."

Bert was preparing to go to dinner with Hugh Gibson and Edgar Rickard. Lou spoke to the men and went to her room to lie down. Bert stepped in to say good-bye and found her collapsed on the floor. The doctor on call at the Waldorf was summoned immediately, but by the time he arrived, Lou was dead.

Bert emerged from his wife's bedroom to face his friends: "She's gone."

CHAPTER 15

No Finer Example

On Monday, January 11, 1944, fifteen hundred mourners gathered at St. Bartholomew's Episcopal Church in Manhattan to pay their respects to Lou Henry Hoover. Bert, Herbert, and Allan stood together, alone, in a front pew. Newspapers reported that over two hundred Girl Scouts gathered to pay their respects. Alex Sampson and Leon Thompson, two African American White House ushers, traveled to New York to say a last good-bye. There was no eulogy delivered at the New York service.

The family accompanied Lou's body to Palo Alto, where she was interred near her home overlooking the Stanford campus and close to the California mountain trails that she so loved to hike.[1] Longtime friend and Stanford University president Ray Lyman Wilbur delivered a brief eulogy to Lou at a memorial service held on January 14 in the campus's Memorial Church.

Lou Henry Hoover "could have fitted equally well into any stage of our American development from the log cabin with its loopholes for a rifle to the most modern dwelling in the largest of our modern cities," Wilbur told his audience.

> Her experience varied from being under fire in Tientsin to entertaining the great scientists, statesmen, authors, and government officials of this and other countries in her own home and in the White House. Wherever she went she made a home for her husband and children. She had great skill in making domestic things simple, in welcoming and entertaining guests, and in providing a background of comfort for the household, particularly for her husband. His friends and associates became at once her friends and associates.
>
> Here in her home community, Lou Henry Hoover had a unique position. She was known to all and loved by all who knew her. . . . Although she no

> longer moves among us as our neighbor, Lou Henry has not left us; she still lives in our hearts. The thought of her will remain forever dear to us and to those who follow us. There is no finer example of how to live than was given to us by Lou Henry Hoover.[2]

As a tribute to Lou's many years of service, the Girl Scouts launched a national conservation project—The Lou Henry Hoover Memorial Forest or Sanctuary. One of the tributes was the designation of the Azalea Trail in Lou's memory in California's San Jacinto Mountains. Today, Girl Scouts in the Colonial Coast Council, which includes southeastern Virginia and northeastern North Carolina, can earn a Lou Henry Hoover Memorial Sanctuary Patch. Requirements for the patch read much like Lou's assignments during her years at Los Angeles Normal School: Girls study soils, identify trees and flowers, watch the clouds, and make observations about their natural surroundings to earn the patch.

However, the greatest memorial to Lou Henry Hoover is the one that does not bear her name.

In 1928, Lou attempted to buy the cottage where Bert had been born, but its owner, Jennie Scellars, earned an income from charging a small fee to tourists interested in the origins of the then-Republican candidate for president. She wanted to hold on to the property.

Mrs. Scellars died in 1935, and her family offered the cottage to the Hoovers. Bert turned down the offer, believing the asking price to be too high. In the meantime, he asked a West Branch friend, Fred Albin, to monitor the asking price on the property. When the price was dropped to $4,500, Albin bought it on behalf of the Hoovers. A few months later, Albin sold the cottage to Allan, who acted as Lou's agent.

Once she came into possession of the cottage, Lou researched Bert's family history and the history of the cottage. Bert's recollections were limited, since he had been sent to Oregon as a young boy. Lou turned to Theodore and to the Hoovers' cousin, Harriette Miles Odell, for help in reconstructing the family history and establishing the original size and orientation of the cottage. As a result of her research, the Hoovers removed all the nonhistorical additions to the cottage and rotated it to its original east-facing position. The Hoovers retained ownership of the twelve building lots which had been part of the purchase.

On March 22, 1939, the Hoover Birthplace Society, the forerunner of the Herbert Hoover Presidential Library and Museum, was incorporated. Both Herbert and Allan took an active role in shaping the direction of the fledgling Society, and they did so at a time when their father's name still evoked negative reaction across much of the United States.

Lou's desire to shape public perception of Bert's career, plus Herbert's and Allan's efforts, provided the groundwork for the property eventually to develop into the historical site and resource it is today—the Herbert Hoover Presidential Library and Museum. The facilities serve as the primary place to research the lives of Herbert and Lou Henry Hoover, and a number of their contemporaries and colleagues. It is the one place where the story of Herbert Hoover's humanitarianism and leadership are routinely celebrated, and the place where ongoing scholarship into Lou's life allows us to see a fuller, truer picture of this remarkable woman.

Following Lou's death, Bert deeded the property at 623 Mirada to Stanford University with the stipulation that it be renamed the Lou Henry Hoover House. Today, the house serves as the residence for the university's president. One of the discoveries made by her family when they sorted through Lou's desk drawers was a large number of checks made out to her that she had never cashed. The checks were from people to whom Lou had loaned small sums of money or to whom she had sent funds to help them through a difficult time.

Bert died on October 20, 1964, almost twenty-one years after Lou's death. He was interred on the grounds of the Herbert Hoover Presidential Library and Museum in West Branch, Iowa. Lou's body was re-interred alongside Bert's. Shortly before his passing, he ordered that Lou's papers remain sealed until twenty years after his death. By the time Lou's papers were opened for research, she had been deceased for forty-five years.

Memorials to Lou live on, even though her name is not associated with them. The Girl Scouts celebrated their one hundredth anniversary in 2012. Women's sports continue to achieve greater levels of respect, even as the women fight for equality in pay and funding. We have become more sensitive to the importance of caring for our environment. Women have pursued and achieved success in the fields of science and engineering. First ladies have taken a larger role in historic preservation of the White House and its artifacts, and we appreciate the quality of life contributed by the arts. In both large and small ways, Lou Henry Hoover had an influence in weaving together the many and diverse threads that comprise the fabric of American life. As Ray Lyman Wilbur observed in his eulogy: "There is no finer example of how to live than was given to us by Lou Henry Hoover."[3]

NOTES

Throughout, "LHH Papers" refers to Lou Henry Hoover Papers located at the Herbert Hoover Presidential Library and Museum, West Branch, Iowa.

Chapter 1

1. M. F. K. Fisher, *Among Friends*, Berkeley, CA: Counterpoint, March 30, 2004, 14.
2. Lou Henry Hoover diary, The Herbert Hoover Presidential Library and Museum.
3. LHH diary, Hoover Library-Museum.
4. LHH diary, Hoover Library-Museum.
5. Calie Cook, "Alumni History of Whittier School."

Chapter 2

1. Florence Henry to Lou Henry, October 30, 1896[?], Lou Henry Hoover Papers, The Herbert Hoover Presidential Library and Museum.
2. Sue Dyer Oral History, LHH Papers, Hoover Library-Museum, 13.
3. "Florence Bascom," *Encyclopedia Britannica*, July 10, 2019, https://www.britannica.com/biography/Florence-Bascom.
4. Herbert Hoover, *The Memoirs of Herbert Hoover: Years of Adventure 1874–1920* (New York: The Macmillan Company, 1951), 30.
5. Hoover, 14.
6. Hoover, 6.
7. Hoover, 12.
8. Hoover, 15.
9. Hoover, 16.
10. Hoover, 16.
11. Stanford University Chemistry, Literature Notes, 1895, LHH Papers, Hoover Library-Museum.
12. Florence Henry to Lou Henry, January 30, 1895, LHH Papers, Hoover Library-Museum.
13. Local historians date the founding of Castilleja to 1907, but the school is named in a letter from Florence to Lou dated September 15, 1895, and in later correspondence between Lou and Jean once Jean has enrolled at Stanford University.

14. Florence Henry to Lou Henry, October [?], 1895, LHH Papers .

15. Florence Henry to Lou Henry, October 3, 1895, LHH Papers.

16. Charles Henry to Lou Henry, October 25, 1895, LHH Papers.

17. Charles Henry to Lou Henry, October 25, 1895, LHH Papers.

18. Florence Henry to Lou Henry, November 19, 1895, LHH Papers.

19. Hoover, *Memoirs*, 27.

20. Lou Henry to Evelyn Wight, June [?], 1898, LHH Papers.

21. John C. Branner to Lou Henry, June 26, 1898, LHH Papers.

22. Lou Henry to Evelyn Wight, June [?], 1898, LHH Papers.

23. "The World of 1898: The Spanish-American War," Library of Congress, https://www.loc.gov/rr/hispanic/1898/intro.html.

Chapter 3

1. Florence Henry to Mrs. Mason, March 12, 1899.

2. John C. Branner to Lou Henry, February 2, 1899.

3. Florence Henry to Mrs. Mason, March 12, 1899.

4. Lou Henry Hoover to Evelyn Wight, February 19, 1899.

5. Lou Henry Hoover diary, The Herbert Hoover Presidential Library and Museum, February 7, 1899.

6. Julian Ralph, *Alone in China; And Other Stories* (New York, Harper & Bros., 1897 [1896]), 10.

7. Glen Shagren, "Tientsin China in 1900," 1976, 5–6, https://digitalcommons.usu.edu/gradreports/727.

8. LHH diary, October 27, 1899, Hoover Library-Museum. Gustav Detring was a German who had served as the commissioner of the Maritime Customs of China in Tientsin. Fluent in Chinese and English, Detring had arranged the introduction of Charles Moreing to Chang Yen Mao; a meeting that ultimately led to Bert's assignment in China.

9. Kenneth Pletcher, "Opium Wars," *Encyclopedia Britannica*, February 5, 2020.

10. John Taliaferro, *All the Great Prizes: The Life of John Hay from Lincoln to Roosevelt* (New York: Simon & Schuster, May 27, 2014), 377.

11. "Cixi," *Encyclopedia Britannica*, April 9, 2020.

12. Lou Henry Hoover, undated/unpublished memoir.

13. Mary Bainbridge to Lou Henry Hoover, June 7, 1900.

14. Lou Henry Hoover, undated/unpublished memoir.

15. Trevor K. Plante, "US Marines in the Boxer Rebellion," *Prologue*. Vol. 31, No. 4. Winter 1999, 1.

16. Undated/unsigned memo, July 1899 [?].

17. Ladysmith, Kimberly and Mafeking were British towns in South Africa which were besieged during the Boer War (1899-1902). Several 4.7-inch cannon from the British cruiser HMS Terrible were removed from the ship, fitted with gun carriages and used in the defense

of Ladysmith and Kimberly. During the Boxer Rebellion, these guns were shipped to China and helped to lift the siege of Tientsin.

18. Lou Henry Hoover to Evelyn Wight, August 8, 1900.

19. Lou Henry Hoover, undated/unpublished memoir.

20. LHH diary, August 4, 1903, Hoover Library-Museum.

Chapter 4

1. Lou Henry Hoover to Evelyn Wight, 1900[?].

2. Evelyn Wight to Florence Henry, November 26, 1900.

3. Jean Henry diary entry, January 1, 1901.

4. Herbert Hoover, *The Memoirs of Herbert Hoover: Years of Adventure 1874–1920* (New York: The Macmillan Company, 1951), 73.

5. LHH to Jean Henry, January 31, 1902.

6. LHH to Henry family, February 7, 1902.

Chapter 5

1. Herbert Hoover, *The Memoirs of Herbert Hoover: Years of Adventure 1874–1920* (New York: The Macmillan Company, 1951), 76–77.

2. "Elegy for the Red House," The Time Machine, the Royal Borough of Kensington and Chelsea.

3. *Times of London*, January 9, 1903, 12.

4. Kenneth Whyte, *Hoover: An Extraordinary Life in Extraordinary Time* (New York: Knopf, October 10, 2017), 93.

5. Lou Henry Hoover to Florence Henry, May 6, 1903.

6. LHH to Henry family, June 7, 1903.

7. Herbert Hoover to Theodore Hoover, July 15, 1903, quoted in Whyte, *Hoover*, 94.

8. Jean Henry to parents, August 4, 1903.

9. Evelyn Wight Allan to Florence Henry, August 19, 1903.

10. LHH diary, December 4, 1903.

11. LHH, "Bombs over Burma," unpublished/undated manuscript.

12. Herbert Hoover, *Memoirs*, 129.

13. "Inductee Database: Hoover, Lou Henry," *National Mining Hall of Fame and Museum*.

14. Raymond W. Rossiter, "Georgius Agricola De Re Metallica" by Herbert Clark Hoover, Lou Henry Hoover, the *American Historical Review*, 19, No. 3 (April 1914), 597.

15. LHH speech to Awards Banquet, Mining and Metallurgical Society of America, March 9, 1914.

16. "History of the AWC," *American Women's Club*.

Chapter 6

1. London *Times*, https://www.thetimes.co.uk/, July 24, 1914.

2. Lou Henry Hoover, "Report of the Resident American Women's Relief Committee of London," October 18, 1914.

3. Hoover, "Report."

4. LHH to Walter Hines Page, September 23, 1914.

5. Hoover Institution Archives Staff, "Register of the Commission for Relief in Belgium Records," Finding Aid Prepared by Hoover Institution Archives Staff, np.

6. Henry Hoover to LHH, October 26, 1914, quoted in Whyte, *Hoover*, 146.

7. HH to LHH, 146.

8. "Register of the Commission," np.

9. LHH to HH, undated, quoted in Whyte, *Hoover*, 147.

10. "Jackson Reynolds Is Named President of New York Bank," Stanford *Daily*. Vol. 60, Issue 81, January 30, 1922.

11. LHH to Jackson Reynolds, November 24, 1914.

12. LHH to Members of Hoover and Henry Families, November 24, 1914.

13. LHH to Herbert Hoover Jr., November 25, 1914.

14. Lou Henry Hoover, "Belgium's Needs," (notes of a talk, October 1915), LHH Papers.

15. Lou Henry Hoover, untitled talk, April 1917, LHH Papers.

16. "Register of the Commission."

17. Lou Henry Hoover, speech, LHH Papers, n.d.

18. Hoover, speech.

19. LHH to the Duchess of Marlborough, May 26, 1915.

20. Charlotte Kellogg, *Bobbins of Belgium: A Book of Belgian Lace, Lace-Workers, Lace-Schools, and Lace-Villages* (New York: Funk & Wagnalls, 1920), 17.

21. Kellogg, 20.

22. LHH to Mildred Hoover, February 1, 1915.

23. LHH to Millard Shaler, October 31, 1916.

24. "Sale of Lace and Medals to Help Belgians," San Francisco *Bulletin*, February 25, 1915.

25. "Lusitania People—People's Stories," Merseyside Maritime Museum, https://www.liverpoolmuseums.org.uk/maritime-museum.

26. "Womanhood Pays Tribute to Bates, New York *Tribune*, June 11, 1915.

27. Jeffrey Miller, *Yanks behind the Lines: How the Commission for Relief in Belgium saved Millions from Starvation in World War I*, 157.

28. "Small Work by Small Men," *The Bellman*, Vol. 19, September 25, 1915, 343.

29. HH to LHH, October 14, 1915, quoted in Whyte, *Hoover*, 169.

30. LHH to Miss Anderson, November 26, 1915, quoted in Whyte, *Hoover*, 169.

31. Miller, *Yanks behind the Lines*, 158.

32. LHH to Herbert Hoover Jr. and Allan Hoover, July 1932.

33. LHH to Herbert Hoover Jr. and Allan Hoover, undated, ca. 1932.

Chapter 7

1. Grace Clark to Lou Henry Hoover, April 22, 1915.

2. Kenneth Whyte, *Hoover: An Extraordinary Life in Extraordinary Time* (New York: Knopf, October 10, 2017), 174.

3. "Telegram with a Translation of the Zimmerman Telegram," US National Archives and Records Administration: DocsTeach.

4. Edgar Rickard to LHH, April 21, 1917.

5. Rickard to LHH.

6. "Wilson Defines Program," *New York Times*, 20 May 1917, 1.

7. "Hoover Suggests Nation's Motto: 'Eat Plenty, Wisely, without Waste'," *New York Times*, May 20, 1917, 1.

8. "Sow the Seeds of Victory! Posters from the Food Administration of World War I," Educator Resources, National Archives and Records Administration.

9. Edgar Rickard to LHH, September 6, 1917.

10. Letter from LHH to Stanford *Daily Palo Alto*, April 12, 1918 (written on stationery from 1701 Massachusetts Avenue, Washington, DC).

11. Alice M. Dickson to LHH, n.d.

12. Alice M. Dickson to LHH, May 4, 1917.

13. LHH to Edgar Rickard, May 15, 1919.

14. Alice M. Dickson to LHH, August 5, 1917.

15. "Broad Scope is Seen for Club," *The Washington Herald* (Washington, DC, November 13, 1919), *Chronicling America: Historic American Newspapers*, 12.

16. "Juliette Gordon Low: A Brief Biography," Girl Scouts of America website.

17. "The Girl Scouts of the District of Columbia," *Girl Scout History Project*, December 1, 2017.

18. Juliette Gordon Low to LHH, December 6, 1917.

19. Anne Beiser Allen, *An Independent Woman: The Life of Lou Henry Hoover*, 90. (Westport CT: Praeger Publishers, July 30, 2000).

20. "Hoover Domestic Menage is Thoroughly Hooverized," *Evening Star* (Washington, DC, February 3, 1918), 4.

21. "Was the 'Trial Goat,' Mrs. Hoover Admits," *New York World*, February 13, 1921.

22. "Mrs. Vanderbilt Sells Flowers on Avenue," *The Washington Times*, (Washington DC, March 18, 1918), 1.

23. "Activities of Women Prominent in the Social Life of the Nation's Capital," *The Washington Herald*. (Washington, DC, August 4, 1918), 15.

24. "Hoover Domestic Menage," *Evening Star*, 4.

25. 'Trial Goat,' " *New York World*, February 13, 1921.

Chapter 8

1. Lou Henry Hoover to Winford H. Smith, November 5, 1918.

2. LHH draft memo, no addressee, December 12, 1918, quoted in Mayer, *Lou Henry: A Prototype for First Ladies*, 186.

3. LHH to Winford H. Smith, November 5, 1918.

4. Herbert Hoover to Charles Gates Dawes, December 24, 1918.

5. Edgar Rickard to LHH, February 18, 1919.

6. Rickard to LHH.

7. LHH to Edgar Rickard, March 5, 1919.

8. Edgar Rickard to LHH, April 23, 1919.

9. LHH to Rickard.

10. LHH to Rickard.

11. LHH to Rickard.

12. Edgar Rickard to LHH, April 2, 1919.

13. LHH to Edgar Rickard, May 17, 1919.

14. Art and Art History Professor Paul Turner, "Mrs. Hoover's Pueblo Walls," lecture at Stanford University, Stanford University Library, published February 20, 2018.

15. Turner, "Pueblo Walls."

16. LHH to Herbert Hoover Jr., August 27, 1919.

17. LHH to Edgar Rickard, November 14[?], 1919.

18. "1,200 Applaud Hoover's Name for President," *The Sun* (New York, N.Y., September 17, 1919), 1.

19. "1,200 Applaud," *The Sun* (New York, N.Y., September 17, 1919), 1.

20. Flora Hartley Greene to LHH, February 13, 1920.

21. Charles K. Field to LHH, February 29, 1920.

22. Field to LHH.

23. Field to LHH, May 10, 1920.

24. Rose Wilder Lane, *The Making of Herbert Hoover*, quoted in Christine Woodside, *Libertarians on the Prairie: Laura Ingalls Wilder, Rose Wilder Lane, and the Making of the Little House Books*, 26.

25. Charles K. Field to LHH, May 10, 1920.

26. Dare Stark to Charles K. Field, May 19, 1920.

27. Lou Henry Hoover (?), "An article written in 1920 by a friend of 'the Hoovers' and sent to Mrs. Hoover," 1920. Evidence is that Bert signed the lease on the Adams's home in Washington, DC. All of the homes bought by the Hoovers in Washington, DC, were titled to Lou or to West Branch Corporation.

28. Lou Henry Hoover (?), "An article written."

Chapter 9

1. Lou Henry Hoover to Mrs. C. Tiru-Navuk-Arasu, February 12, 1921.

2. LHH to Zelma Boeshar, May 26, 1921.

3. Clelia Duel Mosher to LHH, May 30, 1921.

4. Matthew Schaefer, "Lou Hoover Adding Bricks to the Foundation of League of Women Voters," *Hoover Heads: The Blog of the Herbert Hoover Library and Museum*, August 5, 2020, https://hoover.blogs.archives.gov/2020/08/05/lou-hoover-adding-bricks-to-the-foundation-of-league-of-women-voters/.

5. LHH to Alida Henriques, September 4, 1921.

6. LHH to Herbert Hoover Jr. and Allan Hoover, August 21, 1921.

7. LHH to Hoover Jr. and Hoover.

8. LHH to Allan Hoover, September [?], 1921.

9. LHH to Alida Henriques, September 4, 1921.

10. LHH to Allan Hoover, September [?], 1921.

11. LHH to Hoover.

12. LHH to Allan Hoover, September 19, 1921.

13. Charles Henry Trip Itinerary, September 27, 1921.

14. "Fads and Foibles of Cabinet Wives," the *Washington Times* (Washington, DC, March 5, 1922), 22.

15. LHH to Philippi Harding, March 18, 1932.

16. Alice M. Dickson to LHH, January 14, 1922.

17. "Boudoir Mirrors" advertisement, *Evening Star* (Washington, DC, March 2, 1924), 64.

18. Anonymous, *Boudoir Mirrors of Washington*, 250.

19. Mary Austin to LHH, September 29, 1918.

20. Anonymous, *Boudoir Mirrors*.

21. LHH to Jean Henry Large, Herbert Hoover Jr. and Allan Hoover, [?], 1932.

22. LHH to Large, Hoover Jr. and Hoover.

23. "7,500 Girl Scouts Parade Up Avenue with Gifts for the Needy," *New-York Tribune*, (New York, NY) October 22, 1922, 14.

24. Mary Aickin Rothschild, "To Scout or to Guide? The Girl Scout-Boy Scout Controversy, 1912–1941," *Frontiers: A Journal of Women Studies*, 5–6.

25. Edgar Rickard to LHH, April 25, 1922.

26. Andrew R. Boone, "At Home with Mrs. Herbert Hoover: An Interview with the Leader of the Girl Scouts of America," *Stanford Illustrated Review*. April 1922, 359, LHH Papers.

27. LHH to Allan Hoover, March 26[?], 1922, quoted in Kendrick A. Clements, *The Life of Herbert Hoover: Imperfect Visionary 1918–1928*, 182–3.

Chapter 10

1. Lou Henry Hoover, foreword, *Play Day—The Spirit of Sport*, 67.

2. "Passenger List for Warren G. Harding's 'Voyage of Understanding' trip to Alaska on the USS *Henderson*, 1923."

3. LHH to Ethel Bagg Bullard, August 15, 1923.

4. LHH to Bullard.

5. LHH to Florence K. Harding, August 18, 1923.

6. Edgar Rickard to LHH, August [?], 1923.

7. LHH to Frank B. Kellogg, March 1, 1922, quoted in Mayer, *Lou Henry Hoover: A Prototype for First Ladies*, 201.

8. Janlyn Slach, "Bleeding Heart and Lily," *Hoover Heads: The Blog of the Herbert Hoover Library and Museum*, April 12, 2017.

9. Lou Henry Hoover, Draft of Story on Grace Coolidge for *American Girl*, n.d.

10. Hoover, Draft of Story.

11. "National Affairs," *Time* magazine, April 24, 1924, 6.

12. Whyte, *Hoover*, 291.

13. Edgar Rickard to LHH, June 20, 1924.

14. Whyte, *Hoover*, 291.

15. "Girl Scout History Spotlight: Edith Macy, Founder of Girl Scouts University, *G.I.R.L. Talk, The Girl Scouts—North Carolina Coast Pines Blog*, January 4, 2016, https://blog.nccoastalpines.org/tag/edith-macy/.

16. LHH to Edgar Rickard, May 7, 1925.

17. LHH to Girl Scout Executive Board, November 16, 1925.

18. Telegram forwarded from Jane Deeter Rippin to LHH, n.d.

19. LHH to Abbie Rickard, March 28, 1928.

20. Abbie Rickard to LHH, November 12, 1928.

21. LHH to Theodore Hoover, April 15, 1927.

22. LHH to Allan Hoover, March [?], 1928.

23. LHH to Theodore Hoover, August 28, 1928.

24. LHH to Allan Hoover, November 21, 1927.

Chapter 11

1. "Hoover Reaches Flood Zone with 130,000 Refugees," *Evening Star* (Washington, DC, April 25, 1927).

2. "Republicans Who Are Expected to Be Boomed for Nomination for President," *Evening Star*, (Washington, DC, 03 August 1927).

3. Lou Henry Hoover to Herbert and Allan Hoover, January [?], 1928, quoted in Allen, *Independent Woman*, 115.

4. Unnamed secretary to LHH to Lillian Moller Gilbreth, February 18, 1928.

5. Nat Carle to LHH, February 18, 1928.

6. LHH to Nat Carle, February 20, 1928.

7. LHH to Carle, March 8, 1928.

8. LHH to Allan Hoover, April 19, 1928.

9. LHH to Hoover, April 26, 1928.

10. LHH to Hoover, March 2, 1928.

11. LHH to Hoover, March 8, 1928.

12. LHH to Hoover, March 6, 1928.

13. LHH to Hoover, April 14, 1928.

14. LHH to Hoover, June 5, 1928.

15. LHH to Ida Koverman, February 27, 1928.

16. LHH to Rt. Reverend Ramon Mestres, November 18, 1928. Fr. Mestres died as the Rt. Rev. Ramon Mestres, pastor of San Carolos church in Monterey and of the Carmelite Mission, on August 5, 1930.

17. LHH to Allan Hoover, June 28, 1928.

18. Theodore Hoover to LHH, July 7, 1928.

19. LHH to Theodore Hoover, August 28, 1928.

20. LHH to Allan Hoover, July 18, 1928.

21. LHH to Sue Dyer, [?], 1928.

22. LHH to Mrs. Frothingham, August 15, 1928.

23. "1928 Republican Convention," Republican National Political Conventions: 1856–2008.

24. "1928 Democratic Convention."

25. Christopher M. Finan, *Alfred E. Smith: The Happy Warrior* (New York: Hill and Wang, 2002), 211–12.

26. LHH to Edgar Rickard, October 4, 1928.

27. LHH to Rickard.

28. Adela Rogers St. John, "Mrs. Herbert Hoover," The Liberty, October 20, 1928, 12, https://hoover.archives.gov/research/collections/manuscriptfindingaids/univsocal.

29. Zoe Beckley, "Mrs. Hoover: 'American Through and Through.'"

30. David Starr Jordan to LHH, December 31, 1928.

31. LHH to Grace Coolidge, November 11, 1928.

32. LHH to Ethel Bagg Bullard, December 3, 1928.

33. LHH to Allan Hoover, January 3, 1929.

34. LHH to Hoover.

35. "Election Brings Official Hostesses Qualified for Tasks," *Evening Star* (Washington, DC, November 7, 1928).

Chapter 12

1. Lou Henry Hoover to Mary Randolph, May 31, 1930.

2. Lewis L. Gould, "Modern First Ladies: An Institutional Perspective," *Prologue: Journal of the National Archives*, 74.

3. Mary Randolph to Walter H. Newton, May [?], 1929.

4. Annette B. Dunlap, "Tea and Equality," *Prologue*, 18.

5. Dunlap, 18.

6. Dunlap, 19.

7. Dunlap, 19.
8. Dunlap, 19.
9. Dunlap, 20–21.
10. Dunlap, 21, 22.
11. Laurence Gouverneur Hoes, "Mrs. Hoover's Gift to History," November 6, 1932, 8ff.
12. LHH to Edith Galt Wilson, May 26, 1932.
13. LHH to Grace Coolidge, April 11, 1932.
14. Hoes, "Mrs. Hoover's Gift."
15. LHH to James Yardley and Jane Deeter Rippin, February 27, 1929.
16. LHH to Yardley and Rippin.
17. Viola Virginia Rollings to LHH, February 26, 1930.
18. Ruth Fesler to Viola Virginia Rollings, March [?], 1930.
19. Lucy C. Bray to LHH, March 3, 1930.
20. Ruth Fesler to Lucy Bray, March 6, 1930.
21. Christine Vest interview, quoted in Delia Ray, *Ghost Girl: A Blue Ridge Mountain Story*, 257.
22. LHH to Allan Hoover, April 29, 1929.
23. LHH to Hoover.
24. LHH to Hoover, June 17, 1929.
25. LHH to Hoover, September 27, 1929.
26. LHH to Hoover, June 24, 1929.
27. Jane Deeter Rippin to LHH, December 16, 1929.
28. LHH to Edgar Rickard, December [?], 1929.
29. "Dow Jones 100 Year Historical Chart," Macrotrends, https://www.macrotrends.net/1319/dow-jones-100-year-historical-chart.
30. Joel D. Treese and Evan Phifer, "The Christmas Eve West Wing Fire of 1929," White House Historical Association, February 9, 2016, https://www.whitehousehistory.org/the-christmas-eve-west-wing-fire-of-1929.

Chapter 13

1. "Senate Reception Brilliant Event," *Evening Star* (Washington, DC, January 31, 1930).
2. "Unemployment Rate for the United States," FRED Economic Data, Federal Reserve Bank of St. Louis.
3. "Technical Notes: Labor Force, Employment, and Unemployment: 1929–1939, Estimating Methods," US Bureau of Labor Statistics.
4. Grace Coolidge to Lou Henry Hoover, June 27, 1930.
5. LHH to Abbie Rickard, April 7, 1930.
6. LHH to Mrs. William H. Hoffman, April 9, 1930.
7. LHH to Abbie Rickard, April 7, 1930.
8. LHH to Jean Henry Large, April 30, 1930.
9. LHH to Large, June 5, 1930.

10. Anonymous letter to Mrs. William Brown Meloney, February 18, 1931.

11. Unsigned letter to Lawrence Richey, March 14, 1931.

12. Thomas F. Schwartz, "White House Staff Remember Lou," *Hoover Heads, The Blog of the Herbert Hoover Library and Museum*, October 18, 2017.

13. Schwartz, "White House Staff Remember Lou."

14. Poppy Cannon and Patricia Brooks, *The Presidents' Cookbook: Practical Recipes from George Washington to the Present* (New York: Funk & Wagnalls, 1968).

15. LHH to Allan Hoover, September [?], 1930.

16. LHH to Allan Hoover, October 24, 1930.

17. LHH to Jean Henry Large, n.d.

18. Thomas F. Schwartz, "White House Staff Remember Lou," *Hoover Heads*, October 18, 2017.

19. "Real Gross Domestic Product," FRED Economic Data, Federal Reserve Bank of St. Louis.

20. "One County in United States so Rich It Doesn't Want Farm Relief," the *Bismarck Tribune*, (Bismarck, ND), February 26, 1930.

21. "Enigma of the Great Drought," *Evening Star*, (Washington, DC, September 14), 1930.

22. "Technical Notes: Labor Force, Employment, and Unemployment."

23. LHH to Allan Hoover, August 22, 1931.

24. LHH to Hoover, October 29, 1930.

25. Timothy Walch, ed., *Uncommon Americans: The Lives and Legacies of Herbert and Lou Henry Hoover*, 161.

26. "Mrs. Hoover on Radio," *Evening Star*, (Washington, DC, March 24, 1931).

27. LHH to Allan Hoover, October 2, 1931.

28. LHH to Allan Hoover, December [?], 1931.

29. Sue Dyer, Oral History, 66.

30. LHH to Allan Hoover, May 29, 1932.

31. LHH to Hoover, June 22, 1932.

32. LHH to Herbert Hoover Jr. and Allan Hoover, [?], 1932.

33. Mary Austin, *Earth Horizon*, 323.

34. Austin, 312.

35. LHH to Herbert Hoover Jr. and Allan Hoover, July 1932.

36. LHH to Hoover Jr. and Hoover.

37. LHH to Allan Hoover, August 22, 1932.

38. "The Bonus March (May–July 1932)," *The American Experience*.

39. "MacArthur Lauds Hoover in Crisis," *Evening Star*, (Washington, DC, July 29, 1932).

40. LHH to Herbert Hoover Jr., August 1932.

41. LHH to Allan Hoover, [1932?].

42. "Victors and Vanquished in Maine Elections," *Evening Star*, (Washington, DC, September 13, 1932).

43. LHH to Allan Hoover, October 25, 1932.

44. LHH to Hoover, October 30, 1932.

Chapter 14

1. Abbie and Edgar Rickard to Lou Henry Hoover and Herbert Hoover, November 8, 1932.
2. Abbie Rickard to LHH, November 7, 1932.
3. LHH to Allan and Herbert Hoover, November [?] 1932.
4. "Prospect of Cancellation of New Year Reception at White House Stirs Society," *Evening Star* (Washington, DC, December 11, 1932).
5. LHH to Grace Coolidge, January 5, 1933.
6. LHH to Coolidge, January 23, 1933.
7. LHH to Allan Hoover, April [?], 1933.
8. LHH to Hoover.
9. LHH to Hoover.
10. LHH to Edgar Rickard, December 2, 1935.
11. Helen B. Pryor, interview by Raymond Henle, November 2, 1971.
12. Pryor interview.
13. Irwin Hoover, "The Hospitable Hoovers," *Saturday Evening Post*, April 14, 1934.
14. LHH to Grace Coolidge, February 8, 1934.
15. Grace Coolidge to LHH, March 2, 1934.
16. Grace Coolidge to LHH, December 7, 1934.
17. Mary Randolph, *Presidents and First Ladies* (New York: D. Appleton-Century Company, January 1, 1936), 122.
18. Randolph, 124.
19. Alice Morley Cleaveland, May 18, 1934.
20. LHH to Allan Hoover, May 17, 1933.
21. Alice Morley Cleaveland, June 13, 1934.
22. Cleaveland, March 17, 1940.
23. LHH to Grace Coolidge, December 23, 1939.
24. Edgar Rickard to LHH, September 25, 1935.
25. LHH to Edgar Rickard, February 9, 1938.
26. LHH to Mrs. Harris, September 10, 1937.
27. LHH to Warren D. Allen, December 31, 1937.
28. LHH to Nicholas Goldschmidt, March 10, 1941.
29. Herbert Hoover to LHH, June 5, 1940.
30. Carrie Chapman Catt to LHH, June 20, 1941.
31. LHH to Madame Chiang Kai-Shek, June 23, 1941.
32. LHH to Mrs. Ward Bannister, October 5, 1940.
33. Minnie L. Carpenter, May 17, 1941.
34. "The Japanese Attacked Pearl Harbor," *America's Story from America's Library*.
35. Jean Henry Large to Del Large, December 7, 1941.
36. LHH to Herbert Hoover Jr. and Allan Hoover, November 17, 1943.

Chapter 15

1. "On the Passing of Lou Henry Hoover," Hoover Heads, *The Blog of the Herbert Hoover Library and Museum*, January 10, 2018.

2. Ray Lyman Wilbur, Eulogy for Lou Henry Hoover.

3. Wilbur, Eulogy for Hoover.

INDEX